A CRY FOR JUSTICE

How the Evil of Domestic Abuse Hides in Your Church!

Jeff Crippen and Anna Wood

CALVARY

While the principles taught in this book have been derived from actual events, the characters and scenarios are either fictitious or names and specifics have been changed to maintain anonymity.

Calvary Press Publishing
www.calvarypress.com

ISBN-13: 978-1-879737-91-4

Printed in the United States of America

Good people never pretend to be evil,
but evil people love to pretend to be good.
Sheep don't wear wolves' clothing.

This book is dedicated to our brethren in Christ against whom the gates of hell have raged in all their fury and have not prevailed. And to Jerusha, whose story proved to be the beginning of this one.

Table of Contents

Acknowledgments

We extend our thanks to the many people whose contributions have made this book possible. To Lundy Bancroft, whom I met once for just a few minutes, thank you for teaching us through your books. To Andy Wortman of Greenville Theological Seminary, thank you for being one of the first to encourage us to write this book. To the elders and congregation of Christ Reformation Church, thank you for supporting this project. To my wife, Verla, for enduring hours and hours of her husband being present in body, but absent in mind. Many thanks to Craig, Bev, and Verla for reviewing the manuscript.

And special thanks to Barbara Roberts who took time away from her own writing and busy life to edit the manuscript. Her suggestions improved the book greatly, and her cheerleading kept us going.

Thank you especially to the real heroes of this project: the abuse victims who have been brave enough to once more remember the many years of terrorism they have suffered, to talk with us about it, and help us better understand the mentality and tactics of the abuser.

Regarding the specifics of co-authoring: The reader can understand "I" and "me" (first person singulars) in the narrative portions of the book to refer to Jeff. Anna floats in the background of the narrative – but be assured that she is there, and without her writing, *A Cry for Justice* would only be in black and white. Anna brought the book to life.

Preface

Job 19:7 *Behold, I cry out, 'Violence!' but I am not answered; I call for help, but there is no justice.*

Psalm 10:17-18 *O LORD, you hear the desire of the afflicted; you will strengthen their heart; you will incline your ear to do justice to the fatherless and the oppressed, so that man who is of the earth may strike terror no more.*

I (Jeff) am not by nature a radical, nor am I a rebel. I lived through the era of the "hippy" movement, but never became one. I like conformity, trusting those in charge, and supporting "the program." I do not like conspiracy theories that tell us "they" are everywhere, watching us, fleecing us of our money and minds. I am, therefore, the very last person whom I ever thought would be writing a book like this. But then, here I am. I am the one saying that the system is broken and doing great injustice to victims. That system in this case is the portion of Christianity in which I have been a minister for nearly thirty years.

In this book, as the title indicates, I am sounding a cry for justice, and I hope and pray that it will be heard. I am issuing this cry to what I am calling the evangelical church. By *evangelical* I mean churches under the umbrella of Protestantism that embrace the Bible as their sole authority for what they believe and practice. Churches that believe the Bible is God's own Word; inerrant and infallible. Churches that believe a person must be born again through faith in the Lord Jesus Christ if they are ever going to be set right with God.

While this cry for justice also needs to be heard by churches that are more liberal in their theology, we intend to primarily address evangelical churches like our own because these churches are in particular need of a wake-up call. The liberal churches (who may even be so liberal in doctrine that they deny Christ) have often been socially active already, including in the field of abuse. And the Roman Catholic Church needs to hear this cry as well. But I believe there has been quite a lot of speck removing by evangelical Christians in connection with the sexual abuse by the priests of Rome and not enough removing the log from our own eye first (I do not mean to imply that the abuse uncovered in the Catholic religion is a small thing. I merely use the imagery of Christ, Matthew 7:3-5).

Before evangelicals speak against abuses within the Roman system, should we not honestly face up to the timber found in our own eyes?

What then is this injustice I am speaking of, for surely a cry for justice necessarily implies that there is something quite wrong. Briefly stated, it is this:

> The local church is one of the favorite hiding places of the abusive person. Conservative, Bible-believing religion is his frequent choice of facade. Within the evangelical church, women (and sometimes men) are being terribly abused in their homes and marriages. The children of such abusers are suffering as well. And when these victims come to their churches, to their pastors, to their fellow Christians, pleading for help, well….

> ***Job 19:7*** *Behold, I cry out, 'Violence!' but I am not answered; I call for help, but there is no justice.*

Victims of abuse are often discounted by their churches. When they gain courage to seek help, they are routinely given superficial advice, accused of not being good enough wives or children, told that they are surely exaggerating the case, and then sent back home to "do better" and suffer even more at the hands of their tormentor. And when they finally leave their abuser, either by separation or divorce, most often the victim is the one who must leave their church while the abuser remains.

The church, in other words, is enabling the wicked person. In our ignorance of this subject (and please understand, abuse is a unique subject that requires special training and education to comprehend and deal with properly) we arrogantly assume that we know all about it. Pastors, church leaders and individual church members think they are helping victims. Many sincerely want to help them. And yet, because of their ignorance of the nature of abuse, they end up actually being an unwitting ally of the wicked person, adding to the suffering of the victim. We have a serious problem. The liberal churches know that we do; women's resource centers know; prosecutors and judges know – but we have yet to own up to our ignorance and, yes, arrogance.

I do not make these charges of injustice lightly or with pleasure. I do not make them as an outsider looking in, as someone who just has a bone to pick with the Christian church, trying to dig up stones to cast. I make them as a conservative pastor, as one who has not only seen this evil in the church and its grievous effects on its victims, but as one who has also been a victim of such abuse. Not in my marriage (I have a wonderful wife of over 40 years), but in the church itself at the hands of men and women who claim to be in the light, but who hate their brother (1 John 2:9). Sadly, Diotrephes, the power-hungry abuser who dominated an entire church in the first century, is alive and well in our churches today (3 John 1:9-10).

I hope therefore, in making this cry for justice, to be a voice who answers the one calling out, "Violence!" and one who provides some justice to those who are crying "Help!" I pray that many who read this book will join me. I know of one kind of person who surely will – the Christian victim of the abuser. Because as they read this book, they will say, "You are telling my story! Finally, someone in the church understands and believes me!"[1]

---

1 I do not want to sound arrogant, as if I am the "only one left" who understands. There are some pastors who have effected justice for abuse victims and who are not ignorant of the nature and tactics of the abuser. But the truth is that the majority of evangelical pastors are in the dark in this field. Their training in counseling is perhaps one or two semesters of classes most often with very little if any inclusion of domestic violence and abuse in the course. Yet they have been told that they are "competent to counsel" any situation they may face. The result? They are duped by the abuser and unknowingly assist him in his further abuse of the victim.

Introduction

3 John 1:9-10 *"I have written something to the church, but Diotrephes, who likes to put himself first, does not acknowledge our authority. So if I come, I will bring up what he is doing, talking wicked nonsense against us. And not content with that, he refuses to welcome the brothers, and also stops those who want to and puts them out of the church."*

I originally planned to give this book the title *In Search of Diotrephes*, but in the end decided that would convey the notion of some kind of Indiana Jones adventure. Few Christians know who Diotrephes is. He appears briefly in one of the shortest of the New Testament epistles, 3 John. But you can find him in almost any local church. Chances are, in fact, that you know him. If you are a faithful pastor, I am sure you have been introduced. Diotrephes is an abusive man (or, sometimes, a woman). His traits are evident in the Apostle John's description and his fundamental mentality is: he likes to put himself first. We will examine him in chapter 14.

What do we mean when we say that someone is a Diotrephes? What is this thing we are calling abuse? Who is an abuser and who is a victim? Isn't abuse just another word for what the Bible calls sin? Why is it so special and different? Surely the Bible is sufficient to equip us to deal with every kind of sin. If we maintain that abuse is so unique, aren't we denying the sufficiency of Scripture? Isn't everyone an abuser? After all, we all sin, right?

These are the kinds of questions that come up right at the beginning of a consideration of this subject, and they are good questions that need to be answered. Part of the purpose of this book is to educate the reader in the nature and tactics and mentality of abuse and, in doing so, to help us all to come to understand the pathology of this unique sin. Once we understand, we will also realize that there are specific tools God has given us to deal with it. Scripture, it turns out, is indeed sufficient – but our knowledge and understanding of God's Word most often are not, and that is what needs to be corrected. In the end, we will find ourselves saying, "Oh, so *that* is what the Bible was telling us all along!"

Let me introduce you to this subject of abuse as my eyes were opened to it several years ago. Please understand, this is no pleasant stroll in a flower-filled meadow. Abuse is a thing that we all naturally would rather remain ignorant of.

We are much like Scarlet O'Hara in *Gone With the Wind* who decided that she would just not think about such things today. But as long as this evil remains unknown, it retains its power to enslave and destroy. Of all agencies in the world, it is the Christian church that ought to be the leader in exposing darkness with the light of Christ's truth. Sadly, however, this has often not been the case.

As a result of a serious incident of abuse within the church of which I have been the pastor for nearly twenty years, I felt compelled to begin studying abuse. I began by reading specifically about sexual abuse. I wanted to find out if there are specific, recognizable warning signs that would help us identify potential sexual abusers and thereby do a better job of protecting our people. I knew that there are some patterns the sexual predator generally follows because I had seen some of these patterns both in my experience as a police officer and as a pastor. But I only saw them after the fact, and I wanted to be able to recognize them before anyone was victimized.[2] So I read.

The first book I found was a very expensive one, but I bought it anyway – *Physical Abusers and Sexual Offenders: Forensic and Clinical Strategies*, by Scott Allen Johnson. The subject matter was ugly. Most Christians would soon put it down and label it too much information. But I could not. I had been thrust into the middle of this evil, along with the victim, the victim's parents and family, and the havoc wrought in the church by it. I could not put it down because I was finding answers. Here was a man who understood the abuser, the tactics, the deceptions, the terrible damage done, and I liked him. The book itself is not a Christian book. Scott Johnson may be a Christian or he may not be, I don't know. He writes as a secular therapist. But I realized that he knew more about

2 Strangely, as a police officer, my experience with sexual abusers did not come as a result of arresting them, but from working with two sexual predators who were my fellow police officers! One was a well-known official who was highly respected in the county. Another was a uniformed officer. In both of these cases, certain very similar indicators were present. They both sought out young men through becoming foster parents. They both used their authority to influence their victims. I met a third molester who was a professing Christian and church member. He expressed his "heart" for youth ministry and worked hard to gain access to children, offering to take them on outings and so on. The church put a stop to these activities, but only reluctantly and with a degree of guilt. Years later after he had left that church looking for greener pastures, he was caught by the parents of a child victim and, as his arrest was imminent, he took a rifle and killed himself.

this subject than any Christian I had ever spoken with or read. I would continue to find this to be the case. The secular world has more wisdom by far about abuse than does the Christian church. *A Cry for Justice* is a call to the evangelical church to correct this ignorance.

As I continued to read, I began to realize two things. First, as Scott Johnson explains, there are many similarities between the sexual abuser and the domestic abuser. Sometimes in fact, one abuser may be of both types. This propelled me into further study as I broadened my scope to include material written specifically about domestic violence and non-sexual abuse. The lights continued to go on as I learned more.

The second thing that struck me very powerfully was the realization that I myself had suffered at the hands of abusers in the local churches I have pastored. The tactics of these Diotrephes (both men and women) were strikingly similar to the strategies and methods of domestic violence abusers. Furthermore, as I read and learned even more about the effects of such abuse on victims, I came to understand that I have suffered many of the very same effects (false guilt, doubts about my own thinking processes, isolation, etc). There are very few local churches who are fortunate enough to be free of a Diotrephes in their midst. The Apostle John wrote that when he came, he would "call attention" to Diotrephes' evil, exposing him. But this is rarely done today. We need to ask and learn—why?

What, then, did I learn that abuse is? In all of its forms, what are the fundamental elements that are always present? Let's define it. Please understand that abusers may be men or women, but for reasons of simplicity, and because far more commonly it is the man who is the abuser, we will use he/him to refer to the abuser and she/her for the victim. In the church and in the workplace, I have known numbers of women who showed all the traits of an abuser, though once more, they are more commonly men.

A Definition of Abuse

Abuse is sin. Sin is any want of conformity unto, or transgression of, the law of God (Westminster Shorter Catechism). Dead in their sin and apart from Christ, the sinner zeros in on his sin of choice. In the old days, this was called a person's "bosom sin." In some ways, there isn't a whole lot of choice involved in the deal. Sin binds and enslaves.

> ***Romans 1:28-31*** *And since they did not see fit to acknowledge God, God gave them up to a debased mind to do what ought not to be done. (29) They were filled with all manner of unrighteousness, evil, covetousness, malice. They are full of envy, murder, strife, deceit, maliciousness. They are gossips, (30) slanderers, haters of God, insolent, haughty, boastful, inventors of evil, disobedient to parents, (31) foolish, faithless, heartless, ruthless.*

We see the sin of choice idea in Paul's words to the Corinthians as well:

> ***1 Corinthians 6:9-11*** *Or do you not know that the unrighteous will not inherit the kingdom of God? Do not be deceived: neither the sexually immoral, nor idolaters, nor adulterers, nor men who practice homosexuality, (10) nor thieves, nor the greedy, nor drunkards, nor revilers, nor swindlers will inherit the kingdom of God. (11) And such were some of you. But you were washed, you were sanctified, you were justified in the name of the Lord Jesus Christ and by the Spirit of our God.*

Abusers are people who choose to worship at the idol of power, control, and domination over others. Therefore, the abuser's sin has particularly damaging and evil effects upon his victims. World history is largely the story of abusers who have risen to heights of power, and the murderous havoc they have wrought upon billions. One obscure little Bavarian corporal, sociopathic and entitled, thrust the entire world into terrible and bloody chaos.

The abusers we normally deal with operate on a much smaller scale. They terrorize their wives and children, or someone they work with, and very often a pastor or other church leader. Added together, these "little abusers" have worked more grief and evil than Hitler ever did. And these kind love to lurk in the Christian church. Oh, how they love to hide among the sheep.

Abuse then, is a mentality of entitlement and superiority in which an abuser uses various tactics to obtain and enforce unjustified power and control over another person. The abuser thinks that he is absolutely justified in using these tactics to maintain this power and control over his victim. Abuse is effected in many ways: both physical (including sexual) and non-physical (verbal). It can be active (physically or verbally) or passive (not speaking, not acting). Abuse, therefore, is not limited to physical assault. Indeed, the non-physical forms of abuse often are far more damaging, deceptive, and cruel.

Mark these defining terms down very, very carefully. An abuser is a person whose mentality, mindset, and even worldview is dominated by:–

- Power
- Control
- Entitlement (to that power and control)
- Justification (in enforcing that power and control)

This means that, as I learned, it is a serious mistake to assume an abuser thinks like everyone else does. Abuse is rooted in a unique form of the sin mentality. Any method of dealing with the abuser and helping his victim is destined to failure unless we recognize this fundamental fact. Abusers are not like you and me. They do not look at other people as we do, nor do they view themselves in ways that we would call normal. They are not like the common drunk, or the thief, or adulterer. Yes, the abuser can be one or all of these as well, but the object of his craving—power and control and the incredible sense that he is fully entitled to it—fashions him into an especially dangerous and damaging creature.

We should also make a brief note at this point about the term "victim." As Barbara Roberts explains it in her great book, *Not Under Bondage: Biblical Divorce for Abuse, Adultery, and Desertion:*

> Some people may feel uncomfortable with the word victim. They are wary of encouraging a 'victim mentality' – an attitude of chronically blaming others, of stagnating in self-pity and grudging resentment. This book does not use the term 'victim' to promote such attitudes…rather, it calls a spade a spade because people who have been maltreated will do well to recognize the stark, precise methods by which they have been abused if they are to become astute and vigorous survivors.[3]

If the reader would prefer to substitute "survivor" for "victim," he may do so. However, Roberts' point should be carefully noted. Survivors of abuse must come to understand that they have been victimized, and that victimization has had profound effects upon them.

Everyone Will Want to Know, Right?

Have you ever learned something new that was really, really exciting for you?

3 Barbara Roberts, *Not Under Bondage: Biblical Divorce for Abuse, Adultery & Desertion* (Victoria: Maschil Press, 2008), 18.

It was exciting because it enabled you to understand so many things that were a mystery before. Such knowledge is liberating; it is a breakthrough. What was the first thing you wanted to do? Go and tell everyone. "The world is round, not flat!" But what happened? People didn't want to know; they were happy with the status quo. This was my experience. They were comfortable with their flat world.

When I began to share the insights I was learning with others in the church, a few listened, but many did not. Some were even angry that I would speak of such things. I found that the majority of Christians, and perhaps even in particular pastors, do not want to hear about this topic, let alone consider that it is highly probable that at least one abuser sits in their own pews every Sunday, wearing the mask of one of the most godly men anyone has ever known. This subject is a threat to our comfort zone. It rocks our world, and we don't' want to be rocked.

But I was compelled to persevere. The result was that I preached a twenty one-part sermon series on abuse. I entitled it *The Psychology of Sin* because I had learned that abuse is such a perfect illustration of the thinking pattern of sin, of sin's deceptive tactics and cruel weapons. That sermon series was (and is) posted on Sermon Audio at sermonaudio.com/crc and has resulted in numbers of Christian abuse victims contacting me. Not only did they express their sincere gratitude and joy that someone in the church is finally listening to them, but they have helped me greatly in coming to understand both the abuser and his victim to a much deeper degree.

During the sermon series several reactions were evident in our congregation. There were many who were thankful and receptive to what they were learning. A few who had been abuse victims earlier in their lives were very, very excited. And there were others who really wished that this series would soon end, that surely there simply could not be a great need to learn about such unpleasant things. As time passes, I hope that the latter group will come to a better comprehension of how common abuse is and that in fact no one is untouched by it. Other people – visitors on occasion – rejected the idea that a topic like this was properly dealt with from the pulpit. I recall in particular one lady from a conservative, Bible-believing church who literally laughed and exclaimed "he actually preached a sermon series on that!" As we will learn later in this book, it is this very kind of ignorance coupled with arrogance that is largely responsible for the plight of abuse victims in the evangelical church. Until we are personally touched by abuse in our own family relations, we just do not want to awaken to its existence.

What a Victim Can Expect in a Typical Evangelical Church

There is one final matter of introduction necessary before we move on to a study of the mentality, nature and tactics of abuse. It is one of the chief reasons for *A Cry for Justice.* Let me list for you the typical cycle of what an abuse victim can expect when she reports the abuse to her church (pastor, elders), seeking help and justice. Those knowledgeable about abuse know that there is a "cycle of abuse" that describes the abuser's pattern. What I am suggesting here is that there is a "cycle of abuse" effected at the hands of the victim's church. Here is the drama that I have had victim after victim recount to me:

1. Victim reports abuse to her pastor.
2. Pastor does not believe her claims, or at least believes they are greatly exaggerated. After all, he "knows" her husband to be one of the finest Christian men he knows, a pillar of the church.
3. Pastor minimizes the severity of the abuse. His goal is often, frankly, damage control (to himself and to his church).
4. Pastor indirectly (or not so indirectly!) implies that the victim needs to do better in her role as wife and mother and as a Christian. He concludes that all such scenarios are a "50/50" blame sharing.
5. Pastor sends the victim home, back to the abuser, after praying with her and entrusting the problem to the Lord.
6. Pastor believes he has done his job.
7. Victim returns, reporting that nothing has changed. She has tried harder and prayed, but the abuse has continued.
8. Pastor decides to do some counseling. He says "I will have a little talk with your husband" or "I am sure that all three of us can sit down and work this all out." Either of these routes only results in further and more intense abuse of the victim. This counseling can go on for years! (One victim reported that it dragged on for nine years in her case).
9. As time passes, the victim becomes the guilty party in the eyes of the pastor and others. She is the one causing the commotion. She is pressured by the pastor and others in the church to stop rebelling, to submit to her husband, and stop causing division in the church.
10. After more time passes, the victim separates from or divorces the abuser. The church has refused to believe her, has persistently covered up the abuse, has

failed to obey the law and report the abuse to the police; and has refused to exercise church discipline against the abuser. Ironically, warnings of impending church discipline are often directed against the victim!

11. The final terrible injustice is that the victim is the one who must leave the church, while the abuser remains a member in good standing, having successfully duped the pastor and church into believing that his victim was the real problem. One abuse victim (a man in this case) told me that he finally came to the awakening that "I know exactly what my church is going to do about my abuser: Nothing!" He left while she remained a member in good standing, the daughter of a leading pastor in the denomination.

I observed a similar pattern firsthand following an incident of abuse. Over time, concern for the victim diminishes and the primary focus turns to the plight of the perpetrator, the consequences he must suffer now, and how we can help him. At the same time, the victim is increasingly pushed aside and even accused of causing all of this unpleasantness. In Christian settings, the victim is accused of being unforgiving and of refusing to obey Scripture's commands to reconcile. The victim becomes a leper and often is ultimately driven outside the camp. It is horrible injustice. What must Christ think of it?

Does this all sound just too grim to be true? If so, then you need to keep reading *A Cry for Justice*! We all need to, because we live in a culture which is increasingly denying the reality of what was once called sin. We can confidently expect the species of man which we are calling abuser to continue to increase. People with no conscience are quite at home in a society that through the rejection of God's truth, has "tranquilized its spiritual central nervous system," as Cornelius Plantinga put it.[4] Will you hear their victims' cry? Many are sitting right in the pews of our own churches, and their tormentors sit beside them.

Job 19:7 *Behold, I cry out, 'Violence!' but I am not answered; I call for help, but there is no justice.*

4 Cornelius Plantinga, *Not the Way It's Supposed to Be: A Breviary of Sin* (Grand Rapids: Wm. B. Eerdmans Publishing Company, 2010), Location 144 Kindle edition.

CHAPTER 1

A Look Behind the Mask

***Matthew* 23:28** *So you also outwardly appear righteous to others, but within you are full of hypocrisy and lawlessness.*

Pastor Andrews was continuing with his sermon series on marriage. And the congregation was listening, mostly with smiles and knowing, nodding of heads as the Pastor struck upon some of the common difficulties in the home. It was quite a pleasant atmosphere; Pastor Andrews was so good at giving light and humorous illustrations. "You know, Sunday mornings can be really difficult for families, can't they? All the rushing about to get ready and get to church on time. How many of you had some conflicts this morning at home or in the car on your way to church?" Husbands and wives looked at one another, smiled and chuckled. It was all so foolish, but funny too. Yes, they were just human beings with all of their glitches. The Lord knows all about it.

But in this congregation of some one hundred and fifty people, there were two women who didn't seem to be sharing in the joviality. Oh, there were some strained smiles from them at this point or that but for Rose Jansen and Elizabeth Bettson these words hit a little too close to home. Both were distraught and distracted. Rose avoided looking at her husband and fiddled with the pages in her Bible. Elizabeth rolled up the corner of her jacket, unrolled it, then rolled it again as she stared straight ahead. Unlike them, their husbands "got it". Laughing and nodding their heads, they seemed to appreciate the Pastor's point. "It really is funny, you know, isn't it?," Pastor Andrews continued, "how we argue on Sunday mornings and then put on a happy face and come into the church building all smiles." Preparing to wrap up, he smiled at his congregation. "But God understands. Jesus knows we are all fallible and frail. That is why He went to the cross. May He bless each one of you this week. Let's pray." Heads were bowed as the prayer was offered. The amens were said, the closing hymn was sung and people stood to leave. On the way out a happy atmosphere prevailed: hands were shaken, the Lord was praised repeatedly—and the people headed home to their roasts or to meet friends at the Sizzler.

For Rose and Elizabeth it was different. As they left with their husbands, they did so to return to a world that no one in the church knew about or could even imagine. They left with husbands whom everyone thought they knew, but didn't. Welcome to Rose and Elizabeth's world. It is the world of abuse. It is a foreign land to most of us but one that exists right within the church, often in the pew just next to us.

One of the primary reasons for writing *A Cry for Justice* is that I have seen firsthand how abuse is minimized in our churches and our culture. It is minimized largely because the abuser enjoys secrecy in his abuse. Because we are "in the dark" and are ignorant of the abuser's tactics, we are prone to take the word of the abuser himself (while not even realizing that we are doing so) as he tells us how harmless he is. The wolf, in other words, tells us how saintly he is and explains that it was the sheep's fault that it was eaten.[5] And we believe him.

Characteristically, abuse lurks behind a disguise; we fail to see it because we are conditioned to fail to see it. If we are going to get to the truth about abuse, we must humble ourselves and admit that, just possibly, we still have much to learn. In order to do so we must be willing to put aside our own preconceived notions and seek God's help as we delve into Scriptures that we have never truly understood or fully believed. Sin is deceptive, deceitful, and quite capable of putting on a convincing disguise as light and righteousness. Wolves really can

5 With sad frequency even professional counselors and therapists fall for the abuser's explanations of why he abuses. Many fail to even contact the victim and instead rely entirely upon the abuser for an explanation of what happened and why. One reason we are so susceptible to the abuser's tactic of "playing the victim" is that we have been taught that the abuser is the product of his past, having been victimized himself in some manner. Therefore, we accept the abuser's tales and blaming strategies. This is a serious error that only enables the abuser and further victimizes his victims.

dress up like sheep. God's Word exposes these facades, but we must put away our superficial, rushed, and simplistic study of the Bible if we are going to hear what He is telling us.

> ***1 Samuel 16:7*** *But the LORD said to Samuel, "Do not look on his appearance or on the height of his stature, because I have rejected him. For the LORD sees not as man sees: man looks on the outward appearance, but the LORD looks on the heart."*

The purpose of this book is to pull off the mask that abuse wears and look into the world in which the victim lives so that we can be equipped to help the victim and expose the abuser. As we explore this world, we will learn that the abuser feels entitled to possess power and control over his victim. He is convinced that he deserves it because in his world, he is superior and therefore his victims exist to serve him. He is, in his mind, justified in using an array of tactics to enforce this power. His conscience is largely or even totally non-functional.

Janelle and John – A Case Study

Janelle and John are members in good standing of their local church. They met one another 15 years ago in their adult Sunday School class. Janelle was soon swept away by John's charm and style. He listened to her as if she were the only person on earth, something she had never experienced before. John treated her like a queen. He sent frequent cards and gifts and declared his intense need for her in his life. Frankly, Janelle liked being needed.[6]

John cloaked his declarations in Christian words he knew Janelle would accept. He would often assure her, for example, that "God has wonderfully blessed me by bringing you into my life." Janelle was certain that John was a godly man and would make a fine Christian husband. Of course, he had some rough edges, but who didn't? She was certain she would be able to help him

---

6 In our story of John and Janelle, we cannot take the time to go back and examine their earlier lives, upbringing, etc. This subject is however a very important one, particularly in respect to the victim. Victims/survivors of abuse should read and learn about how certain things in their childhood and youth may have shaped them into a more vulnerable target for the abuser. However, abusers are often so skilled at manipulation and deception that any person can be drawn in by them and become their victim, even people who come from a very healthy family background.

improve. He would welcome her help, of that she had no doubt. Isn't that what a wife is for, after all?

Over the course of their few months of courtship, Janelle occasionally experienced tweaks of uneasiness with John's words or actions. He would often become distracted when she tried to talk to him about her interests, but would demand her full attention as he discussed his interests with her. He demanded to pick all of their activities when they were together, even telling her that she didn't really want to see that movie when she requested that they see a certain one. She assumed that these things were the result of him being tired from work and the demands of his life. He started to display some anger when she talked with others, but he assured her it was because he loved her so much that he couldn't stand to share her. By the time of their wedding, he had begun to criticize her choices in clothing, which soon led to him insisting upon selecting her entire wardrobe. After their marriage, it became evident that any article of clothing she had selected would be the object of John's criticism.

The John whom Janelle married disappeared for good within three months following the wedding. The man she now lived with seemed like a stranger. She increasingly felt afraid of him, not unlike a puppy who feels the boot of an evil master for the first time. John, with rising frequency:

- Expected her life to revolve around him.
- Reminded her daily of his superiority to her, and to women in general.
- Indulged his wants while her needs went unmet.
- Expressed his great displeasure whenever he detected happiness in her.
- Mocked the things she loved.
- Told her she was not being submissive enough or obedient enough.
- Kept all of the money under his control. Janelle was therefore required to obtain his permission before she purchased anything.

Understand however that at this point Janelle still did not understand what was really happening. That is to say, the thought did not actually occur to her that what she was experiencing was abuse. She really didn't know anything about the subject. Oh, she had heard of domestic violence and wife-beaters and so on, but in her mind those were things that happened to other people. John had never actually struck her with his fist or anything like that. So, if we had been able to ask Janelle if her husband abused her or if there was domestic violence happening in her home, she would have honestly answered "Oh, no! Nothing like that." Janelle felt like that abused puppy, but she did not know she was being abused. She desperately needed someone to come alongside of her and say, "You are the victim of a very common evil which we call abuse. This is how John thinks about you and about himself. These are the tactics a man like John uses to keep you under his power and control, and if it continues, it will do serious harm to both you and your future children." As we will see in more detail later, the very action of naming the attitudes and actions of the abuser can be immensely liberating for a victim.

Not only did Janelle not yet understand what was happening to her, she did something that all of us do when we are first targeted by an abusive person. She put on the clothing of false guilt and self-blame. Reinforced by John's blaming, Janelle thought she was the problem. Janelle was a Christian. She believed the Bible really is God's Word. And she had been taught from that Bible that God expected wives to respect and honor their husbands and that if she would do this, John would love her (We are not saying this is actually what the Bible teaches. This is simply how Janelle had been taught and it was her understanding of marriage). Janelle spent more and more of her time thinking about how she could be a better wife, and examining herself to find any real or imagined flaws. Never did she think the fault lay with John. She concluded that, if she could just be a good enough wife, John would stop being mad at her. Janelle found a number of Christian books that claimed to teach women how to be a most excellent wife; some that even claimed she had absolutely no right to her own thoughts or opinions and that her husband was to be obeyed no matter what he demanded—all in the name of Scripture. Those books said absolutely nothing, however, about what was really happening to Janelle: abuse.

Sadly, Janelle's understanding of theology was colored by all of this. She extended her "if I do better, then he will love me and not be so mad at me" thinking to her concept of God. A theology that was reinforced by her church.

This Thing We Call "Abuse"

It is vital for all of us to very clearly understand that abuse is a category of sin that is quite unique. While abuse is sin and therefore shares all of the fundamental qualities of sin, like hatred of God and rebellion against the Law of God, abuse is in many ways a very unique manifestation of sin. Its lust for and entitlement to power, control, and domination over others proceeds from a skewed mindset that looks at oneself and others quite differently than non-abusive people do. It is not some general sin that we all commit, at least as we are defining it in this book. Abuse is a sin that in many ways is the very best illustration of the very mind of sin, because it is sin let loose from the restraints of conscience. Abuse, we might say, is sin in a "purer," more cunning and more destructive form.

Yes, we all have hurt others by sinning against them. But we are not all abusers. Abusers share certain kinds of thoughts and tactics that *define who they are.* As two hunters in Montana found out this year, you may shoot and wound a black bear and track him down successfully, but if you shoot and wound a grizzly bear, he may well track YOU down and kill you. Wisdom dictates that we deal with grizzly bears and black bears differently. In the same way, we must deal with abusers differently than we deal with sinners in general. Part of the thesis of this book is that we in evangelical Christianity have been treating grizzlies like black bears, and victims have been getting eaten up as a result. Jan Silvious writes in her book *Fool-Proofing Your Life*:

> ... the skills that work for most relationships just won't work in this one. You must master an alternative set of relational skills if you want to survive the relationship. It is relational suicide to assume you can win over a fool by argument, sweet reasonableness, or any other common wisdom. Even Christian virtues like gentleness, patience, and turning the other cheek may only get you into a deeper mess.[7]

As Silvious points out so well, the Book of Proverbs and other Scriptures make this fact abundantly clear. The fool, as the Lord calls him in Proverbs, is a particular kind of sinner. Paul instructs Timothy (2 Timothy 2:24-26) to patiently correct his opponents, so that God might mercifully grant them repentance. But then, he gives what at first reading seems to be conflicting instruction:

> ***2 Timothy 4:14-15*** *Alexander the coppersmith did me great harm; the Lord will repay him according to his deeds. Beware of him yourself, for he strongly opposed our message.*

7 Jan Silvious, *Fool-Proofing Your Life: How to Deal Effectively With the Impossible People in Your Life* (Random House Digital, 2011), 10.

There is no conflict. Alexander the coppersmith was not the same category of sinner as the typical opponent of the gospel. He must be handled with great caution because he is capable of doing great harm to Timothy, as he had done to Paul.

We repeat then, abuse is a unique and particularly serious category of sin. Thinking that all sin is the same, that all sinners are the same and that the methods of counseling them are all the same, leads to doing what the majority of Christians, pastors and churches are doing today: enabling the abuser and further victimizing his victims. The Bible does not present all sinners and all types of sin as belonging to one uniform class.

The Apostate as an Example

To help us better understand what we mean when we say that abuse is a unique kind of sin, let's consider Hebrews 6:4-8 and think about how it may well apply to the classic abuser.

> ***Hebrews 6:4-8*** *For it is impossible, in the case of those who have once been enlightened, who have tasted the heavenly gift, and have shared in the Holy Spirit, (5) and have tasted the goodness of the word of God and the powers of the age to come, (6) and then have fallen away, to restore them again to repentance, since they are crucifying once again the Son of God to their own harm and holding him up to contempt. (7) For land that has drunk the rain that often falls on it, and produces a crop useful to those for whose sake it is cultivated, receives a blessing from God. (8) But if it bears thorns and thistles, it is worthless and near to being cursed, and its end is to be burned.*

I know a lady who is focused upon her abuser's salvation. She is wise and has separated from him. But she believes Christ is going to save him. May her faith increase, and if she believes this is her calling, then blessings on her. But I would not advise this in general to abuse victims. In fact, most survivors will tell you that their eyes began to be opened to what was happening to them when they came to realize that their abuser was never going to change.

When a person decides to embrace Christianity as a mask to hide behind, they commit a sin that is very odious to the Lord. Consider what the writer of Hebrews is saying in the verses above. There are people, he says, who have been in Christ's visible, local church, people who have eaten the bread and who have drunk the cup of Christ in the ordinance of communion; people in whom the Holy Spirit has worked so that they really know the gospel is true and that the promises of Christ are sure, but who then reject it all. Christians differ a bit on their interpretation of this passage, especially in respect to whether it is possible to be a Christian and then fall away from Christ and end in hell. For myself, I do not think this is possible. Christ does not lose one of His sheep whom the Father has given Him (John 10; 17). But that aside, at least we know that there are people who are in the very midst of Christ's body, His church, who reject what they know to be true.

Now, notice what the Scripture says of them. It is impossible to renew them again to repentance. They are "Esaus."[8] Their end is to be burned. This is why I have often told our people here at Christ Reformation Church that the pews of the Christian church are the most dangerous place in the world if anyone who sits in them, listening to Christ's truth week after week, rejects it.

Yet this is precisely what the "Christian" abuser does! Right? Many Christians who have survived abuse give first hand accounts (and I have heard many of them) of how their abuser played the game in church. How he deceived and even continues to deceive the church. What kind of mind does it take to do that and still be able to sleep at night? It is the mind of the sociopath – the mind with no conscience. In some way, this kind of person is especially wicked in God's sight because he holds up Christ to open shame, just as the mockers did when Christ was crucified. They mock him by their evil facade.

My point is this – the abuser who is pretending to be a Christian is *the* hardest and most treacherous of all abusers. We are told by the Apostle John that there is a category of person for whom he does not require us to pray –

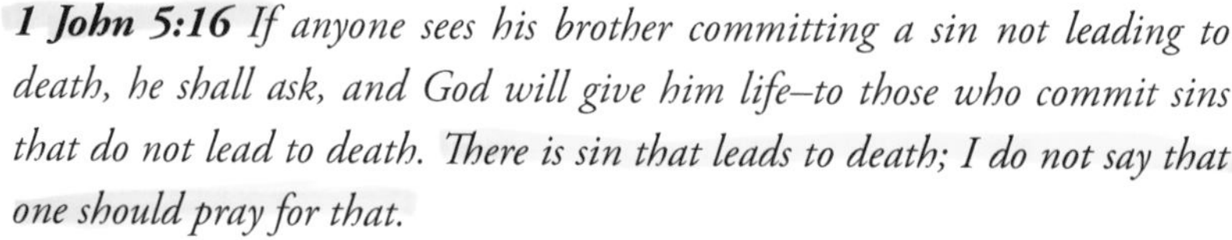

> ***1 John 5:16*** *If anyone sees his brother committing a sin not leading to death, he shall ask, and God will give him life–to those who commit sins that do not lead to death. There is sin that leads to death; I do not say that one should pray for that.*

8 Hebrews 12:16-17 "that no one is sexually immoral or unholy like Esau, who sold his birthright for a single meal. (17) For you know that afterward, when he desired to inherit the blessing, he was rejected, for he found no chance to repent, though he sought it with tears."

I think John is speaking of the unpardonable sin, and I think that this sin is committed just as Hebrews 6 describes it. It is committed by a person who, by the convicting work of the Holy Spirit, has come to *know* the truth of Christ and even, you might say, have been given a glimpse and taste of the glories of heaven, but who, like Esau, despises it. And I submit that the abuser who plays the Christian is exactly such a person.

Now, someone might point to Saul of Tarsus and how he horribly abused Christians, yet God gloriously saved him, and we know him as the Apostle Paul. I would simply answer, "Saul of Tarsus believed and repented when Christ appeared to him." This is something the abuser does not do. Paul even said of himself:

> ***1 Timothy 1:12-13*** *I thank him who has given me strength, Christ Jesus our Lord, because he judged me faithful, appointing me to his service,* (13) *though formerly I was a blasphemer, persecutor, and insolent opponent.*

Paul said he "*acted ignorantly* in unbelief." This is not true of the Hebrews 6 man.

I do not presume to know the final word on all of these things. I do not have a list of people whom theologians call "reprobate." But I do think that I am correct in saying that victims of abuse need to at least have the information that their abuser, if he is playing Christian, is one of the hardest, most evil kinds of sinners. The likelihood that he is ever going to repent and come to faith in Christ is very slim. He has already had truckloads of God's mercy shown to him through hearing the gospel, and probably through the faithful testimony of his wife. Yet he rejects it all. She needs to know these things in order to make an informed decision about her future. Listen to these wise words of a longtime abuse survivor:

> My ex-husband is a reprobate. He abused me for years in the first part of our marriage, in which neither he nor I were professing Christians. I left the marriage and got child custody sorted after a big court battle. I started attending church and became a professing and practicing Christian. I gave him a Bible and witnessed to him many times when our child was being handed over for visitation. He wasn't interested in Christianity until we'd been separated for four years; then he accepted my invitation to come to an evening church service where he responded to the altar call and said the sinner's prayer.

For the next few months he showed quite marked signs of true conversion: he loved to read the Bible and go to church and be with other believers, he heard the Lord speaking to him in his dreams with instructions to read scripture like Matthew 18:3: "I tell you the truth, unless you change and become like little children, you will never enter the kingdom of heaven."

Although at first I hadn't wanted reconciliation, I began to want it after seeing these changes in him. So we reconciled, renewed our vows, and within twelve months he had shed all his Christian coloring and was assaulting me again. Mind you, in those twelve months he'd been very verbally and psychologically abusive, but I didn't *see* it till he assaulted me again. Once during those twelve months he'd even heard God telling him very sternly and specifically "Go and tell your wife you are sorry for treating her the way you've been treating her, and ask her how she would like to be treated." I nearly fell off my chair when came home from work that day and told me what God had said to him. But his brief flash of reform didn't even last twenty four hours.

He remains unrepentant to this day. How do I know? Because he's lied; he's never apologized to me, and he has told others a pack of lies to cover up the real reasons why I separated from him, divorced him, and eventually pulled the plug on all visitation.

Surely this man is exactly what the writer of Hebrews is talking about: "those who have once been enlightened, who have tasted the heavenly gift, and have shared in the Holy Spirit, and have tasted the goodness of the word of God and the powers of the age to come, and then have fallen away…". Like the seed sown on shallow ground: it springs up with great promise but it comes to nothing.

What He Looks Like

What, then, does abuse look like? Listen to these very typical actions of an abuser. Each of them is real. They have been provided to me by abuse victims and are common tactics widely used by abusers. They are not aberrations nor are they unusual. Understand that this list is by no means comprehensive, and we will enlarge upon it later.

- Activities must be according to his desire. Whatever the abuser is presently doing or whatever he wants to do is always to be the most important thing for everyone to do (Even if the activity is entirely illogical).
- He abuses the things his victim owns. Even when he is supposedly out of control in anger, he always seems to only damage her things, never his own.
- He criticizes the physical appearance and attributes of his victim, often using very vulgar language to do so.[9]
- He works to isolate his victim from others. He will, for example, sabotage developing relationships or launch a verbal tirade if he learns she wants to go visit a friend.
- He robs the victim of sleep in various ways. He may demand sex in the middle of the night, awakening her. Or he may keep the children up very late. Sleeping people do not focus their attention on him, and he must have their attention. More than one victim reports that their abuser would often start verbally attacking her while she was asleep, waking her and continuing his tirade.
- He keeps his victim in poverty. This can be a result of his own selfish actions that result in overspending, spending on non-essentials, bankruptcy, inability to keep a job (not due to lack of skills, but lack of effort) or simply not wanting to work.
- He will loudly and angrily complain about any purchases she makes, even if those things are very reasonable needs.
- He, in contrast, can buy whatever he wants, even if there are not sufficient finances for it. Most of what he buys are non-necessities (junk food, lottery tickets, cable TV, etc.).
- He prohibits his victim from obtaining medical care claiming "we just don't have the money."

9 I reluctantly refrain from directly quoting the graphic language victims are subjected to by their abusers. I say, reluctantly because while we have the option of not quoting it here, victims do not enjoy that luxury. It seems to me that if we are to truly bear the burdens of the victim, we must not be naïve to anything that they have to suffer. But, as this book is primarily directed toward Christians, I will refrain so as to not put an unnecessary obstacle before anyone in reading this book. Please realize however that the "saintly" Christian man in your church, who is, in fact, an abuser, uses horrible, ugly, wicked and profane language to further assault his victim.

- The television and remote control are his domain. Sometimes he even hides the remote when he is gone.
- He often insists that his victim get back to the housework and waiting on him or giving him sex, even though she has just come home from the hospital after giving birth, or if she has been ill.
- He often acts in a cruel manner toward the victim's pets. Many abusers are also animal abusers.
- He frequently alienates the children from the victim in many different ways so that the children think the victim is the source of the family problems.

You will notice that to this point, this list of abusive behaviors does not include physical assault. Here is a very, very important fact that many people are absolutely in the dark about, including pastors, Christian counselors, and individual Christians. The abuser carries out his warfare against his victim in a wide variety of ways. Some of these tactics are physical in nature (slapping, grabbing the throat, punching, kicking, using or threatening the use of guns and knives, sexual assaults, etc.). But many weapons of the abuser (in fact probably most of them) are non-physical in nature. And these non-physical tools often have more damaging results on the victim than physical abuse.[10]

As we will see, being a victim of abuse and living with an abuser is very much like being a prisoner of war in a concentration camp. Just as both physical and psychological methods are used by the enemy in those settings, so it is in the experience of the abuse victim. When we deal with a victim therefore, we should not be surprised if she exhibits some forms of mental instability. This certainly does not mean that she is a crazy person, but simply that she is suffering from some of the typical mental effects of longstanding abuse. If we fail to understand this, we will be ripe for the deceptions of the abuser in trying to convince us that the victim is the problem because, "as you can see, she's crazy!"

All abusers do not utilize all of the weapons and tactics of abuse that we are going to discuss in this book. But the ones we will present are common. Do

10 Effects of abuse upon victims include doubts about one's sanity, a sense of worthlessness, false guilt, hopelessness, isolation, fear, a loss of one's personhood and individuality, substance abuse, anger…and many others that we will discuss later in this book. Despite all of these symptoms, the abuser can still announce that he has "never laid a hand on her."

not make the mistake of concluding that a person cannot be the victim of abuse unless she is being physically abused. In particular, let me caution pastors in this regard. It is easy to underestimate the damage that non-physical abuse can have on its victim and, by doing so, fail to have a biblical understanding of how to relate to the victim or what options are biblically open to them. For instance, I have heard and read several well-known and respected pastors make statements that indicate they do not believe a woman can leave her husband unless she is in actual physical danger of physical assault. Over and over and over again, abuse victims are being told that God requires them to stay with their abuser (usually the abuser is called her husband and the term abuser is not used at all). She is told that this is God's will for her as a wife.

Often this advice is coupled with further counsel that if she will persevere in her marriage no matter the cost to her, God will win her husband over. She is told that submitting to the abuser is God's will for her sanctification and that she is a missionary in her home. The reaction of the church at large, coupled with her fear of her abuser, often leads the abused wife to endure a life filled with fear and pain and to do so in solitary silence. Little wonder then that abusers enjoy such immunity from exposure and prosecution in the church, and in fact so frequently select the church as an arena for their evil.

I respect Pastor John MacArthur, Jr. I have read and benefited from many of his books and lectures. But like all of us, Pastor MacArthur is not above the need for correction. It is my opinion that his teachings in respect to abuse contain some common and particularly serious errors shared by many Christian pastors. For example, on his *Grace to You* website, Pastor MacArthur is asked, "What do you recommend in your counseling where there is child molestation or wife beating or extreme alcoholism or some of those situations that become not just marginal but really intolerable for a wife we'll say?" Here are the primary points of his answer:[11]

1. 1 Corinthians 7:10 says that if she divorces, she is to remain unmarried, or be reconciled to her husband.
2. Common sense tells us that the victim can take steps, such as separation, to defend herself and her children.
3. Even if the abusive man has committed incest with or beaten the children, there are no biblical grounds for divorce.

11 John MacArthur, "Dialogue on Divorce," Grace to You Website (1979), www.gty.org/resources/sermons/2221/Dialogue-on-Divorce

4. God will give the victim grace to endure this suffering. But she has no biblical grounds for divorce and it is God's will for her to "hang in there and that will make her a great prayer warrior."
5. MacArthur does not deal with the rest of the 1 Corinthians 7 passage in which Paul does address the right of a deserted or abused spouse to be free from bondage.[12]

At the same website you will find similar teaching by MacArthur entitled "How should a wife respond to a physically abusive husband?"[13] MacArthur limits abuse to physical abuse and counsels abuse victims to remain "... if you are not truly in any physical danger, but are merely a weary wife who is fed up with a cantankerous or disagreeable husband." Apparently, in MacArthur's thinking, there are only two categories: 1) physical abuse, or 2) having a disagreeable husband, the latter not really qualifying as abuse. MacArthur holds to this position at least as late as 2009, as is evidenced in his book *The Divorce Dilemma: God's Last Word on Lasting Commitment.*[14] Anyone who has studied the nature of abuse in any detail will immediately recognize that MacArthur's repeated use of the adjective "physical" in describing abuse betrays the fact that he is dangerously uninformed on the subject.

He is not the only well-known pastor who holds such a belief.[15] Repeatedly I find pastors giving this kind of very bad and even dangerous counsel to abuse victims when in fact they have never studied the nature of abuse in any depth at all nor have they had any real training in the field. No one is qualified to declare what God's instruction is on any subject until they first understand the nature of that subject! God's Word has much to say about the mentality and nature of abuse, but most people simply do not take the time and effort to hear these things before they rush to counsel someone about a topic they do not understand.

---

12 Roberts, *Not Under Bondage.* Roberts presents a biblical argument that abuse is desertion and therefore a valid ground for divorce.

13 John MacArthur, "Answering Key Questions About the Family," Grace to You Website, http://www.gty.org/resources/positions/p00/answering-the-key-questions-about-the-family. .

14 John MacArthur, *The Divorce Dilemma: God's Last Word on Lasting Commitment* (Greenville: Day One Publications, 2009), 86-87.

15 R.C. Sproul, *Now That's a Good Question* (Carol Stream: Tyndale House Publishers, 1996), 404-405. Sproul has helped me immensely in coming to an understanding of biblical doctrine, but nevertheless he is another who forbids divorce for abuse, even though he acknowledges that abuse is a violation of the marriage vows.

Christians really have no excuse for being so naïve about evil. The Bible which we hold to be the very Word of God, instructs us that man, outside of Christ, is a slave to sin. He thinks and lives in agreement with the world (Ephesians 2) and with the god of this world, Satan. Sin is his master. Therefore, every word he speaks, every action he takes, every thought he thinks, is impelled by that master, sin. This means that the abuser, whose addiction is for power and control over his victim, is always functioning according to that craving. He is always on task. The "good" works he does are designed to gain power and control. The zealous service he renders to his church, his apparent love for people, is always online with his "firing solution" to hit his target: power and control. We should know this. But we do not. Or perhaps we know it, but choose not to believe it.

Listen to the following observations from a Christian woman who has experienced decades of abuse and who has often sought help from fellow Christians, pastors and counselors, but in the end received primarily unbiblical and foolish advice:

> In Proverbs we are warned of the dangers of dealing with fools. These are people who have no righteousness in them and who desire none; people who consistently refuse instruction and who flaunt their lack of desire for it; people who ruin others by their failures to prepare, to try, or to do rightly. They are people who are cruel, full of anger, no good, and who use abusive tongues as daggers. Several of the Psalms express David's sufferings at the hands of evil men who wished him harm and he prayed quite strongly against them, that God would deal with them, stop them, punish them, and even kill them! In the New Testament, we are told of several men who caused harm both in the church and to the Apostle Paul himself by their conscienceless cruelty and actions.

The point is, Scripture addresses abuse but we miss it. The failure lies in us: we don't know Scripture or human nature so we can't see what God means or doesn't mean. Why? The probable reasons certainly include that we think too highly of man and too lowly of God. As a result, we fail to interpret these Scriptures as they demand to be interpreted. Then we pull out "God hates divorce" and "women obey" and say that's the end-all; and all the while, we fail to note all of the other things God hates:

> ***Proverbs 6: 18*** *a heart that devises wicked plans, feet that make haste to run to evil…*

Proverbs 6: 17 *...and hands that shed innocent blood...*

Psalms 11: 5 *The Lord tests the righteous, but his soul hates the wicked and the one who loves violence.*

Proverbs 17:15 *He who justifies the wicked and he who condemns the righteous are both alike an abomination to the Lord.*

Countless Christians, pastors, elders and theologians repeatedly make these errors when dealing with this subject of abuse. In *A Cry for Justice*, it will be only after we have thoroughly examined the tactics and mentality of the abuser, the effects of abuse upon victims and their children, and thereby come to an accurate understanding of the nature of abuse itself, that we will turn to the Scriptures and bring them to bear upon the question of abuse as a righteous cause for divorce.

A Matter of Degree

Not all abusers practice their craft to the same degree or in the same manner. In actual practice, one abuser will carry out the tactics and actions of abuse upon his victim to a greater or lesser degree than another. This is essential for us to understand or we might approach the subject with the very wrong and damaging idea that we are only talking about the more "extreme" cases, while anything less than the extreme does not qualify a person as an abuser. Bancroft agrees with this, noting that abusers can be found along a spectrum of abusive tactics. Some of them, he says, will use many more abusive weapons than others. In addition, their mentality will be found on a gradient, anywhere from partial to complete justification or entitlement.[16] What is always shared is that the abuser is identified by his sense of entitlement/superiority, demand for power and control, and his confidence that he is justified in the abusive tactics he uses to obtain these things that are rightfully his.

It is to a more detailed examination of these tactics that we now turn our attention. Let's continue to strip away the disguise of the abuser by becoming wise to his schemes and thereby cease to be used by him in his torment of the victim.

Ephesians 5:7-8 *Therefore do not become partners with them; for at one time you were darkness, but now you are light in the Lord. Walk as children of light.*

---

16 Lundy Bancroft, *Why Does He Do That? Inside the Minds of Angry and Controlling Men* (New York: Berkley Books, 2002), Location 165, Kindle Edition.

CHAPTER 2

To See the Abuser, We Must Admit He Exists

2 Corinthians 11:13-15 *For such men are false apostles, deceitful workmen, disguising themselves as apostles of Christ. And no wonder, for even Satan disguises himself as an angel of light. So it is no surprise if his servants, also, disguise themselves as servants of righteousness. Their end will correspond to their deeds.*

"How the English-speaking peoples, through their unwisdom, carelessness, and good nature, allowed the wicked to rearm." (Winston S. Churchill, *The Gathering Storm*)

In some ways, this is the most important chapter of this book. And yet, it is the most difficult to write. How do you write about something that is a ghost? How do we give substance to something that, when we reach out to touch it, disperses like fog? The power of the abuser lies in his ability to wear a disguise, to play a role, and to "step out of character" into his true abusive self at will. Like the English-speaking peoples Churchill writes about, Christians too often, in "unwisdom" and good nature, allow the wicked man to arm himself.

> The perpetrator often presents to the public as a model, mild-mannered citizen – he seems like a good husband. Yet in reality the marriage is characterized by his selfishness, manipulation and irresponsibility. He lies, minimizes and twists the truth. If the victim declares the relationship over, the abuser often wants the relationship to continue and will say so insistently and persistently. He may appear to be deeply sincere and heartbroken. He will often make a show of conversion or recommitment to Christ and/or

> counseling when his wife separates. But for all this outward display, he will downplay and minimize his responsibility for the situation and subtly make it look like his wife is at fault. [17]

When we study this evil called abuse, we are studying one of the clearest illustrations of the very nature of sin. This is one of the primary reasons that I spent 21 Sundays with my congregation preaching and teaching on this topic. It is not a mere social issue, suitable only for those liberal social-gospel churches. It is the embodiment of so much of what the Bible reveals to us about sin. And one of the things God's Word warns us about in respect to sin is that it is deceptive in its very essence. If you want to meet sin, meet the abuser. Learn about him – how he thinks, what his tactics are, and what he does to his victims. Like a vampire who comes to his victim in secret, he sucks the life out of them when no one sees and no one knows.

You have watched those old vampire movies, right? Bela Lugosi stuff. What happens when sunlight shines on a vampire? He sizzles, and if it shines long enough, he turns to dust. That is what we want to do with the evil of abuse – shine light on it so that its power is no more. This light is the light of Christ's truth. Therefore, the pulpits of our churches are most appropriate places to expose this darkness. Jesus Himself apparently thought so:

> ***Luke 20:45-47*** *And in the hearing of all the people he said to his disciples, "Beware of the scribes, who like to walk around in long robes, and love greetings in the marketplaces and the best seats in the synagogues and the places of honor at feasts, who devour widows' houses and for a pretense make long prayers. They will receive the greater condemnation."*

Jesus exposed abusers. So must we. Jesus gives us no other choice.

What Does a Wolf in Sheep's Clothing Look Like?

That sounds like a stupid question, right? The answer surely is quite obvious. But the reality is that most Christians think that a wolf dressed in sheep's attire is pretty easy to spot. Like the wolf in Red Riding Hood, we fancy that we will be able to say, "Oh grandmother! "What big ears you have!" We are foolish.

---

17 Roberts, *Not Under Bondage*, 25.

A wolf in sheep's clothing looks exactly like a sheep. The Apostle Paul was warning the church at Ephesus of this when told the elders –

> ***Acts 20:29-31*** *I know that after my departure fierce wolves will come in among you, not sparing the flock; and from among your own selves will arise men speaking twisted things, to draw away the disciples after them. Therefore be alert, remembering that for three years I did not cease night or day to admonish everyone with tears.*

What does one of these fierce wolves look like? Just like one of us. If we believed that, we would be on the alert and Paul exhorts us to be. But, alas, we don't. So we slumber on guard duty. The abuser comes along. He's got the same uniform we do. We check his ID. Everything looks in order, so we allow him entrance. "Such a nice chap," we remark.

> Here is a real example of a behavior trait of an abusive man in the church. My ex always, always, always, plans his good works to coincide with holidays so he can get good mileage out of it. For instance, this Christmas, he helped feed the homeless at his church. Now, when he goes back to work or talks with extended family, friends, when they ask about his Christmas, he can tell them how he fed the homeless. Think of all the people he can say that to. It is great PR for him, makes him look like a really good guy. It goes a long way for his facade. (Abuse Victim)[18]

I highly recommend the story of Bradly Morris Cunningham found in Ann Rule's book *Dead By Sunset.*[19] As I read it, I found myself wishing I had a time machine so that I could go back to 1986 and rescue his wife, whom he viciously beat to death. Cunningham's ability to mesmerize women and men with his charm was amazing, and he devastated countless lives. After escaping prosecution for eight years due to a lack of evidence, he was finally convicted of murder and now serves a life term in the Oregon State Penitentiary. The book includes the professional testimony of Dr. Ron Turco, a forensic psychiatrist, who described Cunningham's true self and false self. As he explained the psychopathic personality to the jury at Cunningham's trial, Dr. Turco said that the outward

---

18 Waneta Dawn, *Behind the Hedge* (Xulon Press: 2007). Dawn tells a very similar story.

19 Ann Rule, *Dead by Sunset* (New York: Simon & Schuster, 1995), 415-420.

appearances of a person are only minimally helpful. The exterior represents the false self. To truly know someone, we must observe them in their unguarded, more intimate moments. Cunningham's true self, hidden beneath his false self, was the person who, without conscience, killed his wife. This true self is who Cunningham really is.

I shudder to think what Cunningham could have done in the church if he had chosen a facade of Christianity.

Let's Face it – We've Been Duped

> Roy could charm the birds out of the trees if he tried hard enough. Everyone who meets him, loves him. Until they get used by him, that is; however, even then, they sometimes come back for more and more, not realizing they are being used. There are times I still have to stop and remind myself who and what I am dealing with. It's quite often one of the children will come and say "Daddy's doing better," until they realize they have said that so many times before. (Abuse victim)

We have already examined many of the various tactics abusers use to further their disguise: lying, crazy-making, blaming, and accusing. In fact, we could accurately say that virtually every tactic the abuser uses against his victim furthers his deceptive façade. All he does operates under a canopy of deception. This is how he gets away with it. More than that, playing his chosen role is what gives power to his evil.

> ***John 8:44*** *You are of your father the devil, and your will is to do your father's desires. He was a murderer from the beginning, and has nothing to do with the truth, because there is no truth in him. When he lies, he speaks out of his own character, for he is a liar and the father of lies.*

One of the most important things we must do in fighting abuse is to come to terms with the fact we have been deceived by abusive people. That things are not always as they appear to be. That human beings are capable of incredible degrees of deception. That there are some people whose minds and consciences simply do not operate as ours do, making them capable of living a lie and yet being able to sleep quite well at night, untroubled by any remorse.

You have read, as we all have, the regular news accounts of murders committed by men who are husbands and fathers. A wife is shot. Even children are killed.

Whole families wiped out, and normally the murderer kills himself as well. What do most all of these stories include? Interviews with the neighbors and co-workers. And what do they say? What do WE say? "I just can't understand it. He was always such a nice man and they seemed like a fine family." This should tell us at some point that abusive people are masters at playing their chosen role. As these terrible kinds of events reveal, this man was not a nice man at all. And something was horribly wrong all along in that family. We didn't see it. Perhaps we didn't want to see it.

Jonathan Edwards preached a sermon entitled "True Grace Distinguished From the Experience of Devils," based on James 2:19 ("the devils also believe, and tremble"). Listen to Edwards warn us about how far the disguise of a wicked man can go (I have paraphrased some of the more archaic phrases for clarity) -

> Therefore it is clear, from this Scripture, that no degree of head knowledge of religion is any certain sign of true Christianity. Whatever clear notions a man may have of the attributes of God, the doctrine of the Trinity, the nature of the two covenants, the functions of the persons of the Trinity, and the part which each person has in the affair of man's redemption; if he can preach ever so excellently of Christ, and the way of salvation, and the admirable ways of God's wisdom, and the harmony of the various attributes of God in all of God's works; if such a man can talk clearly and exactly about the justification of a sinner, and of the nature of conversion, and the operations of the Spirit of God in applying the redemption of Christ to us.... if he has more knowledge of this sort than hundreds of true Christians; yet even all of this is no certain evidence of any degree of saving grace in his heart.[20]

Such a person still only does what Satan can do. Satan knows that God exists. Satan knows the Bible is true. Satan is quite an excellent theologian. Yet he remains the essence of evil. Christians, of all people, should know this. Yet somehow, we have not really believed that such deception is possible. We have not been careful to read and believe God's Word to us. And so the abuser continues to hide and deceive and victimize. Like Hitler, he builds his death machine while we slumber.

---

20 Jonathan Edwards, *The Works of Jonathan Edwards, Vol. 1* (Amazon Digital Services: 2009), Location 2980, Kindle Edition.

Serial child molesters are addicted. Just like a heroin addict, they are addicted. Except the object of their craving is not a syringe full of heroin, but children. Specifically, they are addicts to sex with children. They think about it. They plan it. One might say that every move they make is motivated by their addiction. What they need is access to children. That is what it is all about for them. As Carla Van Dam notes, "Their behavior is ruled by their desire to have sex with children."[21] Now, what if a person is addicted to power and control? Simply translated, this will mean that every move they make is going to be motivated by their addiction. They will charm, they will play the victim, they will exert great energy, they will select their vehicle, they will buy a house, they will select a career – all to further their addiction to power and control. And, in the case of the abuser, he will often even profess Christ and put on the appearance of a wonderful Christian, ready to give of himself to Christ's work as no one else in the entire church. In all of these ways and more, the abuser works to gain allies to his side, against the victim.

> Tom rode in like a knight in shining armor. He had all the right Christian clichés ready to lay on me and my pastor and my parents. It was very seductive, this idea of marrying someone who loved and adored me, who really wanted to take care of me. Stupid, naïve girl that I was. (Elizabeth, abuse victim)

Secrets

It is evident that in the realm of deception there will necessarily be *secrets*, and so it is in the world of abuse. Truth does not deceive. Truth is like light. It operates in the daylight. Sin hides in darkness. Sin has secrets.

Now, we realize that there are good secrets. The surprise birthday party or that Christmas present hidden in the closet. In World War II, Corrie Ten Boom kept a secret hiding place where she protected Jewish people from the Nazis. Scripture commends the Hebrew midwives for not being entirely open with Pharaoh (Exodus 1). Good secrets do good. And in most cases, good secrets are temporary. Good secrets are designed to be revealed one day.

---

21 Carla Van Dam, *The Socially Skilled Child Molester: Differentiating the Guilty from the Falsely Accused* (New York: Routledge, 2006), 1.

So, what is a bad secret? It is something that is accompanied by a *threat*, and which is never to be told, else the threat will be carried out. The blackmailer has a secret and makes threats. And in light of what we have been learning about abuse, we should not be surprised to learn that the world of abuse is a world of bad secrets.

How many people in your circle of acquaintances are keeping the abuser's deceptions secret, and doing so out of fear? How many people sitting in the pews of your church next Sunday are going to come there hiding the secret of her abuser's true nature? A secret enforced by threats. He will take the children away from her. He will beat her or kill her. So she doesn't speak. She doesn't tell.

Children are also damaged greatly by the world of the abuser's secrecy. They are sworn to silence about what daddy did to mommy last night and their oath of silence is enforced with a threat. To keep abuse secret, children often must tell lies. That bruise on their arm must be explained. Or that swelling over mom's eye. Or why mother looks like she has been crying. Secrets are also kept because exposure threatens to bring great shame upon the children, or because of their fear of being abandoned by their parents or parent. Keeping bad secrets is always associated with fear, and living in habitual fear is not a healthy place to live.

Probably no type of abuse is wrapped in a greater degree of secrecy than sexual abuse. This is an ugly, terrible world and yet it is one that many, many women and children endure as a way of life. Typically, unless a sexual abuser in the home is exposed while the children are still young, decades go by before the now adult children realize what has happened to them. Abusers make threats to children they sexually violate in order to keep "the secret." Fear, intense feelings of shame, false guilt and more, all work to greatly damage these victims.[22] Many domestic violence abusers also sexually abuse the children in the home.

In many ways, we all aid the abuser in keeping his secrets. Recently, I read an article in a newspaper which reported that a husband and wife had both been arrested and charged with horrendous acts of sexual abuse of their little children. The article was very candid and described some of the sodomizing crimes the parents committed. Then I read the comments posted online in response to the article. Several readers were highly offended that the newspaper would be so graphic in its

22 Steven R. Tracy, *Mending the Soul* (Grand Rapids: Zondervan, 2008), Location 941, Kindle Edition.

report. "Why make us think about such things?" "What good can come of giving all these details?" This is intentional naivety. It is a luxury that those little children do not have. I would not be surprised if some of these objectors were Christians.[23] We must stop covering up for abusers just because our ears are too "delicate" to hear what he is up to. The foul, stinking words he uses. The twisted, perverted sexual abuse he inflicts. His threats. His guns. His fists. We need to drag it all right out into the aisle of our churches, or better yet, up onto the front platform, where everyone can see it. After all, in God's sight *the whole stinking, foul mess is there each Sunday that we allow the abuser to be there among us.*

Feelings and Intuition as Abuse Detectors

Because of the covert, deceptive nature of abuse, it is often very difficult or even impossible to easily point to some objective, observable fact that identifies someone as an abusive person. At least this is so early on in a relationship with such an individual. However, we all have something in us we sometimes call a feeling or intuition. And it turns out that whatever this trait is, it serves us better than we realize. The problem is we have been taught to discount it.

How many times have you said or heard someone say, "Jake seems like a very nice guy, but I just have never felt at ease around him"? Or, "I don't know, I don't want to be judgmental. But there is something about his eyes that unsettles me." Have you ever felt the hairs on your neck "stand up" or been stabbed with that pang of fear in your gut, but you can't point to any specific reason for it?

Gavin de Becker, in his excellent book *The Gift of Fear* (De Becker 1997), encourages his readers to give more heed to these things. He argues that these feelings are really not so baseless after all, but result from our mind very rapidly and almost subconsciously processing certain perceptions that are out of the ordinary. That man standing on the corner ahead of us. The new guy at church who makes you uncomfortable.

Recently, I was trying out a new one-man pontoon boat on the river near our home. It is a rural area and relatively safe, it would seem. But as I rowed the

23 The Bible itself reports upon our sins very graphically. Perhaps these critics would take issue with God Himself and accuse Him of being too graphic in the Scriptures? Do they give the Bible an "R" rating?

boat back to the shore, I saw a man, perhaps twenty four years old, standing by himself off to the side of my landing point. He had a shaved head, was holding a cell phone, and was quite friendly. He asked me how the fishing was and said that he had just seen "a nice one, about 15 pounds" roll in the water just above me. He then wished me good luck and a good day.

I never turned my back on him. Why? It sounds so paranoid, right? Shouldn't a Christian go right over to such a person and share Christ with them? Ask them if they need a ride somewhere? No! And I didn't do any of those things, because I had a feeling about this guy. Did he really see a fish roll? Maybe. But the chances were good that he was merely trying to suck me into whatever plot he might have for getting something from me. That something may have been as little as a handout, but it could have been something far more serious.

Mark this down carefully and don't forget it: the most evil people in the world typically seem, at the first, to be the nicest, most charismatic, most caring people we have ever met. I suspect that we could have met Saddam Hussein or Adolph Hitler, had dinner with them, and come away saying, "you know, he's actually a great guy. He must be really misunderstood." Martha Stout is not sure that the devil exists (I, of course, am quite certain that he does), but she believes that if Satan is real, he would surely try to make us feel sorry for him.[24]

If someone is too good to be true, they probably are.

Young women should never discount their intuition about a man. Young men should listen more carefully to their feelings regarding a woman. It is a very sad state of affairs to hear an abuse victim recount the feelings and warnings of their intuition which they disregarded early on in the relationship with their abuser.

Thinking Outside Our Box

Romans 3:13-18 *"Their throat is an open grave; they use their tongues to deceive. The venom of asps is under their lips. Their mouth is full of curses and bitterness. Their feet are swift to shed blood; in their paths are ruin and misery, and the way of peace they have not known. There is no fear of God before their eyes."*

---

24 Martha Stout, *The Sociopath Next Door* (New York: Broadway Press, 2005), 109.

"I have learned to really pay attention to exaggerated behavior in people. That is something my ex-husband does. I personally believe it is because he does not really feel most emotions, he is just acting them out, and it comes out exaggerated." (Abuse Victim)

All human beings, including ourselves, enter this world as sinners, under God's righteous condemnation, rebels against Christ and against the Law of God. All human beings are sinners. But not all sinners are the same. The category of sinner that we are calling *abusers*, are different than good old Clyde down at the plant where we work. You know, pagan, worldly Clyde with his foul mouth and party-on ways. But Clyde has a conscience that is functional. For all of his sins, Clyde still thinks much like you and me in certain fundamental ways.

Lawrence is different. Raised in a fundamental, very conservative home with a father who was a busy, well-respected pastor, Lawrence has become one of the pillars of the church in which he and his wife are very active. In fact, they are unusually active. When you first meet him, Lawrence is really impressive and you feel as if you are in the presence of an eminent, sold-out-for-Christ Christian.

As time goes along, Lawrence showers you with praise. Your gifts, he says, deserve to be used in a more effective way. He and his wife could really use you in some of their ministries. You feel flattered. This is exciting. More time passes, and as it does, you find that Lawrence has another side. An aspect of his personality that is, well, cold and mean. You find that you don't feel safe and comfortable around him. That somehow if you say the wrong thing or if you don't measure up to his expectation, you will be punished. Lawrence has a way of remembering your past mistakes (those times when you really let him down) and of reminding you of them.

Lawrence is not a Christian, although he is regarded as one of the finest saints in his church and even in his community. Lawrence is an abuser. Lawrence can drive his dagger into his victims in any number of ways, and then go home and sleep very comfortably. Lawrence has no conscience. Lawrence will never admit fault.

We desperately need to come to understand that the Lawrences of this world do not think in the same box that we do. They operate in a world largely or entirely devoid of a functional conscience. Without the hindrance of this God-given inner prosecutor/defender, the abuser is free to see himself as justified in whatever is necessary to ensure his power and control to which he is entitled. While we say "Oh, I don't think I could ever do that," we must also come to the point of being able to say, "But the abusive man can do such things with no remorse at all." There are such people. Many of them, in fact. They,

- Lack shame.
- Have no empathy.
- Experience little or no real anxiety.
- Display false repentance very convincingly.
- Lie, even in the face of plain facts that controvert their lie.
- Use what appears to be real emotion or feeling, but in fact is just an act designed to manipulate.

Christians should know these things. Christ has told us all about such people who claim they love God:

> ***1 John 4:20*** *If anyone says, "I love God," and hates his brother, he is a liar; for he who does not love his brother whom he has seen cannot love God whom he has not seen.*

As George Simon puts it in his important book *Character Disturbance:*

> I have concluded the main reason these predators are so successful in manipulating others: It lies not so much in their highly effective knowledge and use of manipulation tactics, but rather in the reluctance of normal 'neurotic' individuals to make harsh judgments about others, or to trust their gut instincts about the kind of person they are probably dealing with....On top of it all, they're also often blinded by the notion promoted by traditional psychology theories over the years that everyone is basically good (and most especially, just like them underneath their wall of 'defenses').[25]

Martha Stout warns that most of us are far too influenced by outward appearance.[26] The abusive person's very currency of deception lies in such things as a charming personality, handsome physical appearance, unusual holiness in religion, above-average intelligence and eloquent words. So we play right into his system and buy it. Here is a description of a terribly abusive man named Saul:

---

25 George K.Simon Jr., *Character Disturbance: The Phenomenon of Our Day* (Little Rock: Parkhurst Brothers, 2011), Location 1184, Kindle Edition.

26 Stout, 93.

> ***1Samuel 9:2*** *And he had a son whose name was Saul, a handsome young man. There was not a man among the people of Israel more handsome than he. From his shoulders upward he was taller than any of the people.*

The Israelites got just what they deserved – a king like all the other nations around them. But for all of Saul's outward handsomeness, Israel made a really bad deal. Saul was an abusive, manipulative, self-serving man.

Robert Hare notes that normal people have great difficulty believing that anyone could possibly do something that *they* could not even think of doing, let alone do it and not be bothered in conscience.[27] But we must believe it. There is, you might say, more than one operating system among human beings. Abuser's minds speak a different language than those of normal people. We will examine this language in chapters five and six as we try to understand the mentality of abuse. Exactly what is he thinking, anyway?

Elizabeth describes what she eventually learned after surviving a very abusive marriage:

> We view people through our own filters, especially at first. We all tend to evaluate the actions and words of others based on how it would be for us if we were speaking them. So if we hear someone saying the right Christian things, someone who appears to be respectable, we believe them (or at least we give them the benefit of the doubt). So if we are fairly moral and truthful people, *we expect that others are and most people aren't really looking for any warning signs.*
>
> I'm weird, because after being in counseling for a couple of years, and everything I've been through with my ex, I felt like I came wide awake, especially when it comes to other people. My radar is up, all the time. Not looking to find something wrong so much as looking not to be fooled. Knowing where to set boundaries with certain people
>
> Where we are failing, is that we are failing to believe it when people show us who they are. People show you who they are. You need to believe them, when they show you who they are, the first time. They gossip. They grumble. They're overheard undermining a pastor or teacher. They put down their

---

27 Robert Hare, *Without Conscience: The Disturbing World of the Psychopaths Among Us* (New York: The Guilford Press, 1999), Location 2406, Kindle Edition.

wife or kids. They lie about something they don't need to lie about. They say things that don't sound plausible.

And we don't believe them even when they show us who they are.

John and Janelle: inside the mind of an abusive man

Twisted. That's what it is. And mean. She thought she could do me in by fooling me, by trying to act like she was trying to please me, but she was wrong. It's just so twisted. I try and I try to make her see the light. To make her know that there is a right way, one acceptable way, of doing things and if she does like I tell her, she'll be okay. We'll be okay. But she never listens. Like last night when I told her that she isn't going to go to that women's Bible study at church. She didn't like it. She's a real rebel that way. But those women are no good for her and I won't have it.

I think she likes pulling my chains. Or maybe she likes messing with my mind, trying to take me down, trying to make me look small--small to her, small to my children, small in front of everyone. Well, it's not going to happen. I won't be made to look small. I am in charge and I know what I'm doing. She thinks she can handle things? Thinks she can tell me what to do? Fat chance. I'm the Boss and she answers to me. That's what God Himself says and she should know it by now. So that settles it. Besides, she's just a woman. A twisted stupid woman who uses tears to try to control me.

But it isn't going to work. I won't fall for it. I know what she's up to, trying to make me think she wants to please me. She's using me. She's been using me all along. Women are like that and you've got to watch them all the time or they will have you running around while they give the orders. And it's mean, too. Somebody's got to teach her a lesson and since God says I'm her Boss and she has to obey me. I'm gonna straighten her out good. It's for her own benefit. A man has to do what he has to do, even if it is unpleasant sometimes.

CHAPTER 3

How Abusers Deceive Us

"We cannot understand that which has not been given a name."[28]

Jack was a church board member in the most happening church in town. A well-respected professional, husband, father of three fine girls, Jack was surely the model of what a Christian man should be. And yet here he was: *drunk* in front of hundreds of community members that Saturday evening as he arrived at the Christmas cantata. Jack was holding his three month old daughter as he worked his way to his seat. He stumbled. A man in the crowd shouted, "Hey, watch that guy! He's drunk and he's going to fall and hurt that baby!" And Jack was drunk. Somehow, Jack made it to the middle row and sat down, only two seats away from three of his church's board members. Strangely, it seemed that Jack was doing this in front of them intentionally.

The next day at church, Jack said nothing of the incident. No one else said anything either. And if someone had asked Jack about his actions, he would have not only denied it – he would have quickly had them believing that what they thought they had seen was an invention of their imagination. Nothing was ever said about the matter again. Jack had successfully altered reality and history became what he wanted it to be. When actions and words (or, in this case, non-words) deny one another, the truth is obscured, and even completely forgotten.

28 Ann Pike, *Danger Has a Face* (Denver: Outskirts Press, 2011), Location 16, Kindle Edition.

Identifying and naming the abuser's tactics is very important. Giving a name to something identifies and exposes it. You feel a sense of relief, for example, when your doctor tells you, "Well, here is what your problem is. We call it strep throat." Now you know. There it is and you can take steps to deal with it. So it is with the tactics of the abuser. This is incredibly freeing for victims to hear: "This is what he has been doing to you. It is called ________, and this is the reason he is doing it. We've seen this many times before. You aren't the only one to suffer from it and we can help you deal with it."

In this chapter and the next, we are going to identify and define some of the typical weapons of the abusive man. We have grouped them into three categories, though the boundaries of these classifications often overlap and thus are somewhat artificial. Nevertheless, the classifications are helpful. They are: 1) tactics of deception, 2) tactics of shaming, and 3) tactics that instill fear. This chapter addresses deception, while shaming and fear are presented in chapter four. Before we proceed, let me caution you against the temptation to be incredulous and throw up a wall of denial.

Pastor, church leader, church members – these things can and do happen in our churches. Please consider this carefully as you read: do you think that surely no one in your church could possibly be speaking or acting in these ways to his family, to his wife, to her husband? Remember, not everyone who attends church is actually a Christian. Not everyone who seems to have repented and turned from their ways actually has. The wolf in sheep's clothing isn't always one who is seeking to verbally spread false doctrine; often he *lives* a false doctrine (by not living out the truth of what he claims to believe). Often he is a man (or, at times, a woman) who is bent on controlling those closest to him for his own personal gain or to bolster his own weak self-esteem, and he will use whatever means it takes to do so. To deny that this can happen, does happen, and might be happening to "good families" in your own congregation is to embrace a dangerous dream world from which you desperately need to awaken.

When I speak to church congregations and pastors on this subject, I know that I can expect a variety of predictable reactions. These include:

- Surprise/Shock – "I can't believe he's talking about such a thing here in the church. What does this have to do with us anyway? This is really quite inappropriate. We are used to sermons about David and Goliath."

- Gratitude – "Finally someone is addressing these things that have been going on in secrecy here for a long time." These people can be seen nodding their heads in agreement quite frequently during the presentation. Afterward, some of them will find their way to my proximity and as they walk by they look at me and mouth the words, "Thank you! Thank you!"
- Fear – These people usually say nothing. They sit motionless with a confused expression on their face. Some are thinking, "But this doesn't seem to fit with all that I have understood about the biblical doctrine of headship and submission and divorce." Others might be sitting right next to their tormentor, their insides churning from the emotions triggered by the topic of discussion.

And, of course, there may well be an abuser sitting right there in the audience. How will he react? I initially believed that surely such a person would be quite agitated or even angry, and this is certainly a possibility. But his response may be much different. His anger may be directed against "such men" who dare treat their wives in that way! "That woman should divorce the guy immediately!" The log in the eye sees the speck in the other person's eye. Other therapists who are experts in the field of abuse validate this. Bancroft, for instance, notes that he has seen abusive men in a therapy support group come crashing down on another abuser in the group for mistreating their victim.[29] Abusers never see themselves as abusers because part of their mentality is incredible justification for what they do. To them, abuse is something that is worse than their own methods.[30]

Your church will display the very same reactions. Think carefully about this. These reactions prove the thesis of this book: the evangelical, Bible-believing church has been rendering injustice to victims of abuse and enabling wicked, abusive people to continue in their secret reign of terror.

We turn now to those tactics the abuser uses to deceive his victim, and us.

Creating an Atmosphere of Chaos and Confusion

You hate her.

You can't stand her.

29 Bancroft, *Why Does He Do That?*, 35.

30 Ibid., 158-159.

You love her.

She has some power, some romance that draws you."[31]

One of the most common effects of the abuser's tactics is the creation of a cloud of chaos and confusion around him. Victims will tell you what it is like, though early on they can't even articulate it. This is one of the chief reasons why you can spend many hours with an abuser trying to get him to see this point or to understand that fact, and never get anywhere. You can walk away from a session like that with your head spinning. When someone asks you, "Well, what did you talk about?" your answer will probably be, "It's odd but, I really don't know!"

Abusers have many ways of promoting doubt, chaos and confusion for those who are in their world. Of course, as is true of all the abuser's tactics, the purpose of this chaos is quite calculated. Confused people are easier to manipulate. Doubt and chaos take the light off of the real culprit – the abuser – and leave everyone wondering, or even blaming the victim or themselves. In such an environment of doubt, it is very common to see family members fighting with one another while the source of the problem, the abuser, sits back and watches.

Abusers who use the promotion of chaos can be like hyper-active children, firing off in multiple directions, moving from one direction or position to another. Anyone having to deal with them on a day-to-day basis will be left reeling as they never know what the abuser's mood, attitude, actions or even beliefs will be from one day to another. For instance, employees who have the unenviable duty of working for such a person never know what the day is going to hold. They may have made plans for the next day's work, and their plans can be very orderly and logical, even obvious. But when the boss shows up, he throws them a curve by exchanging the well laid out plans with a surprise agenda that has not been planned at all. The employees are left to sort things out while the boss is seemingly oblivious to the chaos he has created. The home of such a man is in a very similar chaotic state. The chaos serves his purpose of forcing his family to keep their focus on him, wondering what he is doing, where he is, and what he is about to do. Since no one can make plans without him (he won't allow that) or act on their own (another thing he won't allow) his imposed chaos insures that he remain the center of everyone's world.

31 Wayne Wang, *Anywhere But Here*. (Twentieth Century Fox. 2002). Daughter describing Susan Sarandon's abusive mother character.

Similarly, some abusers keep the fog of chaos and confusion hovering around them by using what could be called "consistent inconsistency." For example, Bob is a man whose fellow church members say "You never can predict which side of an issue he is going to come down on. His pattern doesn't make any sense. He is so inconsistent." You might find yourself offending him if you talk about a particular movie that you saw, but shortly afterwards he will shock you with his discussion of the new beer he discovered recently. This chaos works to keep others off balance and unsure of themselves around Bob. It works toward Bob's goal of having power and control. Bob is not quite so chaotic after all. He is deliberately using a pattern of conduct that is designed to obtain and maintain control over others, by keeping them off balance.

Crazy-making[32]

Related to the atmosphere of chaos and confusion is the effect which all of this uncertainty has on the victim. Abusers frequently work to make their victims begin to doubt their own perceptions. A person who no longer fully trusts in what their senses tell them is a person who is very easy to control.

For example, many (if not most) abusers play dual roles. One minute they are the attacker and next the victim; so who are they? A man can be charming, thoughtful, giving and kind and in less than a second his voice can suddenly transform into cool, piercing, chilling coldness. Who is he? The truth is that he is a power and control-seeking man who has an unshakable belief in his own personal entitlement: everything and everyone is there for him to use and to do with as he pleases. His conscience is largely, if not entirely, non-functional.[33] But he knows he must work to prevent others from knowing all of this. And so he trades in personas. He wears masks. His victims never know when he might change the current one for an altogether different one. All of this promotes self-doubt in the victim. It contributes to making her believe she is crazy.

32 The reader should be familiar with the term "gas-lighting" as well. It is virtually synonymous with "crazy-making" and is derived from a 1944 movie in which a wicked husband attempts to drive his wife insane. One of the tactics he uses is to dim the gas lights and make her think that she is imagining it.

33 Sociopath or psychopath are the terms variously used to describe a person with no conscience. Martha Stout's excellent book, *The Sociopath Next Door* and Robert Hare's equally fine book *Without Conscience* elaborate on these terms. The reader would do well to read both of these. We will discuss the matter of lack of conscience in the abuser in a later chapter.

Abusers change reality. They deftly and very convincingly "re-write" history. This is another way they convince their victim that only the abuser's recollection of events is to be trusted. As this brainwashing continues over time, victims of abuse will find themselves *apologizing* to their abuser for incidents in which they were truly the victims, but have been convinced that "it just didn't happen that way." Abusers, in other words, are *liars.*

Gary is reminding his wife Tanya of the time she coldly rejected their children's request to read a book to them. "You are not a good mother. You only think of yourself." But this was Gary's fictional history. In fact, this incident never happened. Gary is not simply morphing Tanya's motives and words, he is creating a fantasy event. And he is doing it so convincingly, with such a sense of certainty, that although Tanya does not remember it, she is beginning to believe it. How could it *not* be true? Surely no one would just invent a story like that, right? And yet.... she doesn't remember it at all? Is she crazy?

Helen is the long-time superintendent of her church's Christian Education ministry. Pastor Jackson has been at First Church for 15 years. He has never felt at ease around Helen. It is as if she uses some kind of mental telepathy to communicate to him that behind the smile on her face lies some vicious beast which is always ready to be unleashed if her agenda is crossed. And yet, he feels guilty when he thinks such things because she is often quite nice.

Helen likes to remind Pastor Jackson of his past failures. There was that time when he was far too harsh with Sandy Davidson over the curriculum decision. And then the business of that unkind letter that he sent to Karen and Lou Jacobsen. Pastor Jackson, as Helen has told him more than once, has a problem in dealing kindly with people. The troubling thing for Pastor Jackson is that he doesn't remember being unkind. In fact, he has gone back and re-read the letter he wrote to the Jacobsens and it didn't seem harsh to him at all. Still, Helen is so confident about her version. Perhaps he *is* rather unkind and harsh? He doesn't want to be unteachable or above correction, but this is all so confusing. What really did happen? What was he really thinking?

Helen's confident recounting of these facts is, in reality, fiction. She has actually never read the letter to the Jacobsens, and Sandy Davidson was just having a "bad day" three years ago when the curriculum was discussed. Sandy doesn't even think about it anymore. Pastor Jackson is not too harsh with people and is actually a good pastor who loves his people.

Helen is an abuser who demands power and control to which she sees herself as absolutely entitled. Helen makes people crazy by working to make them doubt their own perceptions. Yet Helen, by her own promotion, is viewed by most of the people at First Church as a model Christian, a true servant of Christ. Unless Christ protects His flock, Helen, if she chose, could destroy Pastor Jackson' ministry and split the entire church. Why? Because most Christians are still children, carried about, as Paul told the Ephesians, by human cunning, craftiness, and deceitful scheming.

> ***Ephesians 4:14***, *"so that we may no longer be children, tossed to and fro by the waves and carried about by every wind of doctrine, by human cunning, by craftiness in deceitful schemes."*

The following is an account given by a victim of long years of abuse. She describes firsthand how powerful this crazy-making tactic is and how, if we are not wise, we will end up contributing to it:

> This is called "crazy making" for it does, indeed, make one feel crazy to deal with such alternate and varying realities, never quite able to come to grips with what is true and what isn't. We ought to trust our own minds, right? We ought to believe our own eyes, our own ears, our own experiences, correct? But what if we got up tomorrow and, suddenly without explanation or warning, the entire world was calling the sky orange: not orange at sunrise or sunset, but orange around the day-lit clock? And, what if, when the sun finally sunk and the "orange" disappeared they tell you the night sky was now no longer dark blue or black but was in varying shades of green? One day you might laugh off as a colossal practical joke but what if you got up the next morning, and the next and the next and the next and every single morning you were told the sky was orange and every single evening you were told the night sky was green? And, yet you see, as clearly as you ever have, that the daytime sky is blue (with the exceptions of dawn and dusk) and that the nighttime sky appears as dark blue or black. "You're crazy!" you are told, "it's orange, I tell you, orange!"
>
> And everyone else agrees. You alone disagree and, because you do, you alone are the one everyone thinks crazy. Over a period of time, these thoughts sink into your mind and you have a choice to make: will you alter your reality and believe that the daytime sky is now indeed orange and the nighttime sky

is green? Or, will you stand alone, all the while being accused of being crazy, all because you won't get on the bandwagon and agree with their new version of reality?

That is the choice abuse victims have to make day-after-day, year-after-year. We are told black is white often enough that we begin to doubt our own version of reality. We can clearly see that the daytime sky is blue but all around us are folks who insist on calling us crazy, and marking us as stupid, for not agreeing that it is orange.

The church itself contributes to this when we tell victims of abuse, "Whatever happened to you, it isn't really abuse; maybe just a misunderstanding?" or "But he's such a nice man, are you sure that's what he meant?" or "It's actually your fault, you know; if you were a better wife, these kinds of things wouldn't happen to you." We assist the father of lies when we engage in such tactics.

Playing the Victim

A visitor, upon entering the safety and solitude of a sanitarium, found himself envying the patients. He remarked that he could enjoy living in such a place. People would come and visit you and they would pity you. "And pity is a powerful thing," he thought.

Abusive people are often wickedly cunning in garnering pity for themselves. One of their favorite methods of choice for garnering this pity is what is called "playing the victim." The abuser's goal is to have people perceive him as the victim instead of the perpetrator. We shelter and join forces with *victims*, and he knows this very well. Listen to this warning from Barbara Roberts:

> Caution needs to be exercised when identifying the victim, for when a victim separates from the relationship, the abuser often portrays him/herself as the victim. This blame-shifting attracts sympathy and attention from bystanders who may misread and even believe the opposite of the true situation.[34]

If you watch the second installment in the *Lord of the Rings* movie series, you will see a classic example of an abuser playing the victim. His name is Gollum.

34 Roberts, 25.

Immediately after he attacks Sam and Frodo in an attempt to steal the ring, he is subdued by them and as he is pinned to the ground we see the expression on his face change from rage to weeping. Poor Gollum. Just look at how harshly he is being treated. He then uses this pity to turn Frodo against Sam.

Fred might strike out at his wife with very ugly and hurtful words. He might even hit her in the face with his fist. But when she confronts him, he turns from aggressor to apparent victim literally in the twinkle of an eye. How dare she speak to him in such a manner or blame him for that. Doesn't she know how hard he works everyday to put food on the table for this family? Dan might have hurt several people in the church with his tactless and unkind words, but when his sin is brought to his attention, he soon has everyone apologizing to him for misunderstanding him or for the way in which they went about confronting him.[35] He has been, after all, horribly hurt by what they have done!

After learning more about this tactic (which I should have been much wiser about long ago because the Lord has laid it out for us in Scripture), I began to employ what I had learned in dealing with people who use it. When I saw a person, for instance, very seamlessly shift from attacker to victim, I looked at them and said "You stop that." I then named what they had done—played the victim. I suspect no one had ever done this to the person before.

Morphing the Victim's Words

If you will study the interactions between Jesus and the religious leaders of the Jews, you will soon understand that *truth* was not the goal of these enemies. Jesus, who is *the* truth, exposed their wicked motives and actions. Did they listen? No. They often "morphed" what Jesus said and launched it back to Him as a weapon. Kroeger and Clark describe this tactic in their book, *No Place for Abuse*:

35 In our years of pastoral ministry here at Christ Reformation Church, myself and our elders have had occasion to deal with such men and women. We now fully expect that one of the first things we are going to hear from an abusive person is "you were not right in how you confronted me." This tactic is designed to take the spotlight off of them and their own sin and shift blame onto others. It also shifts the focus of the issue from the sin of the one confronted to a debate over how his sin was brought to his attention. Abusive people who employ this tactic enjoy a high rate of success in achieving their blame-shifting goal because pastors and Christians are not wise to what is happening. One wonders how many churches have been split or even destroyed by such people using this very device.

> Word-twisting is another technique of the abuser. Victims can be confused and overwhelmed by the adroit manner in which offenders distort what they have said and turn their own words against them.... Another technique is to declare that what was said was only in jest: "What's the matter – can't you take a joke?" In this way the victim becomes even more bewildered as to what is really happening. She doubts her own sanity.[36]

The abusive person is truly adroit in his ability to alter the victim's words, morphing his/her statements into an altered reality that makes her look like a fool, or crazy, or even abusive herself! This is one chief reason that dealing with an abuser requires real wisdom. Very different methods must be used as illustrated by the following example:

Pastor Johnson was once again dealing with George. George was his own church within the church. He fancied himself (although he would never overtly say so) to be the real overseer of the flock. George always seemed to know better than anyone. You could count on him to take an opposite position on most any issue. That was about the only consistent trait in him, and his inconsistencies kept everyone unsure and wondering each time some issue arose in the church.

"George," Pastor Johnson said with the typical uneasiness that swept over him when he had to interact with this man, "George, the elders and myself have decided to turn down your offer to teach the men's discipleship class. We don't feel that your abilities lie in that area." George's reaction was predictable. "So, you guys are saying that I cannot serve the Lord as He has called me to! Are you going to force me to choose between obeying God or man?"

We can pretty accurately predict where this conversation is going to go. Pastor Johnson will try to correct George's twisting of his words, then George will twist those words... and so it goes. George does not need explanations or debate. George needs limits and boundaries. And if George does not humble himself, listen and repent of his ongoing sin, George needs to be disciplined by the church for the protection of the flock of Christ. But when was the last time you saw a church do this? Is it not far more common to see George simply left

36 Catherine Clark Kroeger and Nancy Nason-Clark, *No Place for Abuse* (Downers Grove, Illinois: InterVarsity Press, 2001), 79.

to do as he pleases with the rationale that we are called by Christ to love one another? And yet, God tells us plainly what to do:

> ***Titus 3:10-11*** *As for a person who stirs up division, after warning him once and then twice, have nothing more to do with him, knowing that such a person is warped and sinful; he is self-condemned.*

Gathering Allies

One of the most formidable weapons of the abuser is his ability to use tactics such as playing the victim, lying, and manipulation to win the people in the victim's relational sphere over to his side. He alienates them against her by convincing her relatives, children, friends, and co-workers that *she* is the real culprit in their marriage difficulties. In one recent case, after his victim left him, the abuser began a telephone campaign, contacting friends and relatives to convince them that his wife was mentally unstable. He even phoned the local women's resource centers to "warn" them that she was suicidal.

The abuser's lust for power and control drives his actions, including his choice of the people with whom he associates. He will not condone anyone who resists his ally recruiting techniques, quickly moving on to the more malleable. He will often be successful convincing his own new wife or girlfriend, who then becomes one of his greatest and most devious allies. Even the police, prosecutors, social service workers, counselors and therapists, judges, and case workers can all become his pawns to be used against the victim. The local church is often very fertile ground for the abuser to grow his team of allies.

The church has been failing victims. Pastors and church members, so susceptible to deception because of their ignorance of the abuser's motives, tactics and mentality, become the evil man's ally. Christ's church becomes a place of suffering for the victim. Those who are commissioned by Christ to seek justice end up on the villain's side.

Jared married Judy twelve years ago. They are both members of Christ Evangelical Church and are well thought of. Jared is particularly active, serving on two committees, one of which he chairs.

But today, Jared is in jail.

Last night, Judy called the police after Jared twisted her arm. He has done this before, but this time he went too far and broke it. When the police arrived, Jared was standing in the yard to greet them, cool and calm. One officer stayed with him while the other went inside. Judy was sitting on the couch dressed only in her underwear, holding her arm. The officer gave her a blanket to cover up and asked her what had happened. Jared, she said, often gets violent and this time had actually broken her arm. She felt it break and heard it snap. Judy was sobbing.

While waiting for the ambulance, the officer with her looked out the front window. Jared was still speaking calmly with his partner, even laughing about some joke. The officer turned back to Judy and asked her again what had happened. "I told you. He broke my arm."

Still battling with feelings of disbelief ("This guy is so calm and even jovial") the officer went back outside and confronted Jared. "She's crazy! I have no idea how her arm was injured. I came home from work, ate dinner, and later she came running out of the hallway yelling that her arm was broken." But the fresh scratch marks on Jared's forearms told a different story. The officers arrested Jared and transported him to jail. If it hadn't been for those scratches....?[37]

Jared was trying, almost successfully, to win the police as his allies. He was telling jokes about the fickleness of women, plying on men's common struggles with the female sex, and so on. Before this all sorts itself out, Jared will win numbers of his fellow church members over to his side. Judy will be chastised for causing him so much trouble. Why couldn't she just let bygones be bygones? What of the children? Now their daddy is in jail! And if Judy leaves Jared (which she should!), Jared will become a victim to be pitied by the rest of the church as Christians quote "God hates divorce," a phrase, incidentally, that is not really in the Bible. Check Malachi 2:16 in the ESV for confirmation.

Abusers gain allies to their Axis of Evil and use them to wage war against the victim. Let me encourage the reader to see a real parallel here to what is being called "mobbing" in more and more literature about emotional abuse in the workplace. It is also very closely related to the topic of bullying. In mobbing, an individual in the workplace becomes the target of a bully, who then uses various abusive tactics (many of which are the same as we have been discussing here),

37 This account is drawn from my own personal experience. I was the second officer who went inside the house.

including gathering allies to himself to form a mob. The effects of mobbing on the target are devastating, just as they are in domestic abuse. Really when the domestic abuser uses the tactic of gathering allies, he is using mobbing as his method of choice. For further study on mobbing, see *Mobbing: Emotional Abuse in the American Workplace*, Civil Society Publishing: Ames, Iowa 2005, by Davenport, Schwartz, and Elliott. Just as human beings are easily caught up in the emotion of a riotous mob and join in, so it can happen to us if we are not wise to the abuser's tactic of gathering allies.

Minimizing

> ***1 Samuel 13:11-12*** *Samuel said, "What have you done?" And Saul said, "When I saw that the people were scattering from me, and that you did not come within the days appointed, and that the Philistines had mustered at Michmash, I said, 'Now the Philistines will come down against me at Gilgal, and I have not sought the favor of the LORD.' So I forced myself, and offered the burnt offering."*

Along with other tactics, King Saul (a classic abuser) was minimizing what he had done. "I didn't really want to do it, but I had to. I forced myself." As you can see, minimization is a cousin to blaming. The goal is to make the abuser's deed less serious than it really is. Red-flag identifiers of minimization are "just" and "only." Saul had only done what he had to do. "I didn't mean it," Fred told Linda. "And really, no harm was done. I was just joking. You are blowing this thing all out of proportion."

Another way the gravity of his misdeed can be lightened is for the abuser to speak in the passive rather than the active voice. The passive voice places the abuser into the role of victim or as the one being acted upon by forces beyond his control:

- We *got* into an argument and she *made* me so angry the TV *got* broken.
- *Before I knew it*, my hands were around her throat.
- I didn't mean to say that, *the words just came out.*

Just as the abuser will not accept responsibility for his evil deeds, neither will he acknowledge that they are really all that evil. When it comes to *his* crimes, he minimizes everything, but as he accuses his victim, he raises her supposed errors to the highest level of seriousness. This is especially evident when we consider the abuser's characteristic double-standard.

The Double-Standard

> ***Matthew 23:1-4****, "Then Jesus said to the crowds and to his disciples, "The scribes and the Pharisees sit on Moses' seat, so practice and observe whatever they tell you, but not what they do. For they preach, but do not practice. They tie up heavy burdens, hard to bear, and lay them on people's shoulders, but they themselves are not willing to move them with their finger."*

The abuser's mind exercises amazing illogic in maintaining a flagrant double-standard for himself and his victim. In other words, what is right for him is wrong for her. What is a small slip-up for him is a grossly stupid or even downright mean crime for her. You see this double-standard working itself out in the playing the victim tactic. Here, it is quite fine for the abuser to attack his victim with words or even physically, but when she confronts him or defends herself, suddenly he is the victim and she is completely wrong for treating him in such a terrible manner. The double-standard makes reasoned conversations with the abuser impossible and also promotes the climate of chaos and confusion he desires.

The double-standard is an attitude that is found in virtually all abusive people. Here are some examples:

1. He can spend all the money he wants for anything he wants, but she is highly restricted in these areas, and if she does buy even some small item, he punishes her.
2. He can speak angrily and abusively to her, but if she were to raise her voice to him she is totally unjustified and is being cruel.
3. He can treat the children very harshly and it is called justified discipline they deserve. If she "loses it" with the kids, she is a terrible mother.

In other words, the abuser has a log in his eye, which he ignores. It is the speck in his victim's eye that he magnifies. Such a man may, because of his laziness and refusal to follow instruction, lose his job. He will excuse himself, blaming the whole episode upon his boss who "has had it in for me because I know more than he does." Then, if he comes home and his dinner is a bit overdone, his victim's crime is a capital offense and he executes her with his words or worse.

Changing the Rules

The abuser keeps his victim guessing about what he wants, how he will react, or what time something is going to happen. He can act unpredictably and inconsistently in order to keep her more focused upon him, dependent upon him, unable to make independent plans or have her own thoughts. One victim said that whenever their family was in the car and ready to leave, her husband would do something to delay them. He would go back into the house for something he forgot and sometimes even had them all come back inside to help him look for something. To most people this would appear to be a harmless absentmindedness, but eventually she realized is was quite intentional and was a tactic to keep the entire family in suspense and looking at him. Another victim said:

> He changed the rules all of the time. Sometimes something would make him angry and other times it wouldn't. Sometimes he'd fly off the handle at the smallest thing and other times he was quite calm. I never knew who I was dealing with. One day he'd tell me we had so much in the bank and then, later that day or the next day, he'd tell me it was actually several hundred dollars less than he'd said before... with no explanation… so I never knew whether it was safe to shop or not.

The abuser's rules are often dynamic. They change. They change because he changes them. This promotes the chaos and mystery around him, keeping his victim on edge and looking at him to see what is coming next. We have all heard the saying, ignorance of the law is no defense, but if the law is changing day by day with no prior notification, who could blame a motorist for violating the traffic code? The abuser prosecutes and persecutes his victim in just such a nonsensical and unjust manner.

Intentional, Conscious "Projecting"

The abuser's accusations of his victim are often the product of a dynamic in his mind which may be similar to what psychologists call projection – attributing a person's own undesirable thoughts to another person, so that the projector believes these thoughts are actually originating in the other person rather than from within their own mind. When the abuser accuses his victim, he is projecting his mindset, his worldview, upon her, but he does it maliciously and

with conscious intentionality. Because he is out to use people, she is out to use him. If he is unfaithful in his marriage, she is an adulteress. I believe that, at least in part, this is what Jesus spoke of when He said:

> ***Matthew 7:3-5*** *Why do you see the speck that is in your brother's eye, but do not notice the log that is in your own eye? Or how can you say to your brother, 'Let me take the speck out of your eye,' when there is the log in your own eye? You hypocrite, first take the log out of your own eye, and then you will see clearly to take the speck out of your brother's eye.*

If you want to know how an abuser's mind works, listen to the accusations and blaming he levels against his victim. When he accuses a church leader, for example, of being controlling and power-seeking, his accusation betrays the fact that these very motives are active in his own mind. Here is a very typical rant by an abusive man. Simply apply what he is saying about his wife to him, and you will have a fairly accurate picture of what he has been doing to his wife:

"My wife is a real piece of work! Morally, she is a tramp. And she is a liar. She's good at it too. People believe her when she tells them what a rotten father I am, how I abuse her and the kids. She even tells people that I haven't been faithful to her – anything to run me down. I am the one who really loves the kids and watches out for them and this is what I get for it!"

Let's return to John and Janelle's house. Listen as Janelle tells us through the medium of her journal what abuse looks like and the effects it has on the victim. See how many of the tactics we have already discussed you can identify. Especially notice the lack of conscience, empathy and remorse in John. You will begin to understand that John is no mere cantankerous man who happens to be in a bad mood one evening. Look for his mentality of entitlement, power, control, and justification.

John and Janelle – A Look Into Their Relationship

4/11 - We've been married three months today. What should be a day of joy finds me crying. Tonight we went out to eat. When we came home, the front door lock was stuck and wouldn't open. It's done that before and all it takes is a bit of jiggling. I tried to tell John that, but he yelled at me to "SHUT UP!" The neighbors were in their yard and they heard him yell at me. I was so embarrassed. I was even more embarrassed when he broke the window pane so he could reach in to unlock it. I kept trying to tell him to jiggle it but he pushed me back. I begged him to stop so he started cursing at me. He shoved open the door, stepped over the glass and ordered me to clean it up.

I did what he told me to do then I went to the kitchen where he was. I started to tell him the glass was cleaned up but he interrupted me wanting to know why there wasn't a beer chilling for him. "I'm sorry. I forgot," I said. Usually at this point I'd go to him, we'd hug and make up. Not this time. When I reached for him, he stopped me with his eyes. They were cold. Hard. "You know what?" he asked. I thought it was a game, a way to make up. I tried to smile at him, hoping his eyes would smile back. They didn't. "You're really stupid, you know that? I married you because I felt sorry for you. You are so far beneath me. I did you a favor by bringing you up in this world. And this is how you repay me? By forgetting my beer? I am so sick of your... your stupidity! You can go to hell for all I care!" With that he left, went to the living room and dropped into his chair. He's been there ever since, over an hour, flipping channels and muttering to himself.

I didn't know what to do. I stayed in the kitchen, trying not to cry, praying and washing dishes and doing laundry. Finally, I thought that if I brought him a coke he would calm down and everything would be okay so a few minutes ago I did. "You think that this is going to make up for you being too stupid to chill me a beer? No way. You'd better get your act together, Jan. You're my wife and I'm your head and you have to obey me. You will obey me and that's all there is to it, is that clear? From now on, unless I tell you not to, you'd better have me a beer chilling every single night!"

His voice had been rising; by now he was yelling at me again. He looked at me, so full of anger, then he threw his glass against the wall where it shattered. "Pick that up, you cow!" I did it because I was afraid not to. I just kept telling him, "I'm sorry. I'm sorry." He ignored me. I guess I'm no good for anything. John hardly ever wants to be with me unless we are going out to eat or are going to a movie he wants to see. Otherwise I'm alone. I'm always lonely. I'm trapped. I'm married and I'm alone. There is no one to turn to, no one to talk to, no one who can understand. I am so afraid.

I looked so forward to getting married, to being married. To being a wife. Now I am a wife and it's like I'm single. Except for having to obey every little thing he says. I am miserable and I am terrified.

4/14 - John came home grumpy again today. He was mad because he'd had a hard day at work. When he saw dinner wasn't done he exploded. I tried to tell him it would only be a few minutes, that I got delayed because my mother had called. I was still on the phone with her when he came in. I tried to hold the phone with my hand so she couldn't hear but he insisted I put the phone down and come to him. He grabbed me by the shoulders and held me so tightly that I couldn't move. He told me that I had better never be late with dinner again. That, if it weren't on the table when he came home, I would go to my room and go to bed. Without supper. "Look at me! Do you understand?" By now he was nearly screaming and I was crying buckets. I nodded my head and he said, "Say 'yes, sir', is that clear?" Then he left to go buy himself some dinner.

I was so embarrassed, I knew mama had heard everything. I told her he was playing, that he plays hard and didn't mean the things he said. I tried to laugh it all away. She didn't believe me. I hung up as soon as I could, as soon as she'd stop asking me questions that I couldn't, wouldn't answer, and finished supper. Then I sat there for two hours, waiting for John. I finally put it all up, untouched.

When John came home, he was laughing and talking. He told me about running into Robbie, one of his old friends. He told me he invited him and his wife over for supper some night. He grabbed me in his arms and he kissed me. Hard. Then he went and sat down in his chair and said, "Hey, go fix me a coke." I did and then told him I was tired and I wanted to go to bed. He shook his head and said, "Baby, don't you know a woman's place is next to her man? Now come here and tell me what a handsome man I am." When I told him he was very handsome, he nodded and turned to the TV. That was over three hours ago. It's now after midnight and I sit here writing, trying to keep from dozing off. I've asked him a couple more times if I could go to bed but he said no, I have to wait for him. I hate my life.

4/16 - Today was church. John had told me he'd go with me today but when I woke him up he got mad at me and told me to let him sleep. I reminded him he'd promised. He continued to ignore me so after a minute I left to start getting ready. A few minutes later he popped his head out of our bedroom door, "Jan?" I smiled, "You decided to go with me?" "No, I told you I wasn't going and I meant it. I don't have anything in common with those people at your church. I want you to make me some breakfast. I want some bran muffins, scrambled eggs and bacon. Oh, and some coffee. I'm going to go shower." He pulled his head back in and shut the door. I opened it. "John, if I make all of that, I'll be late for church." "Really? Then you'd better hurry. Cook fast, Jan, I know you can. Now go. Shut the door on your way out. Oh, Jan? Wear the black dress and the black pumps. That way no other guy will be lusting after you." He laughed at my reaction. I was nearly 30 minutes late to church but at least John didn't get upset. It was worth it.

4/20 - A couple of days ago I asked John for a favor. I needed him to change the light in the hall. It's up really high and I can't reach it even on a chair. He first said he'd do it later but he never came I asked him again. "Would you stop suffocating me? I'm not going to let you control me this way. I'll do what I need to do when I'm ready to do it, otherwise leave me alone!" I'm walking on eggshells all of the time now. He's always telling me that I'm "suffocating" him. I'm getting afraid to ask him to do anything or go anywhere. He gets mad no matter what. I'm even afraid to tell him we need coffee or bread because he'll pitch a fit and want to know why I'm wasting so much money on food. But, if I fail to ask him for money for food, he'll pitch a fit and ask why there is "never any **** food in this house?" I can't win no matter what.

4/22 - There was a wedding shower for one of the ladies from church today. I wanted to go, to be with the other young wives, but when I told John about it, he got angry that I needed to buy a gift. I begged for the money, I wanted to go so badly. He finally gave me four dollars. This morning I went all around looking for something the bride could use, something nice. I tried some of the stores but couldn't find anything in my price range, so then I went to the local thrift store. I finally found a plaque that was cute that she can hang in her kitchen. It only cost three fifty. I was feeling rather proud of myself until I got to the shower and she began opening the other presents. Mine was pitiful compared to theirs. When John asked me tonight how it went, I told him how embarrassed I was. "I'm sorry, honey, but if you'd stayed home like a good girl, it wouldn't have happened. Maybe you learned a lesson, huh?" Then he said, "Go make supper. I'm starved."

Is life supposed to be this way?

4/23 - It's really late at night and I'm exhausted. We're watching some old movie and John is laughing hysterically every few minutes. I want to go to bed but he says I need to wait for him to prove that I'm a submissive wife. Today was horrible. We had a potluck at church so John decided to go to church with me. It was awful. He was awful. To begin with, I had to get up an hour early because he wanted me to make banana bread for breakfast, "and it has to be fresh, but I know you like taking care of your man." Then, he picked out my dress, my hairstyle, everything. After I'd gotten dressed, he insisted I change because "you don't look good enough to be with me". While I was changing, he called out and said that, if I really wanted to please him, I'd go to church without any underwear. I was humiliated that he would even suggest that. I told him, "No!" He countered by saying that if he insisted on it, I'd have to in order to be pleasing to God. Fortunately he didn't press it. I would have refused. I just don't know what he would have done.

Then he complained all the way to church: he doesn't like the singing, the preacher better not be long winded today, and so on. By the time we made it to church I was tied up in knots. John was like a child, he fidgeted all during church. He'd draw, he'd tickle me, anything at all to distract my attention from the worship service and divert it to himself. Then he started whispering: this was taking too long, he had things he needed to do after lunch, speaking of lunch it'd probably be cold and so on. Then, as the preacher was wrapping up, he said something that irritated John. He started frowning, then in a stage whisper he said to me "he's being a jerk! See, this is why I don't come with you! Stupid man!" By this time people all around us are glancing back at us. By the end of the service, I was so stressed I could barely think. During the closing song and prayer, all around us everybody else was singing, praying and praising God, and inside I was dying, broken and scared. Getting through lunch made me sick. I could barely eat knowing what was waiting me when we finally left.

Sure enough, as soon as we got in the car, he started. "Did you agree with him?" What seemed to be an innocent question was actually a trap. He already knew I agreed and that was why he was angry with me in the first place. I knew that if I said anything, anything at all, John would explode. "You do, don't you?" He blew up and fussed all the way home. He kept prodding, questioning, demanding answers. If I tried to answer, I was met with accusations and name calling (Stupid, Idiot and such); when I slid into quietness (in a vain effort to protect myself and my heart), he'd quickly pick up on that and start poking me, shoving me and demanding that I answer him. Long before we got home, I was in tears.

6/16 - I haven't written in a while because nothing ever changes. Until now. I'm pregnant. Even John is excited. I hope this changes things. I'm afraid it won't.

7/22 - Things have calmed down a little bit these last few weeks. Mostly they calmed down because John no longer wants anything to do with me. I was no longer a sexy young thing in his eyes. His use of porn has gone way up. He's even trying to insist that I look at it with him. Maybe, since I'm like this, looking at it together will help us, he says. I don't know how to handle it. I want to please him but I know this is wrong. Help me, Lord.

8/12 - We went to visit John's parents today. They were nice, we went out to eat, they gave me some things for the baby. It was a nice day overall. Until we started home. Lately, I have been worried that there might be something wrong with the baby. The doctor says he should be just fine, that the pregnancy is going well but I'm nervous. So, on the way home, I brought it up, trying to reassure myself. I was completely unprepared for John's reaction. Instead of reassuring me, he blew up. He couldn't deal with a child with a mental problem, he said. A physical one, maybe, maybe not. Mental, never. "If there is anything wrong with this baby, he won't deserve to live. And I won't love him." I cried all the way home.

8/18 - John's been nicer since the trip to his parents. I think he knows he crossed a line. Maybe he's really sorry. He's calm, kind, gentle. Maybe this baby is going to change everything. I hope....

9/26 - I went over to John tonight as he watched television and asked him to turn it off so we could do something together. He exploded like I couldn't believe. We fought for over three hours. I didn't even know why we were fighting. One thing led to another, to another, to another. Finally I couldn't take it anymore so I went to the bedroom to get away. I locked it. I slid down on the floor, trying to catch my breath. I was crying so hard, I was hyperventilating. I was scared for the baby. I was praying, asking God for help. Suddenly John started banging on the door, screaming at me to "get the **** out of there!!!" When I didn't answer, he started hitting the door. I screamed at him to stop it but he kept right on. He didn't stop until the door jam shattered. I snapped. "I HATE YOU!!! I HATE YOU!!!" was all I could say. He stopped, looked at me and said, "What's wrong with you? Relax, if you'd calm down, everything would be alright." Later he insisted that I cuddle with him so he could tell me how much he loves me.

I don't know what to think. I don't know what to feel. I don't even know who I am anymore.

Psalm 64:1-10, *"Hear my voice, O God, in my complaint; preserve my life from dread of the enemy. Hide me from the secret plots of the wicked, from the throng of evildoers, who whet their tongues like swords, who aim bitter words like arrows, shooting from ambush at the blameless, shooting at him suddenly and without fear. They hold fast to their evil purpose; they talk of laying snares secretly, thinking, "Who can see them?" They search out injustice, saying, "We have accomplished a diligent search." For the inward mind and heart of a man are deep! But God shoots his arrow at them; they are wounded suddenly. They are brought to ruin, with their own tongues turned against them; all who see them will wag their heads. Then all mankind fears; they tell what God has brought about and ponder what he has done. Let the righteous one rejoice in the LORD and take refuge in him! Let all the upright in heart exult!"*

CHAPTER 4

The Abuser's Use of Shame and Fear

"It's difficult for you when I feel something, isn't it?" (Abusive mother to her teenage daughter)

"Life with Rick has always been about walking on egg shells. I remember telling him, time and time again, that I was afraid of him. He'd tell me that he didn't want me to be afraid of him and that I was overreacting. Later he'd tell me he had this fear that he was going to one day 'snap and kill you and the children.' He told me that for years. Since we never knew what would make him angry, we had to be very, very careful what we said or did." (Abuse victim)

The weaponry of the abusive person is quite an arsenal, and we continue to examine more of it in this chapter. Specifically, we want to consider the tactics he uses to instill fear and shame into his victim. Remember that abuse is all about getting and keeping power and control. A person who lives in fear and who has been shamed into a sense of personal worthlessness is a person who is much easier to control. Abusers know this. They know it by nature. They didn't have to take a course to learn it. It is who they are.

Tactics that Produce Fear

1. Raging

We are calling this tactic *raging* because it is an *extended* episode of physical and/or verbal violence, designed to instill fear. Fear strengthens the abuser's power and control. Susan describes how her abuser would rage:

> His raging was frequent. Through the weekdays when he was at work, we had some peace, but as the end of the workday or the weekend approached the tension would rise. We walked on eggshells constantly. We never could tell what word or even a look from one of us might set him off into a home-destroying rage. This tyranny of shouting and smashing and hurting could go on all evening, or even break out in the middle of the night when we might find ourselves being jerked out of bed. Even the family pet wasn't safe. Sometimes we would sneak out of the house and find a place to hide for hours.

Abusers who rage may often do it simply because they are mean, cruel people who enjoy terrorizing their victims. Their lack of conscience, empathy and remorse permits them to conduct these kinds of rampages, then go to bed and sleep soundly.

Raging may not be as intense as smashing a fist through a wall. It may be of a lower grade and yet still be an extended session of terrorizing. Listen as a victim describes how her abusive husband conducts just such a campaign:

> On Friday, he pitched a huge fit because I fixed leftovers for dinner. He had the little ones scared, upset me, upset the older children, yelled at us all and tried to get our eldest boy to fight him. Then he spent the weekend being moody and grumpy. On Monday, just a few days after his colossal fit, he called from work and acted as if none of it had ever happened. And yet, when he came home, he sat down and started demanding to be waited on: "Where's my dinner?" or "No one brought me any dinner"; "Come over here and take off my shoes for me"; "Go get me some ice and fix me a drink"; "Go get me another drink"; and so on all evening. He yells at the little ones for being little ones: "YOU'RE MAKING TOO MUCH NOISE! GO TO YOUR ROOM!"

Raging can be kindled in a microsecond. It is actually more an act of an evil intent rather than a "loss" of temper or control. The rager can start or stop his tirade when the phone rings or there is a knock at the door, and he can choose to rage about a certain thing one day and ignore it the next.

One victim described how her abuser husband could explode in a surprise attack, and what often set these rages off was for him to see her or the children

happy. Once he walked in when two of them were laughing, really enjoying themselves in a rare moment of fun. He threw his drink across the room, smashing the glass on the wall, and launched into a hellish tirade against them. Happiness and joy in victims removes the abuser from the center of their universe, and he won't have it. A happy person is a free person, and the abuser thrives on keeping his victims enslaved. The thing is from the pit and very much in accord with the very nature of Satan (cf. Revelation 12:9-12).

2. Threats – Overt and Covert

The abuse victim lives in a climate of fear, largely created by her abuser's threats. Threats can be overt and obvious (these are sometimes the easier ones to deal with), or they can be covert and more "felt" than actually heard. How many victims are in our circle of acquaintances and in our churches who are living with these words still echoing in their minds: "If you ever try to leave me or take the children from me, I will kill you"? The abuser typically covets secrecy, so he often threatens his victim with severe punishments if they ever were to talk about their marriage or family to anyone. Or, he might not threaten at all: his explosive behavior might be such a given, that his victim just knows danger lurks behind a sigh, a frown or is being made known through the abuser's momentary silence.

As a result of posting my abuse sermon series on the internet, I have been privileged to read the stories of numbers of abuse victims. So far, all of them have said that when they still lived with their abuser, they felt like they constantly had to walk on egg shells. They all use that exact phrase. Walking on eggshells. Their children felt the same way. The abuser would communicate in various ways that if anyone did anything to displease him, hell itself would break out. This is a climate of threat. To heighten the uneasiness, the abuser quite often leaves the specifics of what really bugs him unstated. He knows their buttons, but he regularly changes his own keypad by changing the rules.

Abusive people employ their tactics, including threats, in our churches as well. We will be discussing the methods of Diotrephes in more detail in a later chapter, but if we are going to be wise in the attacks of Satan upon our churches, we need to understand that abusive people who profess to be Christians are even more deceptive and dangerous than many non-Christian abusers. For example, in respect to threats, the "Christian" abuser will most often utilize covert threats because an outward, plainly-stated threat is too revealing of his real nature.

"Pastor, if you don't deal with this situation properly, then this church is going to disintegrate." By "properly," this pillar of the church was making a covert threat. Translated it means this: "Pastor, if you don't do what I tell you to do in this situation, then I will see to it that your church is destroyed."

3. Physical Abuse

Why have we waited so long to mention physical abuse? There is a reason. We are not trying to minimize the horrid wickedness of this kind of abuse in any way. But to most people, abuse is limited to physical assault. In their thinking, non-physical tactics are not really abuse. A woman is certainly free to leave her abusive husband who regularly slaps, or better, who punches her with his fist.[38] But the woman whose abuser strikes only with words and tactics that don't directly assault her physical person, well, we are much more likely to tell her that it is the Lord's will for her to stay in that relationship and try to be a better wife.

Physical abuse can take many forms, from lesser to greater levels of intensity. (Notice very carefully! If a woman is seeing her abuser's tactics increasing from lesser to greater, she must understand that this is a sign of increasing danger for her). Here are some examples of physical abuse (we include under this heading the abuser's assaults against the victim's possessions):

- Blocking the victim's path.
- Slapping her.
- Refusing to let her see a doctor.
- Pulling her hair.
- Forcing her sexually (this can take many forms).
- Not permitting her to get enough sleep.
- Pushing her.
- Throwing things or smashing his fist on something (holes in sheet-rock are a common sign).
- Violently forcing locked doors open (in a room where she is perhaps hiding from him).
- Kicking things, including pets.

38 Our thinking on these things is remarkably foolish. One victim whose husband struck her in the face and blackened her eye went to her pastor to ask for help. The first question he asked was "Did he have his fist clenched or did he strike you with an open hand?"

- Subjecting her to danger (reckless driving for example).
- Not permitting her to buy adequate food and clothing.
- Pointing guns or threatening with knives (we include these as physical abuse; they are indeed crimes against her person.
- Ripping her clothes or robe off in front of others (such as the children).
- Choking her.
- Holding her down.
- Destroying her possessions.

As wicked and damaging as these things are, we have not yet mentioned the horrific assaults that violent, abusive men commit against their victims. Burning, shooting, stabbing, strangling, vehicular homicide, all of these things and more happen every day. How would your church react to and deal with one of these horrifying scenarios if a member of your church was arrested for such a crime?

I remember many years ago being a relatively new member of a conservative church of some four hundred people. One Sunday morning the pastor announced that a church member was being dealt with by the church board, and reminded all of us that "everyone is innocent until proven guilty." Only later, and then by word of mouth, did I learn that the man in question had been arrested for the drowning death of his small son in the bathtub. It would seem that the very typical "code of silence" had come into play in that church. Nothing else was ever said to the congregation about the situation again. We will deal with this "don't ask, don't tell" code in a subsequent chapter.

Often, people try to explain and minimize an abuser's physical assault on his victim by suggesting that he was out of control, or that he lost his temper. Perhaps, they theorize, he was drunk or the pressures at work and in his life in general just brought him to the brink so that he wasn't himself. As Bancroft notes, such men are not really out of control and in fact are still very much themselves. They can very selectively choose where they leave a mark on the victim or what objects they decide to smash. Perhaps the abuser is actually being very much true to his real character when he is supposedly beside himself?[39]

39 Bancroft, *Why Does He Do That?*, 34-36.

Tactics that Shame

Everything the abuser does to control his victim *shames* her. The tactics that are include here under this heading are particularly designed to shame, but the tactics we have already discussed work toward a shaming end as well. Shame is about a person's personhood. Shame tells the victim that she is worthless. Unworthy of being loved. Unworthy of owning nice things. Unworthy of the "privilege" of being married to the abuser. She is unworthy as a mother, and unworthy as a Christian. This shame is not the kind of shame that is related more properly to guilt. The kind of feeling we get when we do wrong and our conscience accuses us and leads us to repentance. No, the shame instilled by the abuser in his victim is what is often called *toxic* shame. It is poison to the soul and it works very nicely into the abuser's goal of maintaining power and control.

1. Punishing by Silence

The abuser's words are one of his favorite weapons, another is his withholding of words. Many abusive people torment their victims with silence. Jane decided to write to a news columnist for help, the "Ann Landers" type of column we have all read. She said,

> My husband is a very likeable man and a really good father. I love him very much and our marriage is a very good one. But there is this one thing. When we have conflict, I am always the one at fault. And after reminding me of this, my husband won't speak to me for days. He won't smile. He won't answer. He ignores my attempts to make up. Only when he decides that it is time for things to return to normal will he return to his pleasant self. All is well then, until the next time.

The truth is that Jane's husband is not a really good husband and father. He is an abusive man and his cycles of silence are really cycles of abuse.[40] It is simply that he has chosen silence as his favorite weapon rather than some other more obvious one like physical assault. When he sees that Jane is a bit too happy and enjoying her life (thus becoming a person who is less easy to control), he precipitates conflict between them, convinces her that it is her fault (he has many

40 Most books on abuse and domestic violence will discuss what is called the "cycle of abuse." You can find this, for example, in Bancroft's books. It is helpful and important for a victim to understand and recognize this cycle. It may even save her life. You can also find a discussion of this cycle in chapter 10 of this book.

techniques for doing this), and then begins to punish her. In his silence, he demeans her as much as a literal, angry tongue-lashing ever could. In fact, this silence is far crueler than spoken words in many cases. It shames her because it sends a very clear message, "You are not worth my acknowledgment that you even exist."

2. The Tongue – Abusive, Assaultive Speech

> ***Psalm 55:20-21*** *"My companion stretched out his hand against his friends; he violated his covenant. His speech was smooth as butter, yet war was in his heart; his words were softer than oil, yet they were drawn swords."*

Many tactics in the abuser's arsenal use this weapon – words. It is a favorite tool which expresses the evil man's heart (Mark 7:20-23). James says the tongue is set on fire by hell (James 3:6) and the Apostle Paul agrees:

> ***Romans 3:13-14*** *"Their throat is an open grave; they use their tongues to deceive." "The venom of asps is under their lips. Their mouth is full of curses and bitterness."*

The tongue of the abusive man is particularly hellish and shaming. He uses it to deceive, to minimize his evil, and in connection with a host of other tactics. What we want to consider specifically at this point is abusive, assaultive speech regularly and directly launched at the victim's humanity.

Just as a person who is trained in military weapons uses them to hit a designated target, abusive people "shoot" vile names at their select, designated victims. The attack is often, although not always, done in secret, is not always constant (there may be breaks of varying lengths between verbal attacks) and is designed to hurt, control or even destroy. An abusive husband, for example, might tell his wife that she is:

- A typical, stupid woman.
- A cow (very often the adjective "fat" is used before many of these foul names to increase their harm).
- A prostitute (although more typically he will use uglier words such as "whore").
- Good for nothing but sex.
- An abusive mother.
- A rotten mother.
- Sexually incompetent.

- Beneath him, not worthy of him.
- Stupid for being interested in a particular hobby or subject.
- No longer attractive to him due to being pregnant or showing physical results of past pregnancies.
- Crazy/insane.
- No fun.
- Not as smart, as educated, as wise as he.
- A terrible cook and/or homemaker – never measuring up to his mother's abilities.

It is not uncommon for the abuser to use such barbs in front of other people if that furthers his control. For example, he might attack his wife in front of his children (in an effort to undermine her position in the family, her control as mother, her personal dignity) whereas he would perhaps never do so in front of his in-laws (where the advantage may not be in his best interest). Frequently, if she complains, he tells her it was "all in fun" and that she "can't take a joke". The tactic of shame loves an audience.

Remember, the abuser's objective is to maintain power and be in control. Words that assault and tear down the person of the victim rob her of her strength to resist him. A person who starts to believe the labels assigned to them by their abuser is a person who is far easier to control.

3. Blaming

The abusive man refuses to take responsibility for his misdeeds. He will not admit fault, even when the case against him becomes obvious. You can sit down with him, lay all kinds of evidence in front of him, call witnesses, but to no avail. He will not own up. To him, the blame always rests with his victim, or circumstance, or some other source outside of himself. He is very good at manipulating others so they accept his version of "truth" even when they themselves know better.

If the abuser *does* admit to any guilt, it will not be comprehensive. Barbara Roberts describes this tactic of minimal admission very well:

> Some abusers deny all blame; but in my experience an abuser often will (if accused) admit a tiny bit of fault by telling a little of the truth, yet 'he maketh a lie' by omitting the rest of the truth. It gets the church leader off his back if he admits to a little bit of fault. The leader thinks 'I'm getting

through to this guy! He's starting to see the light and repent!' That puts the leader off track because the leader trusts in God's amazing healing power and wants to hope for the best that this abuser is reforming. It also makes things harder for the victim: she hears that the abuser has admitted a little bit of fault, so her hopes rise. And if she complains to the church leaders about how the abuser hasn't fully fessed up, she can easily be made to seem like a professional whinger (a complainer who is never satisified).[41]

Blaming is one of the chief mechanisms by which the abuser traps his victim in false guilt and shame. This is why we feel guilty when he is the one who has done wrong. He is often so masterful at this that his victim actually begins to believe that the fight last night, or the empty bank account, or the adulterous relationship he had—are all fundamentally not his fault. Instead, the victim pushed his buttons, or stressed him out so much he had to go out drinking and spend all the money or she doesn't take care of herself anymore so how could he help not being tempted by that other woman? Like Adam, he may even blame God AND his wife –

***Genesis 3:12**, "The man said, "The woman whom you gave to be with me, she gave me fruit of the tree, and I ate."*

I have seen the intensity of this blame-shifting and denial of guilt numbers of times in my years as a pastor (and in my 12 years as a police officer). While we all have been guilty of blaming and not owning up to something we have done, the intensity of this tactic in the abuser is amazing. Confronting it is like repeatedly smashing into a thick, concrete wall. Abuse victims live with this and often begin to doubt their sanity as a result.

No amount of evidence—even the hard, objective kind—will bring most abusive people to admission of guilt. You can call witnesses to come and recount how the abuser was witnessed acting against his victim. You can try to make him understand how he makes his victim feel. You can produce documents and financial records. But it will all be to no avail. Such approaches simply are not effective in dealing with an abuser and will only result in him accusing you (and his victim), lying to you, hating you more intensely, calling you crazy, and a host of other blame-shifting maneuvers. The abuser's strategies for shifting blame from himself are wickedly ingenious. He gains many allies for himself in this manner, turning them against the victim instead.

41 From personal correspondence with Barbara Roberts, 2011.

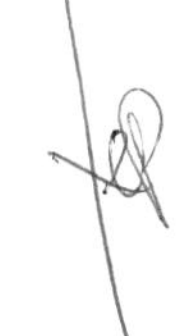

Proverbs 9:8 *"Do not reprove a scoffer, or he will hate you; reprove a wise man, and he will love you."*

Proverbs 17:10 *"A rebuke goes deeper into a man of understanding than a hundred blows into a fool."*

This does not mean that we simply leave him alone! What it does mean is that there are different kinds of strategies to use in dealing with such a person. We will explore some of them later.

4. "Shoulding"

I am indebted to Victoria, a member of the church I pastor, for this term, "shoulding." It is yet another mark and tactic of an abusive person used to shame. We all use this "sh-" word far too often, and the Christian church may be one of the chief places we "should-on" one another. Yes, it is a vulgar concept. But we do it.

Using this weapon, the abuser instructs the victim in what the victim should do, or needs to do, or should not do. "Shoulding," you see. Shoulding extends not only to what actions the abuser insists we take, it invades our very thought lives as he tells us what we should think. Bancroft has learned that abusers not only work to tell their victim what they should think, but also attempts to erode the victim's ability to trust her own senses and conclusions.[42]

Bancroft is relating this to an aspect of crazy-making (causing the victim to not trust their own perceptions). But this tactic extends even further. Because the abusive man has a mentality of superiority over his victim, he is confident that she should see things as he does and do things as he instructs. Being on the receiving end of one of these shoulding sessions (attacks) leaves the victim very unsettled, confused, and stripped of her confidence. Listen to this story from Barbara Roberts' former life with an abuser. He unleashed his "shoulding" upon her, then called in his tactic of threat as backup:

> I remember one time my husband and I were hand weeding the gravel driveway after a good downpour of rain. We each had similar weeding tools. Trouble was, I was using my tool in a slightly different way from how he was using his. The ground was moist and we were both getting the weeds out by their roots successfully, but he insisted that I should be using my tool just the way he was using his. Because I refused, ("I'm getting the weeds out all

42 Bancroft, *Why Does He Do That?*, Chapter 6.

right doing it my way!") he grabbed a big spade, ran up to our car and hit the blade of the spade into the back panel of our car, making a big dent. I was terrified. That could have been me, getting hit. I hurried inside and rang a neighbor to ask if I could borrow some flour as I'd been baking and had run out of flour. I told her I hadn't really run out of flour but could she please bring some up to my place anyway as I really needed someone to visit right now. I knew that if a visitor arrived he wouldn't continue being violent; he was never violent in public.[43]

George doesn't like the way his wife Abby is relating to his mother. One evening, he sits Abby down, telling her that they need to talk. "Abby, you are not treating my mother with love. You need to have a closer relationship with her and you should start working on it right now. I have seen you being cold to her and it's just not right. You should take a gift over to her tomorrow and tell her that you are sorry for not spending more time with her. You are a Christian, and you know that Christ would have you do this."

Of course, this is not the first shoulding conversation George has had with Abby. When George feels that Abby is getting just a bit too independent of him, George pulls out this weapon and goes to work. Abby should read her Bible more. Abby should not watch that movie, but this one. Abby should take more care in her personal appearance.

In the church, the "should-er" works to control those he perceives to be in power; the power that he craves for himself. Many times such a person will see it as his personal mission to see that the pastor or church leaders think and act as he insists that they should. So, he may –

- Tell the pastor what to preach and what not to preach.
- Tell the church board how they should or should not deal with a troubled marriage in the church.
- Critique the pastor's personal qualities, telling him how he should change.
- Announce in a public gathering of the church what specific doctrinal position everyone should hold on some secondary doctrine that is not an essential part of the gospel.

43 From personal correspondence with Barbara Roberts, 2012

Sometimes such a man will even stand up in a gathering of the church body and angrily denounce the pastor and leaders for not doing what he believes they should, or for doing what he insists that they should not. People like this are loose cannons rolling around on the deck of the church, firing off shots as they seek to control. Even more sadly, many times Christians believe them and the sheep are alienated from their shepherds.

5. Violation of Boundaries

Boundaries[44] are lines or limits that protect our personhood. To be healthy, functional human beings, we all need these boundaries and we are entitled to have these limits respected by others, just as we must respect the boundaries other people are entitled to. These boundaries are really set by God Himself and stated very clearly for us in His moral law (The Ten Commandments). Respect of a person's boundaries is the practice of love for our neighbor. We respect his property by not stealing, for example. We respect his life by not killing him or slandering him.

The abusive man is a boundary violator. Crossing the line is still another tactic he uses to destroy the personhood of his victim. His shaming of his victim is very closely related to his violation of boundaries.[45] His boundary trespassing may take some of the following forms:

- Not granting his victim privacy in the bathroom.
- Crossing of sexual boundaries.
- Touching his children in inappropriate ways.[46]
- Reading his victim's personal correspondence or diary.
- Eavesdropping on private conversations.

---

44 For a full treatment of this topic of boundaries, see *Boundaries: When to Say YES, When to Say NO, To Take Control of Your Life* by Henry Cloud and John Townsend.

45 There are a number of good books available on the topic of shame, such as the one by Sandra D. Wilson listed in the bibliography of this book.

46 A victim wrote: "My ex used to tickle our daughter. Most parents tickle their kids in fun, and most parents know when to stop (the child becomes overexcited, or the squeal turns into a scream, or whatever). My ex never knew when to stop. He always tickled too long or too hard, and he never saw that he was overdoing it. Nor did he listen when I told him he had gone too far. Our daughter, of course, didn't have the courage to tell him off."

- Disposing of her personal property.

Often, however, the abuser crosses boundaries in more subtle ways, perhaps most frequently with his words. As Christians, our words must be governed by wisdom, empathy, and tactfulness. The abuser's words are not. They shame, embarrass, violate confidences and generally fail to respect human beings.

> ***Colossians 4:6*** *"Let your speech always be gracious, seasoned with salt, so that you may know how you ought to answer each person."*

6. Isolation

> The money was his, not mine. He would not open a joint account with both of our names on it. I had to go to him and ask for every dollar I spent, and such requests were almost always met with questioning, accusing, and belittling. Since I didn't work outside the home, I had absolutely no source of income of my own. He acted as if we were poor even although I suspected that he had thousands of dollars in the bank. Through economics, he enslaved me and kept me prisoner. (Abuse victim)

This abuser isolated his wife-victim. By limiting her access to funds, he prohibited her from even being able to leave the house that often. She knew that he was her sole support and he wanted it that way. He could totally cut her off from all the finances whenever he wanted and that threat hung over her life like a dark cloud. This is a typical tactic. Isolation shames the victim by reinforcing her growing sense of worthlessness.

Abusers work to isolate their victim in many other ways as well:

- Living the wilderness family life in an isolated location.
- Prohibiting her from working outside the home.
- Insisting upon her home-schooling the children, although he refuses to help in this enterprise and begrudges any money spent on supplies.[47]
- Sabotaging her attempts to attend a church.
- Sabotaging her attempts to take classes or obtain some kind of vocational training.

---

47 Almost all of the members of our church home school. So I am not opposed to this choice at all. We are simply noting here that abusers who choose to embrace Christianity as their façade may with some frequency demand home schooling as still another means of isolating his victim.

- Sabotaging her efforts to operate a home business for supplemental income.
- Employing a variety of strategies to cause her to lose her job if she does work outside the home.[48]
- Employing all types of wickedly ingenious devices to isolate her from her relatives and friends.

Some abusers frequently *move* the household to a new town where the victim knows no one. This severs her previous support system of friends and family, effectively isolating her. And in this era of instant, personal communication, we must also mention how devices such as cell phones and texting can serve the isolating, controlling person as very effective tools. A victim cannot very easily say that she wasn't by her phone. Some abusers will text their victim scores of times each day, demanding overtly or implying covertly that they expect to know every move the victim makes, where she is at every moment, who she is with, and exactly when she will be home. He can interrupt her whenever he wants. With the advent of GPS enabled iPhones, family members can be tracked wherever they have cell reception.

One effect of extended abuse upon victims is the deterioration of their self-esteem. Lacking the confidence they once had, they often become agoraphobic (afraid of being in public) and thus self-isolate. Even if separated or divorced from their victims, abusers frequently continue many of these isolating efforts, including and perhaps especially working to alienate the victim from her children. Abuse takes its toll on the victim's physical health as well, and ill people do not get out much.

> ***Psalm 31:11-12*** *"Because of all my adversaries I have become a reproach, especially to my neighbors, and an object of dread to my acquaintances; those who see me in the street flee from me. I have been forgotten like one who is dead; I have become like a broken vessel."*

7. Accusing

While accusing and blaming are similar, the tactic of accusing is even more

48 One abuser would call his wife's work and ask her boss if he knew where she was at the moment. At other times he would show up at her work and demand that he be allowed to talk to her. He even called anonymously and said she was using drugs and should be drug-tested immediately.

devilish than that of blaming. Satan is called "the accuser of the brethren" (Revelation 12:10). In agreement with "their father the devil," abusers love to charge their victims with sin and guilt. If an innocent person is accused often enough, she can begin to believe the charges against her, even if the accusations are preposterous and have no basis at all.

"You and Phil are sleeping together, aren't you!" Dan coolly remarked while eating his dinner. Mary was dumbfounded. "I saw the two of you looking at each other across the room last week at the school conference. You can't hide anything from me." There was no affair. There was no look across the room. Dan is making a groundless accusation to keep Mary under his thumb.

Abusive people have dysfunctional or even non-functional consciences. In contrast, their victims have very active consciences. And the abuser uses this to his advantage. He can, without any hesitation or remorse, insinuate a horrid charge against her, making her feel the pangs of her own conscience, and causing her to wonder if she really is guilty. A particularly devious tactic is to make accusations against the victim's motives rather than about some observable, outward action. She can say "I did," or "I didn't" in regard to actions. But when it comes to her motives and thoughts, things get much more confusing. "Surely," a normal person thinks, "no one would just invent something terrible like this. He must really believe it somehow. Maybe I have been doing something that has led him to this conclusion?"

Randy came to see Pastor Anderson one day last week. He sat down in the pastor's study, pulled out a sheet of paper, and began to "share some concerns" he had listed on it. "Your sermons are just not interesting. You are driving people away. You aren't personable enough. You need to be a better politician if you are going to succeed in the ministry." Pastor Anderson felt that hybrid sense of fear and nausea in his stomach we have all experienced. As a pastor, he was supposed to be open to criticism and to resist pride. He admitted he was a sinner no better than anyone else in the church. And yet, he felt attacked. "Pastor, you know I share these things with you out of love." And with that, Randy left. After some pondering, Pastor Anderson's thinking slowly changed from defensiveness to increased consideration: "Perhaps Randy was right; maybe the things he said are really true?"

Who is Randy? Is he a Christian who is puffed up with pride? Is he a naïve man who actually believes the things he is saying? Or is he what Scripture describes as a wolf in sheep's clothing whose mission it is to silence the ministry of the Word of God. The power of accusation, you see. Randy is a master at using the very same tactic in his home, as his wife knows all too well. Or does she?

8. Ridicule and Mocking

Matthew 27: 28-29 *"And they stripped him and put a scarlet robe on him, and twisting together a crown of thorns, they put it on his head and put a reed in his right hand. And kneeling before him, they mocked him, saying, Hail, King of the Jews!"*

We have already considered some of the various verbal attacks abusers launch against their victims, but this particular form of verbal abuse deserves special attention.[49] Abusive people mock and ridicule their victims to strip them of their dignity, confidence, joy and self-worth. Once beaten down, the victim is much more controllable.

Jill has summoned up the courage to try something new. She enrolled in a community art class. Lester told her it was a stupid woman idea and besides, she should know that she has no talent for much of anything, let alone art. Encouraged by her friend Carolyn, Jill still pursued the idea. After a few weeks of class, it turned out that Jill actually does have some artistic talent and the instructor told her so. Her first attempt at an oil painting was really quite good and she brought it home and hung it in the dining room.

That evening, Lester threw a fit when he saw it. He launched into a real rage and asked Jill what the _____ she thought she was doing hanging that ________ in their home. It was the most ridiculous and stupid thing he had ever seen and she had better get it down right now before anyone else saw it. Furthermore, he said that if she EVER brought any more trash like that home, she could just forget about continuing in her class. Jill's picture, and her joy, are stored away in the bottom of a box in the back of her closet. If Jill does not get some help, that is where both will remain until the day she dies.[50]

Abusers like Lester sabotage the successes of their victims. Often, they use mockery and ridicule to do so. If, for example, their victim does happen to work outside the home, any achievement will be met with ridicule. A promotion,

49 We emphasize once more – do not think of abuse as only physical abuse. See Patricia Evans' fine book *The Verbally Abusive Relationship*, listed in the bibliography.

50 Dawn, *Behind the Hedge*. This novel tells a very similar story.

an award, a compliment from a fellow worker – all will be beaten down with demeaning language. Why? Because a successful victim is much less a victim. Besides, the universe is all about the abuser, and everyone in his world must recognize this. If they resist, he knows how to shame them into submission.

Janelle's story:

Several years into their marriage, broken in heart and spirit from years of verbal, mental, sexual, spiritual and financial abuse at the hands of her husband, Janelle sits down, wipes her eyes with a tissue, and proceeds to write in her journal:

> 6/3 We had waited so long for the movie to come out on video. It finally did and, yesterday, John checked it out. It's a classic, one our children hadn't ever had a chance to see. "A movie Mommy! Daddy got a movie!! Come see!" Rosie, Jimmy and Peter were so excited they were dancing around the room. Especially Peter! He just bounced up and down, up and down. I loved seeing them so excited.
>
> I knew John was bringing the movie home if he could get a copy so I fed and bathed the children early. John had had a sandwich on the way home so, when he got home, as soon as we could, we settled down with popcorn and watched it. With the children between us, giggling, I almost felt that, at least for a little while, we were a normal family. John laughed and laughed and I kept on thinking, maybe...just maybe, this time, it'll stick for a while.
>
> Far too quickly, it was all over. It wasn't very late yet so we bundled the children up and headed to the car. They chattered among themselves as happily they settled down to be buckled in. Outings, for whatever reason, are always great fun for them but going out in their jammies is especially fun. I had several items in my hand, my purse, the video, a diaper bag, and I laid them on top of the car while I leaned over to buckle my little ones in. Then, once they were secure, I reached up and grabbed everything, tossed them in the back floorboard, climbed in and buckled myself in.
>
> We headed towards the video store. Afterwards, we were planning to head to the grocery store, pick up some ice cream and come back home to make sundaes. As we got near the video store John said, "Get the video ready, Jan". I reached back to get it only to find it wasn't there. Hurriedly

I turned and started searching: I looked through the diaper bag, under the seat, in my purse. It was nowhere to be found. It didn't take my husband long to realize that something was wrong. "What is it?" he demanded. I felt my heart drop to my stomach and I felt sick. I knew he would be angry at my carelessness. Stumbling over my words, I told him. I had expected him to be angry, I didn't expect him to explode. "How could you be so stupid? How?" "I thought..." "You thought? You *thought*? You didn't think anything! You are an utterly stupid woman, do you know that? How could you be so careless? That was so dumb! Now we have to pay for it! And it's your fault… because you are so stupid!"

By this time I was crying. through my tears, I tried to tell him that the children, who had grown silent, were listening. "Let them listen! Then they'll know how stupid their mother is!" Forgetting the other errands, oblivious to our lost fun, he turned around and headed home. "It had better be there," he warned. But, it wasn't. And that set him off again. I forget how many times John told me I was stupid. I can't recall how I settled down the children who were, by now, crying hysterically. I only remember how very, very stupid and how utterly worthless, I felt. I cried for hours last night. John's right. I really am stupid. I don't even know how to pray today. Why would God want to hear from someone as dumb, as useless, as I am?

Psalm 34:15-19 *"The eyes of the LORD are toward the righteous and his ears toward their cry. The face of the LORD is against those who do evil, to cut off the memory of them from the earth. When the righteous cry for help, the LORD hears and delivers them out of all their troubles. The LORD is near to the brokenhearted and saves the crushed in spirit. Many are the afflictions of the righteous, but the LORD delivers him out of them all."*

CHAPTER 5

A Look into the Mentality of Abuse

Jeremiah 17:9 *The heart is deceitful above all things, and desperately sick; who can understand it?*

If someone asked you to define abuse, you would probably go to the visible, outward, acts and describe what it *looks* like; the things we have been describing in the last two chapters: the hitting, mocking, crazy-making, and so on. But these outward tactics are not the real essence of abuse. Rather, it is what lies behind them that we must come to understand. Abuse, in its essential being, is the abuser himself. And even more accurately, it is his mentality, his mindset, the paradigm through which he sees himself, his world, and most importantly—his victim. We cannot help victims and neither can we expose abusers unless we enter the abusive mind.

The Scale of Abuse

All abusers are characterized by certain fundamental attitudes which are the elemental building blocks of what we are defining as abuse. Without these, a person is not an abuser as we have defined the term.

- Entitlement/Superiority
- Power
- Control
- Justification

We will be looking at various attitudes produced by these basic building blocks in this chapter. However, we must first emphasize that not all abusers operate at the same level of intensity. Abuse functions along a scale or range ("spectrum," as Bancroft labels it), from lesser to greater. This is vital for us to understand for several reasons –

1. It will enable us to recognize abuse for what it really is, even in what appear to be the "less serious" cases. We need not find the most severe abusive tactics before we can conclude that a man is an abuser. (While some abusers physically beat their victim, others are passive abusers – refusing to work or take on responsibility for example).
2. We will understand that an individual abuser can advance along this scale and become a greater danger to his victim.
3. We will try to understand what determines where a particular abuser is located within this range.

Jesus said that the man who actually commits murder and the man who hates someone in his heart are both murderers (Matthew 5:21-22). While we would all rather be murdered by the second man than the first, the reality is that the essential heart of murder is present in both men. And so it is with abuse.

Let's review our definition of abuse as stated earlier in the introduction:

> Abuse is a mentality of entitlement and superiority which evidences itself in the various tactics the abuser uses to obtain and enforce unjustified power and control over another person. The abuser thinks that he is absolutely justified in using these tactics to maintain this power and control. Abuse is effected in many ways: both physical (including sexual) and non-physical (verbal). It can be active (physically or verbally) or passive (not speaking, not acting). Abuse, therefore, is not limited to physical assault.

When does a sinful human being become an abuser? It happens when who they are is defined by the mentality of abuse: entitlement, power, control, and justification, although the particulars of how these elements are expressed can vary widely. A boat is a boat because it possesses certain basic qualities of "boatness," though boats may come in many different sizes, shapes, and colors. So it is with abuse.

Jan Silvious, speaking of the abuser in terms of the fool in the book of Proverbs, observes that an abuser is someone who is an abuser by character. His abuse is chronic. Because of this, he never really thinks about what he does so much as merely acting out what he is.[51]

Conscience and the Scale of Abuse

Neil Goldschmidt was a famous figure in Oregon politics and business. His achievements included holding the offices of mayor of Portland, U.S. secretary of transportation, governor of Oregon, and head of the state Board of Higher Education. But Neil Goldschmidt was a lie. Behind this noble façade, Goldschmidt was in reality a sexual predator who targeted a thirteen year old girl. He used her while he was mayor of Portland. An eighth-grade girl! And in the end, his abuse took her life. Drugs and alcohol exacted their toll and she died at a young age. Goldschmidt was never prosecuted. The statute of limitations had run out.

How does the abuser, like Goldschmidt, carry on with the weight of his misdeeds pressing him down? This is the wrong question to ask. It is based upon a failure to understand the mentality of the abuser. The question assumes that the abuser is indeed "weighed down" by his conscience, as we would be if we did such things. The abuser uses this fundamental error in our thinking to his advantage. "Poor man. Yes, he did wrong, but surely he has suffered terrific internal torment all these years. Let's just leave him alone." He plays himself a kind of victim you see, and people fall for it. The reality is that he actually has "carried on" in his life quite nicely, because he does not have a healthy, functioning conscience like non-abusers do.

The abuser lacks a healthy conscience: The internal prosecutor that characterizes a functional, socialized mind is either remarkably weak or non-existent in the abuser. Abusers fall within a scale of abuse, and their specific location in this scale may very likely be determined by the degree to which their conscience is disconnected.

Some abusers, in other words, might be described as remarkably selfish. As we move up the scale of intensity, we might define them as having a narcissistic personality. And as we come to the most severe degrees of abuse, we meet people who are classified as sociopaths or psychopaths. Sociopath and psychopath are terms used more or less synonymously to describe people who, among other traits, have no conscience. But we would suggest that all abusers have seriously

51 Silvious, 29.

dysfunctional consciences at the very least. In other words, something has gone amiss with the process the Apostle Paul described,

> ***Romans 2:15*** *They show that the work of the law is written on their hearts, while their conscience also bears witness, and their conflicting thoughts accuse or even excuse them…*
>
> *Perhaps this is what Paul wrote to Timothy about:*
>
> ***1 Timothy 4:2*** *…through the insincerity of liars whose consciences are seared…*

Martha Stout, in her excellent book, *The Sociopath Next Door*, emphasizes this conscienceless characteristic of the sociopath. She maintains that because conscience is something that we feel, it can only exist when a person is capable of relating to another person on an emotional level. Where there is no ability to love, neither can there be conscience[52]. Therefore, because abusers cannot love, they cannot be prosecuted by a conscience.

George Simon is right on when he concurs:

> Narcissists struggle with forming good consciences because they find it difficult to even conceive of a power or cause greater than themselves. Further, their excessive sense of self-importance and attitude of entitlement make it difficult for them to entertain the notion that anything besides what they want has any real value or importance. So they pay little attention or heed to the wants and needs of others.[53]

Here is an example, related by the victim of many years of abuse, which illustrates the abuser's inability to really "connect" as one human being to another:

> The only compliments I ever get from him (except for my cooking) are physical compliments. "Your hair looks pretty today," or something like that. Most of them are sexualized, even in front of the children. He'll make a comment, designed, in his eyes to be a compliment, that is sexual in nature because he knows no other way to compliment me. I have no real worth in his eyes outside of the fact that I cook, clean and am a sexual object—a woman.

52 Stout, 126.

53 Simon Jr., *Character Disturbance,* 135.

The Bible teaches us that all human beings are born in the image of God. Among other things, this means that our Creator has endowed each of us with the knowledge of certain basic truths:

- We are created beings.
- We did not create ourselves.
- The universe is a created order.
- There is a Creator.
- As creatures, we are accountable to our Creator.
- We owe our Creator acknowledgment that He is God, and thanksgiving for all that He gives us.

The first chapter of Paul's Epistle to the Romans makes this quite clear, as do other Scriptures such as Psalm 100:

> ***Psalm 100:3*** *Know that the LORD, he is God! It is he who made us, and we are his; we are his people, and the sheep of his pasture.*

However, this innate knowledge must be embraced by us. As George Simon maintains, to form a healthy conscience, a person must adopt and accept into their mind the laws of their society, and to do this, he must submit himself to a higher power.[54] The abuser has short-circuited at this point. He becomes his own higher power so that he views the universe and everyone in it as existing for his pleasure, service, and glory. He has no fear of God. It is as if he is self-created and owner of his own pasture.

This is still another example from an abuse victim. She illustrates the abuser's lack of conscience:

> Calvin seems to me to share the traits of the anti-social personality (sociopath). Not in everything, but a lot. I really don't think he has a conscience. He gets really cold eyes when he's angry. Cold. Dead. Like there's nothing there. On the surface he looks like a law-abiding citizen, but the truth is that he acts as if the rules—any rules—don't apply to him. He skirts them as far as he can and gets away with anything that he can. He has no qualms about borrowing and not paying back money. He owes money to quite a few former landlords as well as to the utility companies in every single town we've ever lived in. He owes money to all of his friends and

54 Ibid., Location 1267, Kindle Edition.

family members. He owes several hospitals, and various businesses. He filed for bankruptcy. He sold my wedding rings when he got in a financial bind.

He won't follow the rules in other ways, either: when we lived in another state, he refused to allow me to do all of the testing required by the State for home schooling because it cost money. He expects others to help him when he needs it but I can only think of a couple of times he's ever been willing to help others. When we lived in a small town, he accepted $500.00 from an old lady to clear some of her land for her. He did part of the work and then refused to go back and complete it. The entire time we've been married, I have lived in constant fear of the phone ringing or the doorbell ringing for fear that we're going to be in trouble with someone in some way. But this man is without a conscience; he sleeps just fine! When it comes to consequences, he ensures that I am the one who has to deal with the bill collectors.

Understanding then, that abusers fall somewhere in a range or scale of abuse, and that their particular degree of abuse is largely determined by the dysfunction of their conscience, we can now proceed to consider more specifically how these people think. That is to say, how does the abuser's mindset, largely or totally unhindered by conscience, operate? What thoughts and "emotions" lie behind the visible tactics of the abuser?[55]

Egocentric/Narcissistic

At the center of the abusive mentality that defines the essence of abuse is a monumental fortress of entitlement. The abuser's world is about him and for him. He is ego, and that ego is the center of the universe. He has no mentality to even understand Scripture's instruction:

55 We place "emotions" in quotation marks because it is well established that abusers – certainly those who qualify as sociopaths – do not feel emotion as normal people do. When it comes to emotion, they are color blind. They see situations, but they don't feel the colors, you might say. This was well illustrated in a television show in which a husband simply could not grasp why his wife was so upset after he disregarded their anniversary. A friend, learning of the situation, punched the husband quite hard in the shoulder and then said, "She feels like that inside." The husband acted surprised as if such an experience were entirely foreign to him. Even when they appear in a rage, many abusers are not as infuriated with anger as a normal person would be when evidencing such rage.

Philippians 2:3-4 *Do nothing from rivalry or conceit, but in humility count others more significant than yourselves. Let each of you look not only to his own interests, but also to the interests of others.*

Largely, the abuser's personhood is defined by this egocentric, narcissistic mentality of entitlement, so that it is evident in virtually everything he thinks or does (if we are wise enough to see through his disguise that is). To such a person, there are no darts of conscience for being selfish. The whole thing is quite logical in his mind.

Lance was arrested for domestic violence. He pushed his wife to the floor because the dinner she made did not suit him. As she fell, she hit her forehead on the edge of the table and a large bump formed by the time the police arrived. The next day, his wife obtained a restraining order. Lance was sentenced to thirty days in the county jail and was not allowed to return home for six months. During this period, Lance visited friends and gave them his version of the incident. It was all due to an overreaction on the part of their daughter. There was no need for her to call the police like she did. Now, he can't even be at home. A man has *needs*, he tells his friends. He isn't used to being without sex this long and he is so lonely.

It is all about Lance. His wife and children, even his friends he is trying to win as allies, all exist to serve him.

One very common phenomenon in abusive men is that their abuse will frequently increase when their victim becomes pregnant. The man who is consumed with himself does not like competition, and babies are competition. During the pregnancy, his wife has new needs: vitamins, doctor appointments, more rest, and perhaps a special diet. None of these things fit into the abuser's world. Pregnant women have suffered horribly at the hands of abusive men.

Lack of Empathy

Frequently, abuse victims will describe "those eyes," referring to the blank, cold, soul-less stare in their abuser. Such eyes belong to a person with no empathy for other human beings (or animals). Empathy is that human quality which enables a normal person to identify with the feelings of others. To put oneself in the other man's shoes, we might say. It is that attribute in us that gives us the ability to understand the importance of "do unto others as you would have them do unto you."

Abusers have no empathy. We must, however, guard against being deceived by his tactic of feigned empathy. When it suits his purposes, he can pretend to be quite caring. He can turn on the tears and personal warmth. On other occasions, he may actually sense some pangs of regret regarding how he has abused his victim. But it comes to nothing in the end. It is something like what we are told about Esau:

> ***Hebrews 12:17*** *For you know that afterward, when he desired to inherit the blessing, he was rejected, for he found no chance to repent, though he sought it with tears.*

Barbara Roberts' tells her experience with this:

> Another really tricky thing about the abuser's lack of empathy is that sometimes he seems to show real empathy. He wells up with tears when reading about the plight of poor children in Russia who have cancer because of exposure to radioactivity. He declares that he'd love to drive a bus for disabled children, because he would so like to help them. He may even (very occasionally) come tail between his legs to his wife, asking for forgiveness for hurting her. My ex actually had a revelation from God one day while he was at work (I believe this is true, not just a concocted story). While he was standing in the factory he felt God saying to him "You need to ask Barbara for forgiveness, and you need to ask her how she would like you to treat her." He came home that day and recounted this vision so humbly, so transparently, with such empathy. My heart leaped with hope. I told him "I want you to speak respectfully to me; and I want you not to swear." Not big requests, I would have thought. But no change ensued.[56]

This, along with the absence of conscience, explains why they can launch into a terrible rage against their victim, or deny their wife and children sufficient money for essentials like food and clothing, and then go into the living room, turn on the TV, and never give what he has just done a second thought. "Are we going to have some coffee in here or what?"

Lack of empathy and conscience also explains why the abuser can treat his victim horribly, and then behave as if it had never happened. He might suddenly tell his wife, whom he has victimized shortly before, "Hey, put on your black

56 Personal correspondence with Barbara Roberts, 2012

dress! Let's go out and have a really nice dinner. I love you in that dress!" This inconsistent and logically irrational behavior contributes to the crazy-making climate of chaos we have already discussed.

It is vital we understand that abusers have no empathy because as we will learn when we discuss how to deal with an abuser, efforts to try to reach the "heart" of such a person are going to fail. "Oh, if I can just get him to feel how much he has hurt me," is a flight of fantasy in these cases and worse, the abuser will see such efforts as weakness in his victim and exploit it against her.

Jason is a leading figure in Grace Church. Jason chose this church a number of years ago because of its uncompromising character. Jason is uncompromising. He prides himself in being true to his conscience, and will be very happy to tell you what specific school of eschatology (the doctrine of last things) is correct, what Bible version is the only one approved by God, and any number of other subjects you may require answers on.

But Jason is an abusive and controlling man. He regularly injures people (especially his wife and children) with his words. Jason has no empathy, so he gives no regard to how his words might affect people. He speaks his mind without regard for the consequences and feels quite proud and satisfied that he is not afraid to "stand for Christ."

Jason's behavior one Sunday was quite typical. No one in Jason's church, including the pastor and deacons, had ever confronted him. They decided that they were just called by the Lord to love Jason as he is. Evan, the adult Sunday School teacher, had shown a short video that was an allegory about Christians keeping the gospel to themselves rather than sharing it. Just as the class was closing, Jason stood up and said rather loudly, "That video was inappropriate and full of false doctrine! If I want to watch a video I can do it at home. What we need here is Bible teaching!" The class sat in silence, and then Evan closed in prayer. Jason's wife was once again humiliated and knew she would be in for an extra helping of Jason's verbal abuse when they got home.

When Evan went to the pastor and church board later in the week, asking what was going to be done about Jason's behavior, he was told that the Lord would have us all be patient with people like Jason and pray for him. After all, Jason is a good Christian brother. He just has some rough edges. Evan left confused. It seemed that the Bible had plenty of things to say about how the church is to deal with a Jason. But then, the pastor must know more than him about it.

The next month, Evan resigned his teaching position, another victim of this abusive man with no empathy. As the years roll by in the future, many more names will be added to Jason's list of victims – including the pastor who, in just two more years, will announce that the Lord has "called him" to a new church. In fact, the Lord had nothing to do with the pastor's move. What the Lord has been calling Independent Bible Church to do for a long, long time is to confront Jason with his patterns of sin and, if necessary, to put Jason out of the church. And yet many churches are sinfully permitting men like Jason to practice their abuse in the body of Christ unopposed.

Never at Fault, Never Sorry

If you have ever sat down with an abuser and called their attention to their abusive tactics and attitudes, you already know what a frustrating experience this can be. Largely, this is because the abuser's mindset does not permit him to ever be wrong. He is never the problem. With all probability, if Jason were confronted, even if witness after witness testified to his abusive ways, Jason would not admit fault. He would blame and accuse. He would rationalize (very irrationally), drawing upon his uncanny ability to make excuses.

As we have already learned, abusers have a monolithic and impenetrable mindset of self-justification. He is entitled. He deserves to have others acknowledge his power and control over them. If they refuse to bow to him, then none should blame him if he has to use abusive tactics to make them submit to his rule. If his wife had just done what he told her, none of that unpleasantness last night would have happened.

Closely related to this profound sense of justification for what he does is the abuser's inability to ever truly be remorseful or sorry. This is still another very, very important fact for us to clearly understand if we are to avoid the abuser's deceptions. Abusive people mimic repentance and remorse, but it is an act designed to manipulate the victim, or simply the product of a regret that eventually vaporizes without producing real change. The reader is encouraged to read Bancroft's identification of eight things that an abuser might do or say which are clear signs that he is not repentant and is not changing for the better.[57] (Christians are particularly easily duped by false claims of repentance, though we really have no excuse for it).[58]

An abuser who insists that his victim must forgive him, reconcile with him, and trust him is a person who is in no way repentant, no matter how many "I'm sorry's" he affixes to such demands. Any supposed repentance that connects itself with insistence that the victim "should" or "needs" to do something so that he can change, is false repentance. Even a hint of blaming or rationalizing is evidence that his repentance is not genuine.

Edward has been in counseling for three years, not voluntarily, but because his wife (Lindsey) insisted that unless he obtained counseling for his abusive ways, she was going to leave him. Edward has not changed. Although his counselor (a Christian counselor who has had no training in the area of abuse) is very happy with Edward's progress, Lindsey doesn't see it. She doesn't see it, because there is nothing to it.

And yet, Edward regularly reminds Lindsey how much he has changed. Lindsey wants to believe it, but she can't. One Saturday morning, Lindsey told Edward she has had enough of his abuse and that she is leaving him. He pleads for her to see how much he has changed and demands that she stay in their relationship. When Lindsey stands her ground, Edward's pleading turns to anger. As he storms out of the room, he exclaims "now you won't even be here to see how much better I am!" Edward will be able to garner the sympathy of his pastor, his fellow church members, his children and relatives. Even his counselor will tell him that Lindsey is wrong. Lindsey will have to find a new church. Edward will remain right where he is.

57 Bancroft, *Why Does He Do That?*, 350-351.

58 Christians desperately need to come to a correct biblical theology of repentance, forgiveness, and reconciliation. Wrongly handled, these become some of the favorite topics of the abuser's distortion, permitting him to manipulate his victims with "biblical authority." We recommend Barbara Roberts *Checklist for Repentance* at http://www.notunderbondage.com/resources/ChecklistForRepentance.html. Also see Bancroft's *Why Does He Do That?*, 350-51.

Objectification

A man who thinks of his wife as a "trophy wife" is not commendable. A trophy is not only something that is won, but possessed. When human beings are viewed as possessions, their humanity and personhood are diminished. They become objects. How, for example, could human beings be marketed as slaves, bought and sold like cattle? Largely it is because they were thought of as cattle.

Abusers objectify their victims, making it far easier for them to practice their evil tactics with no remorse. Victims are possessions in the abuser's mentality, much like a car or house. They are objects whose purpose is to bring pleasure to their owner. This attitude is expressed quite clearly in song lyrics by Eminem in which a man calls his girlfriend "My Darling," and tells her that if he cannot have her, no one can. Why? Because he possesses her soul, mind, heart, and body.

Objectification has much to do with what propels an abuser to fight in court for custody rights of his children, even though he has never loved them. But they are his, and he is going to have his rights to what is his! Even more horrible is the frequent scenario of an abuser killing his wife and children, then himself. If I can't have you, no one can. It is incredible how many songs, movies, television shows, and romance novels endorse the mentality of abuse, yet they are rarely criticized for doing so.[59]

You can hear the abuser's objectification in his language about his victim. For example,

- "I told my old lady to...."
- "She's a typical stupid woman..."
- "You have to submit to me..."

And these are some of the least vulgar depersonalizing expressions abusers use. Abusers often work to convince the victim herself that she is not fully human, but rather an object possessed by him. He uses humiliating and degrading words and actions to do this. Just as the Nazis spoke of their Jewish prisoners as non-humans, making it far easier to annihilate six million of them with apparently no remorse, so the abuser speaks of his victim with non-human labels. As the victim becomes increasingly objectified in the abuser's mind, his abuse of her can increase as well.

---

59 Lundy Bancroft, "Domestic Violence in Popular Culture." http://www.youtube.com/watch?v=STQk-dRPQeE

"Get in the bedroom, woman!" Gary told Laura. If Laura objects because it is late and she has worked hard all day, Gary may well step up his degrading speech toward her. He might call her some animal name (e.g., pig, cow, etc.) because animals are not human. Gary does not view Laura as a human being.

James is a professing Christian with a good reputation in his church. But in fact, James is an abusive man. He considers his wife to be his own possession, owned by him with God's full approval. James often speaks of how a man needs to be sure that what is his remains *his.* He has reminded his wife of this more than once – that if she ever tries to leave him, he will never let her go and might even kill her if she forces him. James has a warped view of the Bible's doctrine of marriage.

Ownership, possession, and objectification explain why abusers are often extremely jealous of their victim. While his double standard permits him to flirt or even have affairs with other women, he will not tolerate what belongs to him doing the same. He will often portray his jealousy—even his rages of jealousy—as his intense "love" for his victim. But it has nothing to do with love and everything to do with a mentality of possession.[60]

Objectification also explains why so many abusers work to keep their victim isolated from other people and relationships. This minimizes the abuser's perceived threats to ownership of what is his, and his control underscores that ownership as well.

> Once he actually tried to talk me into allowing him to make a tiny little brand and using it on me so that it would show I was his. Crazy, huh? Actually he talked about this for years. He did extensive research on it as well as on various ways to discipline and punish your wife. (Abuse victim)

Master of the Bedroom

Gary and Laura (mentioned above) have been married for five years. Gary has demanded sex every single night! It does not matter to him how tired Laura

60 Bancroft has an excellent allegorical story at the beginning of chapter 13 of *Why Does He Do That?* It is written to explain how boys are often taught to view women as a piece of property to be possessed. Also see Barbara Roberts' article, "Still Married in the Sight of God" http://www.notunderbondage.com/resources/StillMarriedInTheSightOfGod.html That slogan is used as spiritual abuse to enforce the abuser's ownership of his wife, because he has God on his side!

might be, or that she simply does not have the sexual drive to sustain daily relations (few if any human beings really do). But Gary's purpose in this has little if anything to do with his sexual desire, nor with what Gary calls "love." Instead, it is all about Gary enforcing his power and control over Laura.

Gary claims to be a Christian, and he enjoys reminding Laura of the following Scripture, though he only emphasizes the first half of the verse:

> ***1 Corinthians 7:4*** *For the wife does not have authority over her own body, but the husband does. Likewise the husband does not have authority over his own body, but the wife does.*

Gary also regularly refers to his sexual prowess in the hearing of their children. He wants his children to know that he is master of their mother in every way. Many abusers lack normal modesty and discreetness in discussing sex, or in matters of respecting personal boundaries. Those who claim to be Christians will regularly remind the family that "sex was created by God and is nothing to be ashamed of," to justify his immodesty and inappropriate remarks or behaviors.[61]

Abusers obviously have no real concern about the sexual needs of their victim. As always, it's all about him. If his victim objects to anything he wants from her, he will tell her she is frigid, disobedient, unloving; and perhaps even remind her that he can go out and find another woman anytime he wants. Women in abusive relationships, although legally married, are in fact often rape or sodomy victims. What is rape, after all, if not sex that is *obtained against another person's will?* We think of physical force when we think of rape, but a woman is raped when the rapist uses any tactic to take sex which she does not want to give. These non-physical tactics include threats, but also more deviously subtle devices as well:

- Pressing her to drink alcohol.
- Expressing anger if he does not get what he wants from her.
- Denying her privileges unless she yields.
- Initiating sex when she is asleep.

Many years ago when I was in my late teens, there was a criminal case in Oregon in which a husband was prosecuted for raping his wife. The thing was unheard of and ridiculous in most people's thinking. How could a husband ever

61 In chapter 13 we will discuss the question of whether an abuser can truly be a Christian.

rape his wife? Fortunately our justice system has come a long way since then in dealing with abusers, but still has a very long way to go. How many women sitting in our churches on a given Sunday have been raped by their abuser in the preceding week? What would you tell a woman who is an abuse victim if she came to you and said that her husband forces her? Is it not true that the Christian church quite often tells her that she never has a right to say "no"?

Sex, as the most intimate of human relationships, is one of the abuser's favorite tools for establishing his ownership of, and dominance over, his victim. As created by God, sex is one of the greatest gifts a husband and wife can enjoy. As perverted by the abuser, it becomes one of the most cruel and destructive weapons in his arsenal. Sex is almost always used in an abusive marriage as a weapon of domination and control. And its hard to be delicate telling the stories and make sure the listener really understands the truth. I believe we all need to know exactly what abusers are doing to their victims sexually, and get over our "delicacy." Here is an account from a victim:

> One of the things he was into was "domestic discipline." It is related to sadomasochism though most of its followers/ wouldn't agree. It is tied to forcing submission through pain or punishment and I for one (and many who have written on it) believe that at its base is an intense need for sexual gratification through another's suffering. It's very, very ugly and very, very demeaning to the submissive partner. I remember him telling me how much more a man he felt when he was able to punish me. He would force me to stand at attention while he raged at me or he would brag that he could rip my clothes off and I could never protect myself from him or fend him off (he proved it more times than I can count) or how he'd force me to stand in a corner while he whipped me. It has taken a long time for me to be able to talk about the sexual abuse and grotesque acts such as sodomy and whippings during his fun time, and how he would tell me that he owned me and since I was his slave I had no rights, not even the right to clothing if he didn't allow it. The sexual stuff was one of the worst aspects of abuse with him.

An Exercise

Here is an exercise for you. The following is taken from a response to an article we wrote on the web describing how a Christian victim is often targeted by the abuser simply because the abuser hates Christ. (It is my opinion that this lies at the root of many cases of abuse in which the Christian is persecuted for being the truth and light of Christ, which the abuser detests). Notice how persuasive this man's claims are and imagine how easily he would deceive his pastor and fellow church members, friends, and family members. I mean, who could possibly say these things if they weren't true, right? The abusive mentality can, quite easily. See if you can answer the questions we have inserted between sections of this fellow's letter. Please note that, as we have emphasized in this book, we realize that sometimes women can be abusers too. I include a few of my comments in a footnote following:

> You don't really know what you are talking about and you do not have much discernment. You have been deceived by the lie that all or most domestic violence is perpetrated by men against women. Nothing could be further from the truth. I can also tell you don't have any personal experience in this area, and I do. You, like many others have bought into the lies about DV and you say it's mostly women who have come forward to you, therefore it must be only or mostly women that are abused.

1. What is this writer trying to do in his very first paragraph?
2. What are some aspects of his mentality/worldview that are apparent here?

The writer continues:

> I was married to a woman for years who was an abuser and came from a family of abusers. Her mother was an alcoholic and died early and was abusive...her father was an alcoholic. She tried to commit suicide just like her mother and battered herself and had me charged with assault. I was verbally, emotionally and physically abused for years...she hit me, punched me, broke my things, threw my things in the garbage, swore at me in front of the kids, the neighbors and tormented me. Like most men in this situation, I did not contact you to tell my story...usually only women speak out, the men do not. I tried to fix it, for the kids...I hung in there. She lies, deceives, manipulates. I am the Christian and she unfortunately is not, I suggest her Catholic upbringing may have something to do with that. Her family are liars and deceivers...she would come to you and say how I beat her, the kids, control the money and more...and you would believe it...like her

family and few friends...but most neighbors, our children and their friends know the truth. I have been thrown into the world of family court and domestic violence. She stalls in court, and denied me access to our children for months. The courts, media, government and educational institutions are full of radical feminists who hate men, keep the lies alive and fool men like you. Yes, we need women's shelters, but we need men's shelters too.

1. What tactics are being used by the writer here?
2. What attitude toward women do you see expressed here?

The writer went on in his conclusion to claim how the Lord had wonderfully worked in his life to help him forgive his ex-wife and commit his entire life to God. He now prays that someday she will repent and be saved. He included quotations from the Bible.

1. Do you think his claims to be a Christian should be believed? Why or why not?
2. What is more probable: a) That he is a Christian and she is not, or b) She is the genuine Christian and he is not.[62]

62 The key characteristic of this writer that identifies him as an abuser in a not-so-good disguise is his arrogance and entitlement. He opens with an attack against our knowledge, not so subtly implying that we are fools, in contrast to his vast wisdom and knowledge. Genuine abuse victims do not do this. If anything, they are confused about what is happening to them. And their experience certainly is NOT that they have thousands of people agreeing with their position – it is the very opposite in fact. It is the abuser who normally gains allies, not the victim. We need not doubt that this man is the abuser, that the things he accuses his ex-wife of are actually things HE has done to her, and that she is probably a Christian, while he obviously is not. His final "testimony" of God's wonderful work in his life is false.

CHAPTER 6

What Else is He Thinking?

1 Samuel 9:1-2 *There was a man of Benjamin whose name was Kish, the son of Abiel, son of Zeror, son of Becorath, son of Aphiah, a Benjaminite, a man of wealth. And he had a son whose name was Saul, a handsome young man. There was not a man among the people of Israel more handsome than he. From his shoulders upward he was taller than any of the people.*

Saul was a spoiled rich kid. In human terms, he had it all. Born into wealth. Tall and handsome. Surely this fellow was destined for great things. Great and *infamous* things as it would turn out.

King Saul is a classic biblical example of the abusive man. There is probably no combination more dangerous than a sociopath (a person who lacks conscience) in a position of absolute power. When Saul perceived David as a threat, David became this abuser's victim.

1 Samuel 18:8-9 *And Saul was very angry, and this saying displeased him. He said, "They have ascribed to David ten thousands, and to me they have ascribed thousands, and what more can he have but the kingdom?" And Saul eyed David from that day on.*

For the abusive man, life is about power and control and winning. He is constantly scanning his horizons for the slightest hint of a challenge to his kingship. When he perceives someone as such a challenge, he marks them as his target. The abuser lives a paranoid existence, and that makes him very unsafe for those around him.

> ***1 Samuel 18:11-15*** *And Saul hurled the spear, for he thought, "I will pin David to the wall." But David evaded him twice. Saul was afraid of David because the LORD was with him but had departed from Saul. So Saul removed him from his presence and made him a commander of a thousand. And he went out and came in before the people. And David had success in all his undertakings, for the LORD was with him. And when Saul saw that he had great success, he stood in fearful awe of him.*

Notice what these verses tell us about Saul's mindset toward his victim. He was:

- Murderous
- Fearful
- Avoiding
- Envious
- Aware that the Lord was with David and had a fearful awe of him.

When a person is in some type of relationship with an abuser (marriage, inter-family, church member, fellow employee etc.) the victim should consider that these may well be some of the thoughts and attitudes their abuser has toward them.

We continue now with a consideration of more traits of the abusive mentality.

A "Must-Win" Competitiveness

A very common scenario experienced by victims who have separated or divorced their abusive spouse is the subsequent turmoil that the abuser stirs up through the justice system. It can very accurately be called "legal bullying." Most often, this occurs in respect to child custody issues. Abusers do not really love their children, but they will go to remarkable lengths to retain custody of them. The abuser's children are his property and he is going to fight and win for his property rights. In addition, by prolonging court battles he can perpetrate continued abuse upon his victim and force her to submit to his power. One victim's abusive ex-husband has kept the court battle alive for years. When asked "Why do you think he keeps fighting you in court?" she replied:

> Why do they keep pressing this you ask? George loves to fight. It is like he is addicted to conflict. It is George who is driving this completely. It is the only thing left for him to fight about so he is doing all he can to stay at

> war. He doesn't know peace, nor does he know the joy of it. He only knows war. I remember when we fought he seemed to be so addicted to the kill (fight). If I would comply and resist a fight, he hated that. It was like the only way for him to come off of the building up to an all out attack was for me to end up in the middle of the floor in a heap sobbing hysterically. If he didn't get me to that stage, he would keep attacking in various ways. Once he accomplished that he seemed to ease up and be somewhat pleasant and then the cycle would start all over again.

What George really loves is to win. Winning preserves his control and power over his victim. While non-abusive people would leave a conflict that had brought another person to a breakdown, the abuser takes great delight in knowing that he has emerged victorious. That is what life is about for him. Of course, where there is a victor, there is necessarily a loser, and his victim is always that loser. Yet he has no empathy for her whatsoever.

This also helps us understand why dealing with an abuser as we would deal with more normal people is simply not going to work. Most people, when they realize that they have hurt us, empathize and seek forgiveness. Not the abuser. If you try to show him your hurt, if you weep and "share your heart" with him, thinking that he will come to feel your pain, he is only going to take satisfaction that he has won. He sees such things as weaknesses for him to capitalize upon. This is one reason that couples' counseling is not a wise option in the case of abuse. Anything the victim shares in that setting will only be used against her later. The abuser will always approach couples' counseling as another contest from which he must emerge the victor. Peace in a relationship is something he neither knows nor desires. Elizabeth, for instance, finally understood. Tom did not want her to be happy. He wanted her to be happy with what *he* wanted her to be happy with. For Tom, she was only good to the extent that she made him feel good about himself. And that is plainly a formula for a counseling failure.

> ***Psalm 120:6-7*** *Too long have I had my dwelling among those who hate peace. I am for peace, but when I speak, they are for war!*

Lack of Fear

Ray is a dangerous person to be around. He is a danger to himself and to others. Everyone who has known him very long realizes this, although they probably don't understand the reason for it. They mark it up to stupidity, but Ray is actually not stupid at all. Lacking a conscience and devoid of empathy for others, coupled with his narcissistic self-promotion, Ray does not have the ability to feel fear.

Ray works in construction and operates various types of heavy equipment and tools. Ray scoffs at safety regulations and has been warned by his supervisors that if he continues to disregard safety guidelines he will lose his job. In fact, Ray has been fired from another similar job before but managed to modify his job application to hide that fact. Ray's fellow workers avoid being around him especially after he turned a bulldozer on its side last month and nearly crushed a co-worker.

Ray's lack of fear extends to his other relationships as well. At home, his family knows that to work with him on projects around the house means putting one's life in danger. For example, last summer Ray insisted that his son help him re-roof their triple story house. When the boy suggested they use safety lines to prevent a fatal fall, Ray mocked him for being afraid. "If you think about that stuff then you can't get your work done! Stop thinking about it!"

Ray's wife tells us about another time she and her children were endangered by Ray's lack of fear. "Ray decided, without consulting me, to renovate the laundry in our (my) house. He savagely pulled down the ceiling, wall panels and electrical switch covers, exposing bare electrical wires at arm level. We could have been electrocuted by simply brushing against an exposed wire. When I saw it I yelled at him, 'Aren't you going to turn off the power at the fuse box?' 'No! It's fine; don't be stupid!' he snarled. I ran to the fuse box and turned off the power, saying, 'Well, I don't want a dead husband!' I then wrapped lots of supermarket bags around the exposed wires and held the bunched up bags in place with loads of masking tape. We lived like that for several months, while the renovations went on. There was never a breath of apology or thanks from him."

Fear of violating safety rules, civil and criminal laws, or even moral codes is greatly diminished or even non-existent in the abuser because, at least in part, such fear arises out of an appreciation for the consequences of what one's actions might do to other people. Because the abuser lacks empathy for others and really loves no one, He fears no consequences. In addition, his self-indulging desire for immediate gratification of "doing what I wanna do" takes priority over concern for the outcome of his actions. Ray's apparent "skill" on heavy equipment is actually his lack of common sense that would cause most people to hesitate before jumping onto a piece of equipment they have never used before. But to listen to Ray tell you about it, he is an old pro who knows everything there is to know about this machine.

> ***Proverbs 1:7*** *The fear of the LORD is the beginning of knowledge; fools despise wisdom and instruction.*

The Abuser and the Law

When it comes to obeying the law, Ray's defiance is evident as well. He does not fear the consequences of breaking the law. If he decides to build a building at home, he never obtains a building permit. Fishing and hunting regulations mean very little to him. He enjoys driving recklessly to frighten his passengers, and particularly uses this tactic against his wife. Once, Ray was driving his wife and children over a long eight-lane bridge in heavy traffic. For no reason whatsoever (except he'd just felt angry with his wife for some insignificant thing) he braked the car to a sudden stop. The lane behind them was brought to a standstill until he decided to start driving again. Imagine the fear and humiliation felt by the family!

When Ray is caught violating the law, getting a speeding ticket for example, suddenly he invokes a double standard. Now the police are guilty of violating his rights, of falsely accusing him, of not following the proper regulations.

The abuser's relationship to the law is external in nature. Respecting only his own rules, he resents having anyone impose laws upon him. Some abusive people are members of anti-government organizations that paint themselves as true patriots whose intent is to defend the rights and liberties of the constitution. Of course, the abuser grants no bill of rights to his victim and strips her of her freedom and humanity.

God's Law (The Ten Commandments) was written on tablets of stone. In Christ and the New Covenant, God promises to write that Law upon the hearts of His people (Jeremiah 31:31ff; Hebrews 8). Through a normal conscience, even a non-Christian has *some* capacity to sense God's restraints. Out of the common grace God extends to a fallen world, most people agree that it is wrong to murder, to steal, to slander and so on, at least in part. But the law never seems to reach the inside of the abuser. He sees it as an opponent and his goal is to conquer it.

So, for example, when an abused wife tells her abuser that if he ever lays a hand on her, she will call the police and he will go to jail, what does the abuser think? Victims report that telling their abuser this does have a restraining effect upon him, at least in some cases. But we must understand that his subsequent obedience to the law does not proceed from an *inner* acknowledgment that it is wrong to strike his wife. The law only provides an external restraint and threatens him with unpleasant consequences should he violate its prohibitions.

> ***1 Timothy 1:8-9*** *Now we know that the law is good, if one uses it lawfully, understanding this, that the law is not laid down for the just but for the lawless and disobedient, for the ungodly and sinners, for the unholy and profane, for those who strike their fathers and mothers, for murderers…*

Bancroft has concluded that abusers do not see themselves as abusers.[63] Even when arrested, they regard the whole thing as ridiculous and unfair. It is always some other guy that the law should be after, not him. The law is just out to get him. And so he blames and plays the victim.

Only as Deep as His Words

The abuser's entitlement mindset turns history and facts on their head in ways that are absolutely remarkable for the apparent sincerity in which they are presented and their complete lack of foundation. Abusers can present myths in a way that causes most listeners to believe them. What is such a person thinking when presenting fiction as fact? Such a person's reality is only as deep as the words that come out of his mouth.

Ken is a hollow man. He is quite popular with people who know him only casually. He can seem very caring. He is known for his apparent love for children and his interest in them. At social functions, it seems that Ken knows just what to do and say, unless you watch and listen to him closely. Ken's words are just that: words. Words are symbols that are supposed to represent something with substance or which consist of genuine feeling or emotion. Things like trees, love,

63 Lundy Bancroft, *When Dad Hurts Mom: Helping Your Children Heal the Wounds of Witnessing Abuse* (New York: Berkley, 2004), 296.

color, beauty, grief, and so forth. Ken knows the words, but he has no clue of the reality behind them. His inner man is an emotional monotone.

Ken has abused his wife for their entire 20 years of marriage. He has the fundamental mindset of the abuser: entitlement, power, control and justification. Ken is currently dealing with the fact that his wife is not being romantic toward him, and he has been accusing her of being frigid. Tonight, Ken is demanding that she tell him how she wants him to love her. "Show me!" he demands. The problem is, as his wife knows, any attempt to "show him" will end in failure because Ken only uses the word love, but will never come to a real knowledge of it. Ken does not feel and therefore love is unattainable for him to express or to receive. Ken knows the outer form, but he denies the reality.

Abusers like Ken try to mimic what they see in other people. And they can become very convincing mimics, but that is all they will be: actors reciting the lines of a script. Inside lurks the real person they are. "What is empathy?" a sociopathic man asked his friend. "Empathy is a quality in a person that enables them to feel the pain that someone else is feeling," his friend answered. After striking a confused look, the sociopath replied, "Then why would I want it?" This interchange was in a comedy script. But in real life, it is no comedy.

Desire to be Unknown

The abuser's answer to the offer "A penny for your thoughts" is "Keep your penny!" To support his creation of chaos and deception, the abuser works very hard to prevent people from knowing who he is and how he really thinks. Keeping people guessing is habitual for him. He likes to know that he is unpredictable. All of this confusion keeps his victim confused, and confused people are much less of a threat to his control and power.

This desire to be a mystery, to be an unknown, is related to his use of a façade by which he appears as Dr. Jekyl (respectable, nice-guy) but in reality is Mr. Hyde (a cruel abuser). The façade creates confusion about who he is while his unpredictability produces mystery when it comes to knowing what he is going to do.

When you talk to Stuart, you come away wondering if anyone is home. Not because Stuart isn't intelligent, but because he doesn't seem to originate thoughts. Having a conversation with Stuart is somewhat like talking to yourself in a mirror as

Stuart becomes your reflection, parroting back to you. As a result, you never really know what Stuart is thinking, nor what he might do in a particular situation. Some therapists have called Stuart the drifter personality who is not necessarily an abusive personality. But some drifters may well be abusers, or even sociopaths. Stuart's concept of power and control is simply not has high as that of many other more intensely abusive people. And yet he is characterized by the very same fundamental qualities of the abuser: entitlement, power, control, and justification.

To some degree, every abuser is a mystery. To remain an unknown, abusive people may:

- Rage one evening about the meal his victim prepared, and then praise her for the very same dish next month. What *does* he like?
- Express drippingly sweet romance to her, and the next day tell her she is the worst wife a man could ever have. Which is it?
- Pretend to be the most eminent Christian saint, a picture of Christlikeness, and at other times seem to be the devil himself. (When a person displays two different personalities, as most abusers do, always conclude that the evil one is the real person. Good people do not pretend to be bad. Bad people very often pretend to be good. Most abuse victims will agree that had they realized this years ago, they would have come to understand what was happening to them much sooner).
- Not talk at all.
- Be a loner. Make himself hard to reach by, for example, never having a phone.
- Communicate in half-truths or use statements that are ambiguous.
- Make statements that leave it to his victim to complete the thought.
- Stare and look "through" the victim without saying a word.

All of this mystery and confusion-making is quite intentional, serving the purposes of the abuser very well.[64]

> ***1 Timothy 5:24-25*** *The sins of some men are conspicuous, going before them to judgment, but the sins of others appear later.* (25) *So also good works are conspicuous, and even those that are not cannot remain hidden.*

Listen to Dostoevsky describe just such a man:

---

64 Bancroft, *Why Does He Do That?*, 18-20. The abusive person's tactic of being a mystery is discussed.

I've known Rodion for a year and a half: sullen, gloomy, arrogant, proud; recently (and maybe much earlier) insecure and hypochondriac. Magnanimous and kind. Doesn't like voicing his feelings, and would rather do something cruel than speak his heart out in words. At times, however, he's not hypochondriac at all, but just inhumanly cold and callous, as if there really were two opposite characters in him, changing places with each other. At times he's terribly taciturn! He's always in a hurry, always too busy, yet he lies there doing nothing. Not given to mockery, and not because he lacks sharpness but as if he had no time for such trifles. Never hears people out to the end. Is never interested in what interests everyone else at a given moment. Sets a terribly high value on himself and, it seems, not without a certain justification."[65]

If you find that description foggy and confusing, then you are feeling the same confusion an abuse victim lives with. Abusers infect victims with a kind of mental, emotional, and spiritual glaucoma so that life with them is like living in a steam room where nothing is clearly seen.

Boredom

Imagine this person we have been describing. He has no empathy, nor does he really love anyone. He has no conscience and is to a lesser or greater degree emotionally numb. As we have expressed it before, his life is a monochromatic painting, lyrics without music. And this all translates into boredom. Many abusers are impulsive and constantly seeking some new form of stimulation. (Perhaps this is why so many abusive men pursue pornography.)

In attempts to alleviate the boredom, abusers create that chaos we have already discussed. They make things happen, but there is little logic to those things. In fact, they very often despise the discipline of a regular schedule, of thinking things through carefully ahead of time, and certainly do not value the thoughts and input of their victim. Life with such a person can be like having a constant tornado roaming to and fro through the house.

Bored people blame other people. They look to those around them for a solution to the monotony of their life. And when that solution isn't found, they

65 Fyodor Dostoevsky, *Crime and Punishment* (Public Domain Books, 2001), Location 3038, Kindle Edition.

punish. "You're no fun anymore!" Rages can be the result of a person who is just sick with the drudgery of his life and who just has to stir things up in some way, normally to the hurt of others.

Abusive, bored people are starters, not finishers. The evidence of Tom's boredom is strewn throughout his home. There are the expensive mountain bikes he purchased last year, ridden one time, without maintenance or repair, and now in shambles. Then there is the $2,000 Browning rifle with a long-range scope that he just had to have last fall. He went hunting twice, never cleaned the rifle after the last hunt, and now it sits rusting in the corner.

The abusive person's mentality of superiority and entitlement enables him to be a user, but in his mind, it is the job of his wife or children or employees to clean up after him. Responsible stewardship of the things he owns is just too boring for him to be concerned with, even if it means his family suffers from lack. Besides, he must move on in his quest for meaning, which he will never find because he refuses to embrace responsibility.

> ***Philippians 3:19-20*** *Their end is destruction, their god is their belly, and they glory in their shame, with minds set on earthly things. But our citizenship is in heaven, and from it we await a Savior, the Lord Jesus Christ...*

The Mind of a Two-Year Old Terror

Imagine the average two-year old with the resources (strength, money, experience in using others, etc.) that an adult has. Imagine that they are still age two in their emotional makeup and social skills and development of conscience. Imagine them with a gun. Pretty scary, right? If we are going to understand abusers, it is vital that we comprehend their immaturity. Abusers are very baby-like, but unfortunately are not harmless like a baby.

For example:

- The abuser is so self-consumed that if he suffers any illness, minor injury, or inconvenience, he will demand that the world focus upon him.
- When he does not get his way, which most often means when he is opposed in his quest for power and control, he throws a tantrum of some type. A two-year old throws himself down on the floor. An adult abuser may throw his victim to the floor.

- When confronted, he blames and plays the victim.
- He has no problem with contradictory and irrational statements.
- He lacks self-discipline and perseverance.
- Like a little spoiled child throwing a tantrum on Christmas morning because he didn't get what he wanted, the abuser only thinks of himself. Carol said that her ex-husband/abuser always ruined holidays by going into a rage. That is unless it was *his* birthday or Father's day. Another victim describes a similar typical tactic her husband would subject the family to on a holiday:

> On Christmas, when the children were opening their presents, my husband kept interrupting us to read to us from his book, which was totally unrelated to Christmas. We'd have to have the little one's stop everything (we open one at a time so everyone can see) and we'd all have to listen to him read or expound on what he'd read. This self-centered behavior stems from his jealously that anyone else would be the center of the family's attention.

If you are a parent, think for a moment about what it means to train up your children so that they become functional, responsible adults. Fundamentally, it means helping them put away childish things. To be self-giving rather than self-serving. To stop thinking so highly of themselves and instead think of others. It means to love other people rather than themselves. To have empathy toward others. Maturity is loving God and loving our neighbor.

The abuser fails in all of this because he remains a child. And this means that in many ways we must deal with him as we would deal with a child. Parents, you know that it is rather futile to try to "reach the heart of your child" when he is two years old and has just ripped his sister's teddy bear out of her hands. Of course, we should instruct their mind and heart at such times as much as is possible, but if we expect a two-year old to break down in tears out of empathy for his sister at that point, well, we have a lot to learn about parenting! So it is in dealing with the abuser. We must deal with him in terms of consequences and strength.

Virginia is an adept manipulator of her co-workers. She is very capable of using cruelty and rage to punish them into compliance with her demands. Of course her supervisor is oblivious to this and sees her as one of his very finest employees. Virginia appears, on the surface, to be a solid, skilled worker and a real asset to the company. In fact, she has been driving the truly valuable employees out of the company for many years now. No one, except those who have to work with her, understands why there is such turnover. Virginia blames it all on others and those in authority believe her. In reality, in Virginia, the company has a two-year old tantrum-throwing emotional child running amok doing serious damage. In emotional maturity terms, Virginia isn't even potty trained. As Robert Hare puts it in his insightful description of a psychopath, Virginia has:

> ... a narcissistic and grossly inflated view of [her] self-worth and importance, a truly astounding egocentricity and sense of entitlement, and see(s) [herself] as the center of the universe, as (a) superior being who is justified in living according to [her] own rules.[66]

In other words, an emotional toddler. This is why so many abusers intensify their abuse when their wife is pregnant: they can't handle the prospect of anyone other than themselves getting the attention. It's a kind of sibling rivalry: the toddler is jealous of the new baby.

What He Thinks About Women

> ***2 Samuel 13:14-15*** *But he would not listen to her, and being stronger than she, he violated her and lay with her. Then Amnon hated her with very great hatred, so that the hatred with which he hated her was greater than the love with which he had loved her. And Amnon said to her, "Get up! Go!"*

For purposes of brevity, we will deal only with the question, what does the abusive man think about women? We could just as profitably examine the answer to what does the abusive woman think about men? But because most scenarios are of an abusive man (at least in the home), we will limit ourselves to the first question.

Abusive people think in grandiose terms about themselves. They are entitled. They are superior. They are like the little girl with a personality disorder who told her doctor that she likes to think of herself standing on a high mountain looking down upon all the other people—the little people—and they had to do what she said or she would smash their heads!

We are not surprised then that the abusive man extends these attitudes toward women as a whole and toward his victim in particular. Thus the very

66 Hare, Location 471, Kindle Edition.

common practice of male abusers using pornography. Notice what the following account tells us about this abuser's mindset toward women:

> Much of the porn he liked was violent in nature. It bled over in the names he would call me (especially when he was feeling "in the mood"), his roughness towards me, his understanding of what a wife wants and needs. He came to believe that a real man puts his wife in "her place" through physical force. I cannot count the number of times that he told me that he felt more like a man when he was able to "give you what you deserve". The fact that I didn't like that, didn't want it, did little to change his mind. He'd get angry at me for not being "submissive enough" or not "obeying" him as "you ought to" and so forth. (Abuse victim)

This next account comes from another abuse victim. It illustrates very clearly what the abusive man's attitude toward women is. Alex's façade of choice is Christianity, and this makes him one of the worst kinds.

> Alex is and always has been a strong believer that a man needs to keep a woman in her place and to do that requires physical force at times. However, he was raised with the idea that it is never right for a man to hit a woman. How could he combine the two? By convincing her, through twisting Scripture, that he has a right to punish her, humiliate her, dominate her, and that, according to Scripture, she has to "obey" him no matter what he demands of her and no matter what he does to her. [67]
>
> Well, that's just what he did. Many nights, over many, many years, I went to sleep with cuts and bruises from his rough treatment that I felt I deserved.[68] And, since he hadn't beaten me in the classic sense (he wasn't violently out of control as my father was when he beat my mother) I never

67 When I was the pastor of a church in Alaska, a rather sophisticated sounding man phoned my office. He wanted to know if God authorized him to give his wife a spanking. His "reasoning" (which seemed very logical to him) was that if God instructed him to spank his children, then since the Bible says a wife is also under the authority of her husband, it follows that her husband can spank her for disobedience. What do you say to such a fool? As he refused to give me his name or come in and see me, I told him that he needed to remember that if he ever laid a hand on his wife, God has a much bigger stick to strike him with!

68 In our chapter on helping victims, we will discuss this matter of shame and false guilt which the abuser instills in his victims. It is one of the first things the victim must be freed from if she is to recover.

gave any thought to the fact that he was physically abusing me. But he often referred to it himself as "a beating" or "a thrashing" but then he'd turn around and say he would never beat me because that just wasn't right. Then he'd turn again and say that he wanted to "punish you until you cry and then keep on punishing you for a long time afterwards because tears of submission are good for you".

Alex was much stronger than I was and would make a point of demonstrating it regularly (he'd grab me, hold me down, refuse to let me move, back me into a corner or refuse to let me out of the room when I needed to go to one of the babies or something so I'd know enough to be afraid of him) plus he dominated me emotionally (he made me feel that I was never "good enough" for him and, worse, that I wasn't being obedient to God) so anytime I tried to take a stand, I'd end up crumpling. I hated what he was doing but he wouldn't listen and, inside, I feared that what he did would escalate if I took a stand. He was always telling me he was afraid that one day he'd "snap and kill you, me and the children".

He made extreme physical and emotional demands upon me. On top of it, my life was to revolve around him in all ways so he'd schedule me things to do that really made no sense and then get mad if they weren't done; other times he'd "forget" that he'd demanded them and I'd have to bring it up "because, if you were a good wife, you'd want to submit to your husband" and that meant "reporting" to him. He wanted what he wanted when he wanted it and, as a good wife, it was my job to serve him...no matter what he wanted.

He only gave me attention when it meshed with his ideas of controlling a woman. He had these fantasies that he would go on and on about that always revolved around hurting women; one involved him having fun with other women while he encouraged other men to punish me or beat me while he and the women watched. It was sick the things he would think about and insist on talking about. He'd turn any subject into one about beating me, punishing me or about how women, in general, needed to be "dealt with" by their men; every time we talked...literally every single time...he'd take the subject back to this. He even told me he hoped our daughters married men who would "do the things for them I do for you" because it would be "good for them." He told me daily that he was "the Lord of my castle" and as such he could demand anything of me...anything at all...and I'd have to comply (he never tried to demand I submit to his vile fantasies and such, but always insisted that he could if he wished to).

He wouldn't let me go to bed at night until he was ready (which was in the early hours of the morning). He wouldn't let me go to sleep until he was ready to sleep and, if I fell asleep, he'd wake me up and insist on having one of his talks or tell me he was going to have to punish me for some infraction. He had very long lists of rules "designed so you will fail" so that he could ensure I was "dealt with regularly." He'd often make me sleep without enough covers so that I would be cold and remember "that I am your Master because I am disciplining you even in your sleep." Then he'd get tired of it all for a while and he'd drop it and I'd think I could finally relax because it was all over only to have it all start again a few days or a few weeks later. It was never ending.

Isaiah 10:1-3 *Woe to those who decree iniquitous decrees, and the writers who keep writing oppression, to turn aside the needy from justice and to rob the poor of my people of their right, that widows may be their spoil, and that they may make the fatherless their prey! What will you do on the day of punishment, in the ruin that will come from afar? To whom will you flee for help, and where will you leave your wealth?*

CHAPTER 7

Effects on Victims: Abuse as Murder

Psalm 10:10-12 *The helpless are crushed, sink down, and fall by his might. He says in his heart, "God has forgotten, he has hidden his face, he will never see it." Arise, O LORD; O God, lift up your hand; forget not the afflicted.*

If you knew that a man was slowly poisoning his wife and children with mercury in their food, what would you do? They are growing sicker and sicker. Symptoms progress through unexplained loss of peripheral vision, strange tingling "pins and needles" sensations, loss of coordination and muscle weakness. You see it happening and you know that if it goes on, this woman and her children are going to die. What would you do?

Would you tell the woman that God requires her to remain married to her husband? To submit to him? To be a better, more obedient wife in order to make him stop the poisoning? Would you write a book that claims the Bible prohibits divorce in *all* cases and that if this woman divorces her husband, she is forbidden by God to remarry? Or perhaps you would tell her that this poisoning is a trial that God has brought into her life to make her a better Christian, so she just needs to endure and trust the Lord? Or perhaps we would simply deny the facts and tell her that this entire poisoning business is the result of her overactive imagination with no basis in reality at all. In other words, we would tell her that she is crazy. Is that what you would do?

Of course not. You know what you would do. You would take action against this murderous man and rescue his victims from him. You would report him to the police and announce his evil to the church. Why? How do you know this is what you would do? Simply because, you know what mercury poisoning is and what it does: It kills, and murder is against the law of God.

Sadly, we cannot say that we are as wise when it comes to the poison of abuse.

There are two primary reasons why the evangelical church has failed the victims of the abuser: 1) Christians rarely know what abuse *is* in all of its ugliness, and 2) Christians rarely know what *effects* abuse has on its victims. Yet, in spite of this ignorance, we are confident that *we know*, and that we are sufficient to pronounce God's word on the matter. The material we have presented to the reader to this point will go far in correcting the first deficiency, and it is to the second that we now turn – what abuse *does* to its victims.

Abuse as Murder

> ***Matthew 5:21-22*** *You have heard that it was said to those of old, 'You shall not murder; and whoever murders will be liable to judgment.' But I say to you that everyone who is angry with his brother will be liable to judgment; whoever insults his brother will be liable to the council; and whoever says, 'You fool!' will be liable to the hell of fire.*

Consider these words of Christ once again. Insulting, malicious treatment of a person is the spirit of murder. It violates the sixth commandment, even though the victim is still physically alive. Abusers are murderers. Far too often this is true *literally*, as you can read about in your newspaper almost every day; but abuse is always a murder of the victim's personhood. Like lead poisoning, it gradually and progressively erodes her life.

> He always worked to destroy my self-confidence. Gradually I found myself dropping things that had been my interests as I came to believe that I was not good enough to pursue them. I could never please him, never do anything that was good enough for him. Eventually I had no individuality as a person. My life was totally about him. All color and fragrance left my life. (Abuse victim)

The destruction of the victim's personhood is really very similar to what must happen in concentration camps. Through a steady campaign of de-humanization, the prisoner comes to be a mere number, indistinguishable from all the other numbers wearing the same uniform and the same shaved head. As we consider the specific effects of the abuser on his victim, we will see how each is really an aspect of murder. M. Scott Peck confirms this when he writes that evil has to do with killing, but not just killing of the body. Evil kills the human spirit.[69]

Identity Theft: Loss of the Sense of Self

> "I KNOW about feeling a million miles away from the person I once recognized and valued myself to be.…You lose yourself. You remain vigilant. You monitor his moods, actions, and reactions as a meteorologist might study changing weather patterns."[70]
>
> "I used to be putty before God started healing me. I'd go out to dinner with someone and they'd have to order for me. I couldn't even make that kind of decision." (Abuse victim)

Whenever I visit a large hospital, I have a relatively easy time finding the room I want to visit. Check the graphic map in the main entryway ("You are here"), take the right elevator to the correct floor, follow the signs this way and that, and there you are. But then, it's time to leave and I have a problem. Now I have to backtrack without the assistance of all those tools I used to get there. I'm lost. Did I come from that way, or this way? I should have dropped bread crumbs along the way or brought my GPS. I can't trust my perceptions. I can't trust myself.

Life as an abuse victim is much like this. As the abuser constantly works to erode his victim's sense of self: self-esteem, self-confidence, self-care, self-development, the victim's ability to navigate through life deteriorates. She trusts her perceptions of reality less and less. The confidence she once enjoyed in making decisions diminishes. As she is devalued, she may give less attention to taking care of herself, physically, emotionally, mentally and spiritually. She becomes, in her eyes, less and less of a *person* and her abuser is quite happy to reinforce this conclusion.

Many Christians erroneously believe that "self" is always a wicked thing; something to be eradicated. Self-esteem is thought to be evil because it is equated with pride and haughtiness. And, after all, didn't Christ teach that we must

69 M. Scott Peck, *People of the Lie: The Hope for Healing Human Evil* (New York: Touchstone, 1998), 42.

70 Sarah Braun and Bridget Flynn, *Honeymoon and Hell: A Memoir of Abuse* (Self-Publishe, 2011), 363.

die to ourselves, deny ourselves, take up our cross and follow Him. Didn't He? However, the Bible *never* teaches us that following Christ, dying with Him, being raised with Him as new creations, *means we have no individual identity.* On the contrary, Christ knows us each by name. The Holy Spirit joins us to Christ's body, but each of us is given a unique function. It is as individuals that we will be rewarded by Christ on that Day. In fact, it is in Christ that a person becomes really *fully human*. It is living for self, without regard for God or neighbor, that is condemned by Scripture.

As the abuser violates his victim's boundaries, tells them what they should and should not think or do, condemns their decisions, contradicts their perceptions, mocks and ridicules their achievements and interests, the victim progressively jettisons the likes and dislikes, the dreams and hopes, and anything else that served as expressions and extensions of her *self.* Like a country with no borders, she effaces herself to comply with her abuser's world and increasingly ceases to *be.*

Silvia's abuser husband worked to reduce her freedom. He told her "you're just a woman. You don't need freedom. You need to obey me." This man professed to be a Christian, thus the use of Scripture to justify his abuse. Silvia told me that it became harder and harder for her to be able to leave the house unless he wanted to. It grew increasingly apparent that the lives of her and her children would revolve around him. He reminded her regularly that he was better than she was, that *he* would decide what the family would do each evening, *he* would select her friends, *he* would handle all the money, *she* would wear used clothing; all of which (and more) stripped away who Silvia was. The confidence and hope that once characterized her outlook on life melted away and the person she used to be became a stranger to her. Bancroft has found in his experience of working with abusers that they often use degrading words that they know particularly hurt a woman. Such terms attack her very person, label her as an animal, a worthless object, or other vile thing. (Bancroft 2003)

Through the spectacles of the abuser mentality, the victim is not even a human being, and this depersonalization gradually infects the victim's own concept of herself. *Shame*, the feeling that she as a person is one big *mistake*, worthless and not someone to be loved, infects her. Jane Middleton-Moz describes shame as a belief that we are unlovable and alone in our undesirable uniqueness. The shamed person feels helpless, worthless, and hated. She even hates herself. The shamed person does not live her life. It just happens. (Middleton-Moz 1990)

In the end, the victim may come to believe that what she feels, thinks, desires, perceives and hopes for is of no value or importance. It is only what *he* feels, thinks, desires, perceives and hopes for that is true and worthwhile. And a person with no valid feelings or thoughts or hopes is, well, a non-person.

> When I was with my ex-husband I was washing dishes one night and thought "I'm like those cardboard cutout dolls that I used to play with when I was a girl." My father used to bring home occasional treats, and sometimes the treat was a book of cardboard press out dolls, with press out clothes that you could dress the dolls with. Each piece of clothing had little tags at certain places on the edge of the garment; you would fold back the tag to hold the garment in place on the doll. I felt like one of those dolls: two dimensional, lifeless, wearing garments that were as lifeless and two dimensional as myself. Presenting well to others, but utterly devoid of substance. (Abuse Victim)

Doubting of One's Sanity

To be mentally and emotionally healthy, we need to be able to orient ourselves to what is happening around us. We need to have a sense of "the lay of the land" and how we fit into all of it. If you have ever been out in the woods and found yourself "turned around," you have an idea of what this means. You have been absolutely certain that the car is "that way," but the tracks in the snow tell you that it can't be. But it must be! Yes, those tracks have exactly the same tread design as your own boots, but they must belong to someone else. Some people in these kinds of situations refuse to believe their compass because its indication of where north is doesn't fit their idea of that direction.

An abuse victim, as long as she remains uneducated about the nature and tactics of abuse, is much like a person who is disoriented in the woods. She has come to distrust her own perceptions of reality. She doesn't remember denting the car, but he is so confident in his denials of it…perhaps she did do it. She thought…but he said. She saw…but he denies. She heard…but he didn't say that.

Abusers are quite capable of assaulting their victims with intense rage or ridicule, and the next morning behaving as if the event never happened. The victim, still depressed and downcast over the shame heaped upon her, is met

by a smiling, cheerful man. "Hey, babe, it's a beautiful day!" When she fails to respond with a similar sunny disposition, he goes to work on her. "You are always so negative. No wonder the kids are so messed up!" If she reminds him of the evils he attacked her with the previous evening, he gives a radically different version from the one she saw and heard and felt. *And he does so very convincingly.*

- "There goes your wild imagination again."
- "Aw, that didn't happen. This is what happened…"
- "Losing your memory, are you?"
- "You always think the worst of what I say and do."
- "That's not what I said and you know it."
- "I was only having fun with you."
- "You're always twisting things to make me look bad."
- "Everyone else thought it was funny except you."

Over time this kind of denial and lying takes a toll on the victim over time. Constant questioning and confusion about what really happened or what was really said or what one's motives really were gradually drains the victim's confidence in her ability to trust her own perceptions. She becomes increasingly disoriented about what is happening in her life. At times, she wonders if she is going insane. She is constantly ruminating with self-doubt.

> I remember being extremely disoriented when I first lived in London. I'd never realized it, but all the years I'd grown up in Australia, I'd learned to unconsciously figure out where north was by the direction of the sun, since the sun is always slightly to the north in the southern hemisphere. In Europe, the sun was to the south. In London, I always got north and south round the wrong way until I figured out what was going on. This is like domestic abuse. Everything is round the wrong way. That's why the photo which I chose for cover of my book, *Not Under Bondage,* seemed so appropriate (the photo is rotated 90 degrees).[71]

When victims first come to realize that what is happening to them has a name, abuse, and what it's tactics and mentality are, it is like someone is shining a bright light into their darkness. This knowledge serves as a GPS, complete with topographical map that shows them, "This is you, here is where you are, and this is the way you need to go. And by the way, you aren't crazy after all."

71 Personal correspondence, Barbara Roberts, 2012

Traumatic Bonding

"You are devaluated and mistreated by the same person that can often act as if they worship and adore you."[72]

Also known as the *Stockholm Syndrome*, traumatic bonding is a real "wrench in the works" of abuse. It is very important for us to understand it because it will enable us to better comprehend why it can be so difficult for a victim to leave her abuser.

In a relationship of ongoing abuse, the victim can become more and more dependent on her abuser. As she is subjected to ridicule, physical attacks, and other forms of cruelty, her need to be comforted and shown kindness increases. Here is the irony of traumatic bonding: her abuser is the one who offers her this kindness. The very man who beat her the night before is the one who brings her breakfast in bed or promises to make it up to her by taking her out that night.

Her need for receiving human kindness overrides the fact that the one giving it *is the one who causes her trauma in the first place.* So a kind of bond is produced. An astute abuser knows this, and successfully alternates periods of traumatic abuse with seasons of apparent kindness, increasing the strength of this bond and her need for him. The confusion and loss of orientation that is caused by this alternating cruelty and "kindness" produces an even stronger bond between the victim and her abuser, making it even more difficult for her to escape. The isolation of abuse victims only exacerbates traumatic bonding. The humiliation they have endured, the regrets they feel about what they have done or allowed, causes them to avoid people, so that their opportunities for healthy relationships are limited or non-existent.

Traumatic bonding also explains why even the "normal phase" of the cycle of abuse is in fact abusive. The abuser can make his victim feel grateful to him by temporarily releasing her from some of his stringent demands. A kidnapper who forbids his hostage to go to the toilet unless he permits it elicits intense gratitude in the hostage whenever he permits her to go to the toilet. And so it is in abuse. A reprieve from active abuse produces gratitude in the victim and thus the bond between her and the abuser is strengthened.

72 Braun and Flynn, Location 70, Kindle Edition.

Physical Ailments

> "My blood pressure goes up to 225/127 when he rages at me. I am afraid that I will have a heart attack or stroke. I do not feel I can physically survive this much longer." (Abuse victim)

In the three years that I have studied this subject of abuse, *every one* of the victims who have contacted me and shared their stories suffers from poor health. This should not surprise us, given the huge levels of stress under which victims live. Depressed, hopeless people with little sense of self-worth do not look to their own health as they should. They may abuse drugs or alcohol, or not eat as they should. Victims often do not get adequate sleep and, needless to say, being physically assaulted does not help one's health either.

As another means of power and control, abusers quite frequently deny their victim access to adequate medical treatment. One victim told how her husband refused to let her get a recommended surgery because it cost too much, even though he had more than adequate funds to pay for it. Another described how she and her children suffer from poor dental health with multiple cavities, but her husband will not permit them to go to the dentist.

Child-bearing is hard enough in a healthy marriage, but in an abusive one the suffering is multiplied. Numbers of victims tell how they came home from the hospital after giving birth (some even had a C-section delivery) and were made to cook their abuser dinner and clean up the house as soon as they walked in the door. Abusers also often insist on having intercourse with their victim very shortly after she has gone through childbirth, before she has even healed.

Abusers can be slave-drivers when it comes to household chores. Mick lived to hunt. He moved his family into a small cabin in a remote area and made certain that his boss laid him off each fall just before hunting season. While drawing unemployment, Mick hunted and spent his money on himself. The property on which their cabin was located did not yet have electricity or a well. This meant a huge addition to his wife's workload. In addition to homeschooling the children, she had to haul fuel for the generator. Water had to be packed in five-gallon cans from a stream even in the deep snows of winter. Mick was able to buy himself a snowmobile, a pickup, and all kinds of outdoor toys, but it was years before he finally paid for a well to be drilled. During these years, his wife's health deteriorated. She has ongoing back problems and her untreated diabetes has taken its toll as well.

Some abuse victims turn to substance abuse themselves to alleviate their pain. In other cases, the abuser pressures them to use alcohol or drugs, accompany them to bars, and do things they would never do themselves. Abuse also promotes sleep deprivation and nightmares, which detract from good mental health as well.

Fear

Fear. What is it like to live in an atmosphere of constant apprehension, being afraid every single weekday as the clock nears 5:00 pm and you know *he* is coming home from work? This is the typical abuse victim's world.

Abusers use fear to dominate and control their victims. They communicate verbally and non-verbally that *anything* the victim does, or does not do, or thinks, or says, could spark an attack. Fear of what he will do if he finds out she made a purchase, fear of what he might do to one of the children, fear of him finding out she is thinking of leaving him, fear of what he will say if she visits a friend, fear that he will alienate or take her children from her, fear that he won't like the dinner she prepared, fear that he will hurt or kill her dog: fear, fear, fear. This accounts for the "walking on eggshells" environment we mentioned earlier. (Female victims typically say "I live in fear." Male victims don't say that nearly so often. Male victims often say "I live with this crazy woman" but they don't always say, "I live in fear.")

Victims do not even necessarily have a reprieve from this fear *while they are sleeping.* Many report having nightmares regularly. Others try to fall asleep, but know that even if they do, the abuser may drag them from the bed in the middle of the night in one of his rages. One woman always slept with one foot on the floor, because her husband would unpredictably kick her in the middle of the night.

And then there is the fear of what other people think of you. A victim of decades of abuse at the hands of her husband related how she was enjoying a budding relationship with a woman at church. Her hopes were abruptly deflated when, after she mentioned researching the subject of domestic violence, the other woman quickly turned cold. Victims often live with a constant fear of abandonment.

Let's not forget the ever present fear *of being killed* that many victims live with every day. Mick's wife once told me "If he ever thinks that I am going to leave him or report him to the police, I know that he will kill me. No restraining order will ever stop him." The reality of these fears is confirmed by our daily newspapers.

What are the effects on a person who lives in an atmosphere charged with fear? To an uneducated outsider, a victim's behavior may seem odd, unstable, or self-defeating, but many people (including victims) don't realize how much victims resist the abuse. An act of resistance may be covert or overt. Walking on eggshells, the victim is constantly making micro decisions trying to minimize the pernicious effects of the abuser's conduct. Given the crazy-making, unjust, cruel, dangerous and illogical treatment being dished out by the abuser, the responses of the victim to the abuse are usually pretty sensible. The abused person will respond judiciously, tailoring her conduct to the circumstances in which she finds herself, with the aim of maintaining personal integrity even if only within the privacy of her own mind and conscience. An abused person's resistance to the abuse may be indiscernible to the uneducated bystander, but it can be discovered and validated by a discerning supporter who understands abuse dynamics.[73]

Poverty

> ***1 Timothy 5:8*** *But if anyone does not provide for his relatives, and especially for members of his household, he has denied the faith and is worse than an unbeliever.*

Not all abusers are sociopathic CEO's drawing in huge salaries. Many are people with average or below average earning skills, or even if they are *able*, their selfish and even childish absorption with themselves results in them not holding down a job for very long. It is common for abusers who do have sufficient income to refuse to share it with their victim, putting them into a poverty level of existence.

This victim describes how her abusive husband plunged her and her children into poverty:

---

73 Calgary Women's Emergency Shelter, "Honoring Resistance: How Women Resist Abuse in Intimate Relationships," www.calgarywomensshelter.com.

I remember times when I have had to pull bugs out of food in order to serve it because there just wasn't anything else to eat. We have had to endure winters with no heat in the house. We have to wear threadbare, stained clothing to church because that was all that we had. For months we have had almost no protein in our diet; lots of biscuits and gravy.

Most people, including our fellow church members, just don't relate to our experience at all. We go to church hungry in our junker car, and everyone else there is dressed in nice clothes, driving new cars, headed for Sizzler after church. Once when the church did "help" us, they made us feel very small. A couple of ladies were appointed by the deacons to take us shopping and spend five hundred dollars that had been donated for us. They patronized us, directed us as to what we should and should not buy, and simply had no clue at all about what it is really like to be poor. For the most part, we were ignored at church.

I know that for me and for some other women I know who have been abused, our husbands would keep moving us around so that we had no time to make friends. They also purposely chose older, run-down houses and furnished them with worn out furniture…all of which produces embarrassment that makes inviting other people over very difficult.

I am not trying to be overly critical of the church (although we all deserve some rebuke in this area), but to encourage Christians to give some real thought to this whole matter of poverty: what it does to a person, what our attitudes are toward the poor, and how we would want to be treated if we were poor.

Poverty reinforces other harmful effects of abuse: low self-esteem, shame, isolation, physical illness, and many others. Here is the account of a victim whose husband's abuse includes failing to provide adequately for his family and take on his responsibilities as a husband and father:

When he fails to provide, as he always does, I'm left to pick up the pieces in caring for our children. I have to try to figure how to keep clothes on their backs, food in their tummies and so forth...while still doing silly things like keeping the power on. Like right now, I'm having to explain (again) to the little ones why we can't do some of the things that they want to do, things that aren't expensive but, for us, are like reaching for the moon. When every single dollar needs to be spent in ten different places and the landlord is breathing down our necks wanting his money (now, please), there is little or nothing left...and that is my husband's fault but, nonetheless, it affects all of us. And, it adds to my busyness in so many ways. It's a lot easier to plan anything when there isn't the fear of a knock at the door or a phone call... endlessly.

Alienation From Others

I have been a pastor for nearly thirty years, and to one extent or another, I have been the target of abusers disguised as Christians for most of that time. I am convinced that many of them have been sociopaths, on the extreme right hand side of the no-conscience scale.[74] This is one of the primary reasons I have been able to identify with abuse victims and to call on the church to wake up to the havoc these kinds of people are causing among us. Let me explain from my own experience how abuse works to alienate the victim from people and society in general.

After my first eight years of pastoral ministry, I was already deeply affected by abuse. Of course, I didn't understand what was really happening, but as I look back on that period of my life, I can plainly see that such was the case. (I could write another book entitled "Abusers and Sociopaths I Have Known!")

One Sunday, about this same time in my pastoral experience, a very wealthy man who had purchased a ranch in the area where my first church was located, visited the church. Afterward, he spoke with me and apologized for having driven the past year to another church sixty miles away rather than come to ours. One of the main reasons for his decision was that one very abusive man who had been in our church and whom I had confronted with his sin, had convinced this fellow that our church, and myself in particular, were very harsh and judgmental. After hearing me teach the morning class and preach in the worship service, he realized

74 I do not believe that all abusers are sociopaths, but all abusers do have a largely impaired conscience. Perhaps this is giving them too much credit. I have known abusers whose abuse seems to originate in their desire to control others. Others may well have been abuse victims themselves and then embraced abuse of others as a defensive technique. See Bancroft, *Why Does He Do That?* "Note on Terminology." Every abuser I have met however lacks *empathy.*

that he had made a great mistake in being swayed by this man. (Two days later he visited that man and rebuked him for slandering our ministry!). He then invited me to spend the next day with him as he had to drive north for some supplies.

During that next day, at this man's request, I recounted our experience of pastoral ministry in that small, mountain church. I preached every Sunday for eight years in an old log community hall with a moose head on the wall and a big wood-burning barrel stove! Ministry there had been a constant battle. Very few of the professing Christians there were truly regenerate people. And we had a number of very abusive, if not sociopathic people as well.

When I had finished telling him my story, he re-affirmed my call to the pastoral ministry, encouraged me in regard to my ability to preach and teach, and then he said something that seemed odd to me at the time. He said, *"You and your wife are incredibly wounded people and I will pray for you regularly."* In my naiveté about abuse and its effects, I did not see what he knew had to be the case. Abuse wounds. And one of the ways it wounds is, it alienates its victims from other people. Not just in the sense of isolation, but in robbing the victim of his confidence that other people will ever want to have a relationship with him.

To illustrate this, let me share another experience that happened about the same time. The early years of our present pastoral ministry were similarly difficult. Abusive men and women dominated the church. As with all abusers, they saw themselves as entitled to power and control and felt fully justified in using whatever means were necessary to maintain it. A new pastor can be quite the threat to such people, and they bristled. Gradually, one by one, they departed.

About three years into this ministry, my wife and I took a vacation back to Montana. We checked into a motel in the Bitterroot Valley south of Missoula and the next morning I drove to the grocery store to pick up some breakfast items (i.e., doughnuts). I parked in the lot, got out of the truck, and started to walk toward the front door. Some people who had just come out of the store looked at me and said, "Hey, we see you are from Oregon. Where do you live?" I told them, we visited for a bit, and then they left. I had a very strange feeling at that point, but couldn't nail down what it was. But as I got back into the car to leave, it struck me. It had been a long, long while since anyone other than my immediate family had shown me kindness. So long in fact, that the thing hit me as strange and foreign.

Now, imagine what the cruelty of abuse does, year after year, to a victim *married* to an abuser. Beaten down, shamed, plotted against, she loses the very experience of *normal* social interaction. Lacking self-confidence and self-worth, she will begin to fear venturing out into society. Even going to the grocery store can be a fearful event. And trusting a pastor, or church members—these people who seem to live in another world from hers? Forget it.

False Guilt

> ***Revelation 12:10*** *And I heard a loud voice in heaven, saying, "Now the salvation and the power and the kingdom of our God and the authority of his Christ have come, for the accuser of our brothers has been thrown down, who accuses them day and night before our God.*

The self-doubt and distrust of one's own perceptive abilities produced in abuse victims by the abuser's distortion of reality, lying, accusing and blaming produce a profound degree of guilt: *false* guilt. This promotes an even greater sense of shame and loss of personhood. If the victim is a Christian, she may come to feel alienated from God as she concludes that she is not being the kind of wife and mother the Lord requires.

As we have already seen, abusers lack, to one degree or another, a functional conscience. Guilt is the last problem they struggle with! Ironically, the healthy conscience their victim has is turned against the victim by the conscienceless man. Greta, for example, has been verbally abused by her husband James for many years. James frequently makes false accusations against Greta to control her. At one level of her thinking, Greta feels that these charges are false, but Greta is a genuine Christian and she takes Christ's call for humility very seriously. She knows she still sins and that without doubt she has not always acted rightly toward James. Her conscience is sensitive, *and James uses this (which he sees as a weakness in her) against her.* As a result, Greta wears a load of guilt that does not properly belong upon her.

In dealing with an abuser, we must realize that we need to flatly deny his accusations against us and refuse to wear the false guilt he would use to manipulate and control us. Nehemiah understood all of this and was able to answer his accusers properly:

> ***Nehemiah 6:8*** *Then I sent to him, saying, "No such things as you say have been done, for you are inventing them out of your own mind."*

Such an answer is a right, just and powerful response to the accusations of the abuser. If you are a Christian, you need to realize that there is nothing godly about a naïve humility that makes you listen to false charges and wear false guilt. We are to put up the shield of faith and wield the sword of the truth of God's Word when these accusations come.

Professing Christians who tell us that we are required by the Lord to give a hearing to every criticism and charge brought against us are only enabling the enemy (and may well be the enemy themselves!). Would such people require us to listen to the devil himself? Such thinking would condemn Nehemiah's response to the false charges of his enemies.

> ***Nehemiah 6:2-4*** *Sanballat and Geshem sent to me, saying, "Come and let us meet together at Hakkephirim in the plain of Ono." But they intended to do me harm. And I sent messengers to them, saying, "I am doing a great work and I cannot come down. Why should the work stop while I leave it and come down to you?" And they sent to me four times in this way, and I answered them in the same manner.*

How much of the Lord's work is being hindered because pastors feel that they are bound to listen to and meet with every Sanballat who comes along, believing that Christian humility requires us to conclude that there is some truth in every accusation?

Injury and Death

How many days go by in which we do *not* read multiple stories in the news about a woman being horribly injured or, it seems more often, murdered by her abuser? Almost none. Here is some data to consider. You can easily verify these facts by reading from the bibliography of this book, or by simply investigating the many websites devoted to stopping abuse and domestic violence. The following statistics, reflecting abuse in the United States, are taken from http://www.thehotline.org/get-educated/abuse-in-america

On the average, more than three women are murdered by their husbands or boyfriends every day.

- 92% of women say that reducing domestic violence and sexual assault should be at the top of any formal efforts taken on behalf of women today.

- 1 out of 3 women around the world has been beaten, coerced into sex or otherwise abused during her lifetime.
- 1 in 5 female high school students reports being physically and/or sexually abused by a dating partner. Abused girls are significantly more likely to get involved in other risky behaviors. They are 4 to 6 times more likely to get pregnant and 8 to 9 times more likely to have tried to commit suicide.
- 1 in 3 teens report knowing a friend or peer who has been hit, punched, slapped, choked or physically hurt by his/her partner.
- As many as 324,000 women each year experience intimate partner violence during their pregnancy.
- Violence against women costs companies $72.8 million annually due to lost productivity.
- Ninety-four percent of the offenders in murder-suicides were male.
- Seventy-four percent of all murder-suicides involved an intimate partner (spouse, common-law spouse, ex-spouse, or boyfriend/girlfriend). Of these, 96 percent were females killed by their intimate partners.
- Most murder-suicides with three or more victims involved a "family annihilator" — a subcategory of intimate partner murder-suicide. Family annihilators are murderers who kill not only their wives/girlfriends and children, but often other family members as well, before killing themselves.

Seventy-five percent of murder-suicides occurred in the home. (used by permission)

Constant Anxiety about her children

We have not mentioned *children as victims* of the abuser specifically to this point because this is a huge and important topic in itself. I suspect that abuse victims who are mothers and have been reading this book have already been asking, "When are we going to talk about the children?" Chapter eight is devoted entirely to the abuser's distorted parenting of his children and his tactics to use them against their mother.

The effects of abuse on children are profound even if the abuse is primarily directed against their mother. This weighs very heavily upon the victim. Their welfare is one of the chief reasons she is torn between leaving the abuser or staying. Having children by such a person is an enormous complication not easily sorted out as we are about to learn. And watching an abusive man torment her children day after day is torture. Some mothers even live in fear that their children will be murdered. Quite often it is the abuser's attacks upon her children that ultimately confirms the victim's decision to leave.

Signs of Abuse

Can we identify abuse victims by any visible behaviors or attitudes that result from abuse? Bruises and broken bones are more obvious signs, but what about cases where the abuser is not assaulting the victim physically? This is a difficult question to answer and one that requires much prudence and wisdom, lest we find abuse behind every bush and shrub. However, many abuse victims who have come to understand what has happened to them and what the mentality and tactics of the abuser are, tell us that they believe they can "spot" abusers and their victims with some accuracy. Here are some indicators they suggest we watch for to identify possible victims:

- Victims may be trying very hard to keep up the appearance that they have a wonderful marriage and family. Abused women tend to be quiet, careful, and may choose to remain in the background in a social situation, letting their husband do the talking. At church, the victim and her children are on their best behavior.
- Some victims may try to appease their abuser by dressing in inappropriate, immodest ways in public. If she is a Christian, this will weigh upon her conscience and add to her sense of shame.
- A victim may "talk up" her husband in exaggerated ways and may be extremely defensive of him if anyone were to imply he is abusive. One victim (still in denial) told her women's Bible study group (she was the leader) that none of them could ever be married to her husband. She went on to say, in a boastful tone, that he sends her to her room when she sins.
- She may be her abuser's "spokesman," functioning as his ally in his attacks against others. This serves to make him happy with her and her suffering may be lessened for a time.
- Because abuse is very traumatic, we should not be surprised to find a

victim exhibiting symptoms of Post Traumatic Stress Disorder (PTSD). There are many websites available that describe the symptoms of PTSD.

- If the victim is a Christian, especially as long as she is still "in the dark" about what is really happening to her, her growth in Christ may well be hampered. She may not feel the love of Christ for her. She may even show signs of spiritual rebellion and have difficulty receiving love from others.
- Victims often are self-demeaning while, at the same time, exalting of their abuser. This stems from all the false guilt and shame the victim wears.
- Her defensiveness of her abuser may exhibit itself in a surprising and perhaps even inappropriate display of anger toward anyone who is perceived as being critical of her abuser. If you don't understand what is really happening, she may well convince you that you have unjustly demeaned her abuser.
- Watch for fear and its effects in the victim and her children. Victims really can never fully relax. When they enter a room, you may even be able to feel a level of tension yourself. When you ask them what they think about a subject, they will become silent and uncomfortable if it is something they think their abuser would not want them talking about.
- The children are usually very well behaved, because if they are not, there will be real trouble for them when they get home. In public settings the children are at a heightened "level 3" alert because they have a secret to keep. Imagine what the effects this fear has upon their ability to really "connect" with others. It makes it almost impossible. They can end up being regarded by others as "difficult" or "odd."
- If the victim's abuser is away from home for a time, on a business trip for example, you can often see a degree of joy and ease return to her. This disappears the moment he returns. I have heard friends of such a victim remark "You know, I really liked her better before George sold their old house and moved here too."

And what about the identifying traits of an abuser? Here are a few characteristics to watch for. This is by no means a comprehensive list:

- "Over the top," excessive helpfulness to others *when he will be seen*.
- Flattery and charm. Elizabeth (after surviving an abusive marriage herself)

describes how she recognized another man who in fact did turn out to be a sociopath:

- He struck me as sort of a peacock. Like, he was nice but kind of too nice. And full of himself. We walked into the church to meet with the pastor and he went to the piano and started showing off. I can't really explain it, but it was such a striking feeling. His wife isn't like that at all and beside her husband, sort of shrinks a bit and is quiet, so it wasn't a couple of preeners, just one.
- In contrast to his wife and children's quiet, watchful behavior, the abuser desires to be seen and praised.
- Demeaning language toward his wife (often couched in contexts that allow him an excuse if he is confronted). He may often do this through humor.
- A lack of respect for boundaries of others.
- In unguarded moments when he thinks he is not being watched, you may hear him show contempt toward others.
- In a church setting, he can embrace a showy "godliness."
- Resentment toward those in leadership (but often veiled by flattery toward them).
- Contemptuous view of women.

Even if the children in such a home are not directly abused (though they usually are), the fact that they witness one of their parents being abused (usually their mother) still has very damaging effects upon them. We now move on to consider in more depth the effects of all of this upon the victim's children.

> ***Psalm 28:1-4*** *Of David. To you, O LORD, I call; my rock, be not deaf to me, lest, if you be silent to me, I become like those who go down to the pit. Hear the voice of my pleas for mercy, when I cry to you for help, when I lift up my hands toward your most holy sanctuary. Do not drag me off with the wicked, with the workers of evil, who speak peace with their neighbors while evil is in their hearts. Give to them according to their work and according to the evil of their deeds; give to them according to the work of their hands; render them their due reward.*

CHAPTER 8

The Devastating Effects of Abuse on Children

Matthew 18:5-6 *"Whoever receives one such child in my name receives me, but whoever causes one of these little ones who believe in me to sin, it would be better for him to have a great millstone fastened around his neck and to be drowned in the depth of the sea.*

"My son is really struggling right now as a result of his father's abuse of all of us. For years, everything my son would attempt would be met with 'That is really stupid. You can never do that. It won't work.' He is broken in pieces inside and has a lot of trouble believing that God could ever accept him. My daughter craves the attention of men and tends to dress provocatively to gain it. The chaos my husband produced in our home has made her a controller and if anyone gets in her way she steamrolls right over them. Sadly, my younger son is turning out to be a copy of his father. He is only interested in what he wants from someone and it is difficult to even talk to him." (Eileen, Abuse victim)

"He would attack me by being very hard on the children. At other times he would give preference to one child over the others to turn them against one another. I stayed in this horrible relationship for years in order to let my children grow old enough so they could protect themselves against him. I do not know how many times during these years the children witnessed him raging: ripping out phones, smashing holes in the wall, screaming obscenities at us all. We all lived in constant turmoil. He used the children to spy on me, interrogating them for information about what I had been doing through the day. They were made to feel like they betrayed me and at other times they seemed alienated from me,

wondering why I did not rescue them from this terror." (Jillion, Abuse victim)

Abusers damage their children directly by using many of the same tactics against them that they use against the mother. They cause great harm to the children indirectly as well by attacking and demeaning their mother in the children's presence. Children suffer neglect because the effects of abuse on their mother diminish her parenting skills and energy.

> How often I had to send my children to bed hungry because my husband would not give me sufficient money to buy enough groceries. We all felt like Oliver in Dickens' novel when he asked, 'Please, Sir, can I have some more? (Carol, Abuse victim)

In this chapter, we are going to discuss some of the common effects abuse has on children. Even if the primary target of the abuser is the children's mother rather than the children themselves, the children are still very much harmed. And, of course, it would be a rare if not non-existent scenario in which the children received no direct abuse themselves.

> Psychopaths are always poorly qualified to effectively parent. Psychopaths' relentless criticism teaches the child they can never be good enough and this becomes a way for the psychopath to demand more and more from your child. This leads to self-esteem issues as the child matures.[75]

While not every abuser is a psychopath, Anne Pike's observation can accurately be applied to abusers. An individual with little or no conscience who is animated by a mentality that exalts itself above all others is certainly not compatible with healthy parenting.

A Shaken Faith

> ***1 John 3:10*** *By this it is evident who are the children of God, and who are the children of the devil: whoever does not practice righteousness is not of God, nor is the one who does not love his brother.*

From the Christian's perspective, one of the worst effects upon children by an abuser who claims to be a Christian is the erosion of their faith in Christ as they see this rank hypocrisy. At church, the abuser wears his disguise as a model

75 Pike, 103.

of piety. He is affirmed as such by his fellow church members who are absolutely taken in by him. He may be a member of the church board, or even the pastor himself. At home, he is someone entirely different.

Nancy was finally able to break free from her husband of twenty five years after enduring tremendous abuse. "Free" is most often not absolute however, as Nancy knows far too well. Frank, her ex-husband, has visitation rights with their two children and recently, during a weekend stay with their father, the children accompanied Frank to church. It was the same church Nancy and they used to attend before she left Frank. Now Nancy is gone and Frank remains a member, highly thought of by many. In fact, the prevailing notion in the church is that Nancy left Frank without biblical reason. Frank has his issues, they admit, but no one is perfect.[76]

Nancy reports that her children, who know very well that Frank is a truly abusive, mean man, are struggling in their faith. They see Frank in church, holding a Bible and praying when called upon in Sunday school class. What they do not see is the church confronting Frank for his wickedness and defending their mother, whom they have witnessed being attacked many times by their father. They also have seen the continued abuse directed at them and their mother through Frank's regular manipulations of the court system and by his unwillingness to pay a fair amount for their support.

Children in such settings will certainly be left wrestling with questions like:

- Why doesn't God defend us and punish the wicked?
- If my father is a Christian, why would I want to be one?
- How can I believe the Bible if this is what Christians do?
- Why is the church so hypocritical?

When the church fails victims of abuse as in Nancy's case, the abuser's hypocrisy is endorsed and his abuse is enabled. As a result, neither the victims nor their children see justice rendered. The church becomes a co-agent with the abuser in alienating children from Christ. The very typical result is that such children want nothing to do with their father's religion as they grow into adulthood. They do not understand that their father's religion is not that of Christ.

76 We must cease from using the catch-phrase, "God hates divorce." It is based upon a wrong translation of Malachi 2:16, and does not even appear in numbers of translations, including the ESV. See chapter 8, *Not Under Bondage*, by Barbara Roberts. God hates treachery is more accurate.

Damaged Self-Esteem and Worth

One of the greatest benefits of knowing Christ is that the Christian is given a new identity. He is made to be a new person, a new creation. In union with Christ, every Christian possesses God's own name, is adopted by this new Father, is washed clean from the stain of sin, set free from condemnation, given a place in his Father's house, and much, much more. As we will consider in greater detail later, these are some of the fundamental reasons that Christ is *the remedy* for the effects of abuse.

Children of an abusive parent suffer the erosion of a healthy self-esteem and self-worth. They do not feel valued because the abuser does not value them. Love is not to be found in an abusive individual. Life is all about *him*. The universe must revolve around *him*. At best, his wife and children are objects owned, existing to serve him. All of this is plainly conveyed to the children day after day. Their development as individual human beings with thoughts and gifts is seriously hindered as they learn that they must give their minds and abilities to pleasing *him*, or suffer the consequences. I have seen children of abusers stand in front of a McDonald's hamburger menu, unable to make a decision about what to order. Decision-making is very difficult for a person who has spent their life wondering only "what would *he* want me to do?" Similar results will be observed if such a child is asked about their own personal likes and dislikes. They grow up without the freedom to be themselves, to have their own preferences or make their own decisions. All must be in conformity to the abuser.

> My father was a physically abusive drunk, my mother was verbally and emotionally abusive. They both attacked each other and each attacked me. Both, according to them, were Christians. I grew up afraid of everything and desperately afraid of displeasing them. I remember not being able to make up my mind about anything. I didn't even know for sure what my favorite color was. I was never allowed to know. (An abuse victim)

As Christians, we know that our true worth flows from who we are in Jesus Christ. It is true that when we enter this world we are dead to God, rebels against Him by nature, and under His just condemnation. And yet, even before we come to faith in Christ, how does God relate to His sheep? By *grace*—undeserved, free, *grace*:

1 John 4:10 *In this is love, not that we have loved God but that he loved us and sent his Son to be the propitiation for our sins.*

The abuser as parent, however, does just the opposite. His purpose is not redemptive, but self-serving. *His* needs are the real needs. He insists upon receiving regular recognition, but he gives none. He lets his victims know that he expects the worst from them, that they are not to be trusted, and that even their right to continue to be in his house is questionable. Gary describes how his abusive father would tear him down:

> My father would interrogate me and my sister for hours at a time. He would accuse our mother of all sorts of plots against him and demand that we tell him what we knew. At these times, I knew that the best thing for me to do was to just be quiet and say nothing. This made him even angrier, and he was very practiced at posturing and intimidating. Even though we would eventually be visibly shaking, he would accuse us of being liars, traitors, and generally worthless children. We heard over and over again how we would never amount to anything in life, how ugly we were, and how stupid we were if we thought that anyone was every going to love us.

One does not need a degree in psychology to realize that the shame and sense of worthlessness such abuse produces in a child is going to cause serious harm in that child's life. Unlike Christ, who tears us down by bringing His holy law as a mirror, showing us our sin and condemned condition, but then pointing us to the remedy of the cross, abusers have no remedy to offer. Worse, the condemnation they bring to their victims is a false one meant only to control and to destroy.

This survivor offers us insight into her life, being victimized by both her abusive mother who was still alive, and *also* from her own abusive husband:

> Growing up, my mother was my life. Pleasing her was everything. I learned to lie in order to please her, because she would never believe the truth...no matter how benign. My mother professed to be a Christian. We went to church regularly. Everyone there was her friend. She often told them of her woes in having to raise a child like me: one who was not to be trusted, who was selfish and cruel towards her. They began to see me as she saw me. It was not uncommon for the good women of the church to come to me and

castigate me for the way I treated her. They let me know that God was going to punish me for what I was doing. Trouble was that I wasn't doing any of the stuff she said I was. It was all in her mind. But if I tried to tell anyone that she was wrong, I was called a liar.

I grew up ignored and pushed aside by all of the good Christians who just knew that my Mom was "the sweetest little Christian lady in the whole world." Even as an adult, after I married and had children, I had to deal with her effect on me and my family in the churches we attended, because wherever we went, she would follow and begin to spread her lies. We'd change churches only to have her change also. She was so good at wrapping folks around her little finger. What she said was always accepted as truth. As a result, until she died, I was known as a heartless and cruel daughter and no one wanted anything to do with me. My husband wasn't a Christian, though he claimed to be, and rarely attended church.

However, on those occasions he would attend with us, he would openly let it be known he didn't want to be there, even act up, get angry, and talk during the service. This was very embarrassing to me and to our children. Consequently, between my mother and my husband, my children and I had no friends. It's not that I didn't try: for the first several years, I would try to join the ladies at the ladies Bible study, only to discover I was the topic of discussion; I would offer to babysit, even for free, just to try to get an "in" on making a friend but the offers weren't accepted; I would invite children to come play at our house but they were never allowed to. My children were always excluded from special events. Once, my children were the only children in the entire church who weren't promoted in Sunday school because the lady in charge of promotions was my mother's best friend and disliked me so very much. Later, after years of this, I finally got to the point where I never tried any more. There was no point in doing so.

On top of the issues we faced at church, we dealt daily with walking on eggshells with both my husband and my mother. There was no pleasing either one of them and both of them let me, and my children, know what a failure I was both as a daughter and as a wife. My mother would regularly tell the children "Your Mama's being mean to me again" and then go on to tell them in detail how I was being "mean." My husband would often tell them how "not fun" I was or "how unreasonable" he thought I was or that he "cares more about your school than your Mama does," even though I was homeschooling them with absolutely no input or help from him. It was also quite common for him to come to me and tell me how the children were "afraid of you" and that they had come to him to "protect them." Then he'd turn around and rage at us all for interrupting his show or talking too loudly. Sometimes his raging would venture into the physical realm. There was no peace anywhere: none at home, none at my Mom's, none at church.

Fear of Harm to Themselves or Mother

Just as their mother exists in a pervasive atmosphere of *fear*, so it is with the abuser's children. Much of their time is necessarily spent in calculating how to simply "stay out of his way" so as to not set him off. Of course, they really cannot make such calculations, no one can. The abuser *likes* his victims to be afraid. That fear serves him well.

What happens to children who grow up in fear? Whose formative years are filled with constant tension? Experts in child development could no doubt provide us with a long list, and nothing on it would be good.

Fear *enslaves.* Fear is effectively used by tyrants to subdue even entire populations. Notice these elements in the following passage from Hebrews:

> ***Hebrews 2:14-15*** *Since therefore the children share in flesh and blood, he himself likewise partook of the same things, that through death he might destroy the one who has the power of death, that is, the devil, and deliver all those who through fear of death were subject to lifelong slavery.*

Power! There it is. Power and control are the fundamental elements of the abuser's mentality and tactics. The one who has power instills fear in his victims and thereby enslaves them. Children of an abuser grow up in an environment of slavery.

What kind of people do children who are raised in such fear become? Consider these suggestions:

- Fear instills *distrust* of others and subsequent relational failures.
- Fear of being abandoned: *"if you ever tell anyone, I won't have anything to do with you again"*.

- Fear leads to various physical ailments and associated stress.
- Fear leads to even more false guilt and self-condemnation.
- Fear produces shame.
- Fear leads to embracing various kinds of self-protective devices, most of which are damaging in themselves.
- Fear can even make its victims *become tyrants themselves.*

When I was in elementary school, over fifty years ago, the cold war was raging. We lived with the constant fear that the Russians could drop "the bomb" on us at any time. These fears were reinforced by regular drills in our school. A blaring siren would go off (I can still picture the thing, a red, megaphone-shaped device on the wall at the end of the hallway), and we were required to get down on our hands and knees under our desks, away from the windows. I look back on this now and realize that the whole thing did more harm than good. If an atomic bomb fell, no one was going to survive anyway! The drills really just instilled more fear in us as children. It is very hard for me to attempt to describe to you how that fear *felt.* Even looking at that siren in the hall or hearing talk about a bomb *alienated* me from that school building, from my teacher, and from my classmates. It made the place fearful and I just wanted to go back home where we didn't talk about such things or listen to screaming sirens or crawl under tables.

Now, think of a child in the home of an abuser living under the constant fear that "the bomb" could fall at any time—and often does. Imagine that child identifying, in his childish reasoning, various "sirens" around him that blared "the bomb is coming!" There is the look on his mother's face or the tone in her voice, or the clock that said "He's going to be here soon!"

I have a friend who fought in the Vietnam War. Among the stories he tells (all true) is the account of the numbers of times he and his fellow marines had to dive for cover into bunkers because the enemy was shelling them with artillery. He said those times were the most fearful of his entire experience there, including the times when he was wounded. As you lay there in the dark, unable to do anything, and you heard those shells screaming in and then exploding and feeling the horrendous concussion—that was *fear.* I suspect that a child experiencing the raging of abuse against his mother is much like that. It is an artillery barrage of explosive words, of things being smashed, and perhaps even of fists and feet punching and kicking. Should we be surprised if children in such circumstances evidence signs of post-traumatic stress syndrome, and more?

Have you ever noticed how quickly your fear can transform into anger? A child runs away from home and causes her parents great fear and anxiety, but when she is found her mother might grab her and angrily shout at her, "If you ever do that again….!" In the same way, the family members of an abuser can find themselves angry with one another whenever one of them is perceived as "rocking the boat" by somehow upsetting the abuser. We will find in a later chapter that this same dynamic is responsible for the denial and cover up of abuse when it turns up in the church. Fear is at the root of it.

> Stupidly, no matter what my husband did to us, I felt duty bound to let our children know how very blessed they were to have him as their father. Sometimes they'd just look at me as if I were crazy. Other times, when he was being really nice to them, they'd get so lost in this momentary display that they mistook for love, they would end up loving him, trusting him, much more than they did me even though most of the time he was either mean to them or ignored them. (Abuse victim)

Alienation from their Mother

Abusers directly and covertly strive to alienate children from the victim (normally, their mother). The dynamics of abuse alienate people from one another in many ways. Not only does the mother suffer being estranged from her children, but children are harmed by this distancing as well. Consider some ways in which this alienation works, and why. Abusers:

- Erode the children's respect for their mother by shaming words and attacks upon her, or telling jokes at her expense.
- Tell the children that their mother is weak and foolish.
- Tell the children their mother is a super-woman, so they take her for granted and treat her as their slave.
- Show camaraderie and warm affection towards the children when they join him in mocking and ridiculing her.
- Promote doubt in the children about their mother's love for them. If she loved them, wouldn't she stop this abuse?

- Blame their mother for his raging or any of his moods.
- Erode the children's respect for their mother's authority.
- Undermine and contradict the way she disciplines the children.
- Leave all the disciplining of the children to the mother, making her out to be the bad guy.
- Discipline the children excessively, and make it look like their mother won't protect them.
- Play Father Christmas to the children with gifts, treats and liberties, making the children prefer him over their mother.
- Promise children treats, and then blame their mother for his failure to deliver the promises.
- Disclose to the children facts of a personal and private nature that the mother had confided to him
- Some of the above tactics can be used to alienate one sibling from another as well, so that no-one in the family can trust or respect anyone else. Divide and rule is the abuser's motto when it comes to his own family.

Now, consider in what ways this will affect the children. Without a healthy, trusting, respectful, loving relationship with their mother, children are bound to suffer a host of symptoms, develop skewed attitudes toward women, and seek out other relationships or things to fill the vacuum in which a healthy maternal relationship is designed to be.

> I always wanted to be able to be the nurturing mother, tender and loving. But, since my husband refused to do so, I also had to be the disciplinarian for our children, setting the limits, enforcing the punishments. My husband, who was also emotionally and verbally abusive, kept our home in an uproar. What he wanted and what his opinions were changed from day to day. Because he was the way he was, some days he was very hard on the children (yelling at them, calling them names, whipping them much too hard, insisting that they follow a strict code of conduct) and other days, he was way too soft on them, not demanding anything from them or of them. This was easy for him since he demanded so little from himself. On those days, he would get mad at me for setting limits of any kind (about bedtimes, chores, school... anything). "Life is for fun," he'd tell the children, "and your mother doesn't know it." Of course, they readily adopted those ideas and it made it even harder for me to be the nurturing mother I longed to be. (Abuse victim)

False Guilt

Children of abusers blame themselves. This happens for a number of reasons, one of which is the blaming tactic of the abuser we discussed earlier. The abuser overtly blames them for his raging. When five-year old Jimmy spilled a bag of peanuts in the car, his father raged at him and then at the entire family. For the next hour, everyone heard how stupid and worthless they were, how much of an annoyance and inconvenience to his life. "Here I take you out for this trip and how do you repay me? Do you know how much I am giving up for you today?" And on and on it goes. Why did it happen? Because Jimmy spilled the peanuts? Hardly. Yet that is how Jimmy will see it, and so will everyone else. Even if the event results in Jimmy's mother being punched in the face, Jimmy (and his siblings) may very well conclude that *it was his fault she got hit.*

But victims are weighed down with false guilt in other ways too. The terrible *deceptiveness* of abuse plays a major role in leading victims to condemn themselves. This deceptiveness was described very well in the following paragraph sent to me by a mother who, along with her children, has suffered abuse for decades at the hands of her husband, a professing Christian:

> I think that, when we love God, we want to pretend that everyone else who says they love Him actually does. Unfortunately, it isn't so. Because of this, it is easy for abusers to hide in the church. WE don't lie, so why would we believe that THEY would? Also, because we are conditioned to see family life from a biblical point of view, to think that someone who seems so godly, isn't, somehow threatens all that we hold dear. It is then easier to disbelieve the victim (and accuse her of lying) than it is to conclude that what we have seen and what we have believed is not, in fact, true.

And for victims, including children, it is easier *to blame themselves.* We must remember that children are children. Their reasoning processes are still developing and therefore they can easily come to false conclusions about who is guilty and who is innocent. They may blame themselves for not intervening and rescuing their mother because they don't fully understand that to do so would have been a physical impossibility. An eight-year old boy cannot stop a raging thirty year-old man. But eight-year old boys need help in understanding this. The fiction of superheroes they see on TV or read about in comic books is *fiction.* The effects of all of this guilt, unjustly borne, are far-reaching *and none of them are good.*

Depression and Suicide in Boys

I am receiving regular reports from abuse victims with sons that the abuser/father specifically targeted the boys as they grew older. The abuser will watch for opportunities to precipitate a conflict with his son, daring the boy to strike back and even threatening to kill the boy if he does. Listen to Mary and she describes what her abusive husband (Lance) did to their teen-age son, Michael, one evening:

> Lance came down real, real hard on Michael in the name of "defending my wife". Yeah-right. He misinterpreted something that happened and then jumped all over Michael. He accused him of being rebellious, said he was "just like all of these punks today", and accused him of being disrespectful. Michael was furious. I stood up for him and told Lance that he hadn't a clue what he was talking about and told him that Michael is a good and respectful son.
>
> Lance has been doing that a lot lately. Michael despises him for it. He and I talked quite a bit afterwards; he was very upset. As he pointed out, Lance tries to be the husband or the Dad when it suits him, when it's inconvenient he ignores all responsibilities. Plus, Lance is, far more often than not, the one who causes any angst present among our family.

Other mothers have reported the same pattern, with the abuser/father raging with even greater intensity. In some cases, the son has become very depressed and, as the mother learned later, had even come to the point of deciding to sacrifice himself so that his mother and siblings could escape their abuser. These boys may have thoughts of killing their father, even if it means they must go to prison for the rest of their life. Others become suicidal.

Do abusers regularly target their sons as the boys grow older? I would have to leave that question to professional researchers to document. But I can say that several cases I have been involved with do support this theory. And of course, the question is: why? I suspect it has to do with the abuser seeing his son as competition for attention, especially if the boy is a responsible, kind young man. Such a boy upstages the abuser and he grows jealous. If he can provoke the boy into a fight, he thinks he can then portray his son as rebellious and wicked, making himself look better in the eyes of the rest of the family. Abusers look for opportunities to play the hero who protects his beloved wife.

Behavioral Aberrations

Whether delivered directly to children or indirectly by abusing their mother in their presence or in their hearing, abuse has terrible results upon them. Children who are doubting the truth of Christ, who are weighed with shame, false guilt, doubts about their mother's love, and subjected to constant fear, are certain to evidence varieties of abnormal behavior. It is incredible however that very often *abuse* is the last cause considered. We are not being too critical of the evangelical church to say that it is among *ourselves* that abuse as a cause is least likely to be suggested or even imagined.

Here is a list of just some of the negative and harmful behaviors that can be caused in children by direct or indirect abuse:

- Violence or bullying toward other children.
- Wetting the bed or not making it to the bathroom.
- Rebellion against authority.
- Drug and/or alcohol abuse.
- Promiscuous sex.
- Running away.
- Eating disorders.
- Depression and anxiety.
- Becoming non-communicative or withdrawn.
- Emotional numbing.
- Confusion.
- Conflicted ambivalence toward the abuser evidenced by defending the abuser even when the abuse is evident.
- Development of a fantasy, magical world.
- Anger and volatility.
- Addiction to violent computer games, with propensity to act them out.
- Stealing, fire-setting, and torturing animals.
- Inability or unwillingness to engage in conversations of substance. A sense of hiding some secret.
- Sexual abuse of other children.
- Hesitancy to make a decision or to stand firmly in an opinion.
- Unreasonable and inappropriate apologizing.
- Reckless and dangerous behaviors.

- Defiance of the law.
- Inability to see God as their Father.

Among those children who are raised in such an abusive atmosphere, there are some who truly are drawn by God to Himself. Even these, though they might know the truth of God's Word mentally, fail to accept it emotionally; thus, they have trouble relating to God, have difficulty feeling accepted by Him, and feel the need to repeatedly repent for past sins (those that have already been repented of) over and over and over. If they can't trust their parents, whom they see, to accept them, love them and forgive them when they fail, how can they trust God, Whom they can't see?

In a later chapter we will work to provide *hope* for abuse victims, including how they can help their children overcome or even avoid these things. For now, let me challenge all of us to carefully evaluate our thinking about abuse and abusers. I suggest the following questions be put to ourselves:

1. What does the Lord think about abuse, particularly in relation to how it hurts children? What is His attitude toward an abuser of children?
2. Do I see abuse in the same light as the Lord does, or have I been guilty of minimizing or even denying it?
3. Is it really true that children are *always* better off with both a mother and a father, and therefore divorce is *never* a good option for abuse? Have you ever considered that the Pauline exception of abandonment just might include the emotional, spiritual, or financial abandonment often faced by victims of domestic abuse?[77]
4. Have I really taken a hard, serious, studious look at the Bible's teachings about the nature and psychology of sin? Do I think that God's Word says that all sinners are the same and should be treated the same? Do I really understand how incredibly deceptive the sinner can be?

> The difference between truth and fiction is that good fiction must sound as though it could be true. That's not so with the truth. The stories told in our offices sound like they couldn't possibly be true, even though they are. (Divorce lawyer to an abuse victim)

77 Barbara Roberts in her book *Not Under Bondage* has an entire section devoted to the nature of the "leaving" in 1 Corinthians 7.

Abusers as Child Sexual Molesters

More often than we might realize, these effects of abuse upon children are the result of one of the most secretive, devious, and evil actions of many abusers – child sexual abuse. We would expect men who see their wife and children as owned property who exist solely for the abuser's service and pleasure, to be prone to sexual abuse of children. I estimate that about half of the women whom I have interviewed say that their abuser also molested her children. Many were never charged with a crime.

Because of the powerful shame dynamic involved in sexual abuse, victims do not readily report it. Children, when they do talk about being molested, minimize what happened, often telling only a small portion of what was done to them. Even adults who are victims of sexual abuse find it no easy thing to face it and speak about it. Abusers use this shame and fear to their benefit. If the truth does eventually come out, it may be decades later when the criminal statute of limitations has passed and prosecution is no longer possible.

James hates his ex-wife. In fact, James speaks with contempt of all *three* of his ex-wives! But he is particularly vicious when the subject of his last marriage comes up. It seems that James ended up in jail for a few days until his brother could bail him out. His wife had gone to the police and reported that James had sexually molested her 12 year old daughter (from a previous marriage). James is proud today. He was exonerated of all charges. "That stinking _______ trumped up all those charges just to get back at me and take everything I have in the divorce!"

James' current friends, who never knew any of his ex-wives, believe him. They think they know James, and the James they know could never do such a thing. Besides, James has since become a Christian.

But James *did* sexually molest that girl. And in the next few years, James will marry still another woman and abuse her. She will divorce him after James, in a rage, threatens to kill her. James is married *again* at present. He found himself "a wonderful, sweet Christian woman" who is nothing like his previous wives.

In dealing with abusers, we must attune to the frequency with which they sexually abuse children in their home.

> Multiple studies have demonstrated that men who abuse their partners are far more likely than other men to abuse children. Incest perpetrators are

> similar to partner abusers in both their mentality and their tactics....[78]

And even in cases of abusers who do not overtly sexually abuse their children, their refusal to respect appropriate boundaries of family members is certainly a form of sexual abuse. Walking into bathrooms unannounced when a daughter is showering, making fun of a child's developing body at puberty, refusing to practice modesty himself in front of the children, or making overtly sexual remarks or actions toward their mother while the children watch are all examples of sexual abuse.

When a victim leaves her abuser and enters into a court child-custody process, it seems that all too often mothers are being forced by the courts to permit the abuser to have the children for specified visitation times. Put yourself in the place of a mother who *knows* that this man sexually molested her children, but she can't prove it. Now they are ordered to spend time with him.

It is common to find both secular and Christian counselors, pastors, domestic courts, and other authorities who embrace the theory that it is always best for children to have relationships with both their mother and father. Thus the ongoing battles in courtrooms over child custody and visitation when a divorce is filed. While this thinking may be true in non-abusive divorce cases, such ideas are highly questionable (many victims will say they are just plain foolishness) in the case of an abusive spouse. Here is the experience of one abuse survivor, and her story is very common:

> When my daughter and I left the abuser, life was initially pretty chaotic due to litigation, the need to monitor our safety and remain vigilant at all times, the judgments of our church, the upheaval of regular visitation; and the abuse he did to her and me via visitation including turning her against me. Life started to become normal only when my daughter's visitation to him ceased. She could then begin to recover from the nightmare. Her emotional state improved, her sleep improved, her schoolwork didn't suffer so much, and she developed deep and healthy friendships. And her relationship with me was able to be repaired.

Janelle, writing in her diary:

> I couldn't sleep tonight so I got up and read. I checked out a book from the library yesterday on abuse in marriage. I wanted to prove to myself that what

78 Bancroft, *Why Does He Do That?*, 245-246.

was happening wasn't abuse but something else entirely. But the more I read, the more it makes sense. The more sense it makes, the more the tears come.

John has abused me? How could that be? I thought he loved me, I mean, I know he loves me. At least, I think he loves me. He said he did. He vowed to cherish me. Abuse doesn't fit into that. But the book makes so much sense. His demands to be in control, his belief that the world, my world, ought to revolve around him, the right to hurt me... just because I'm his wife... because I'm his wife! Just so he will feel like a man. His lies. He's broken so much. He's broken me so much. What does this all mean? Where does this leave me? What do I do now?

Dear Lord, what do I do?

Exodus 3:7-9 *Then the LORD said, "I have surely seen the affliction of my people who are in Egypt and have heard their cry because of their taskmasters. I know their sufferings, and I have come down to deliver them out of the hand of the Egyptians and to bring them up out of that land to a good and broad land, a land flowing with milk and honey, to the place of the Canaanites, the Hittites, the Amorites, the Perizzites, the Hivites, and the Jebusites. And now, behold, the cry of the people of Israel has come to me, and I have also seen the oppression with which the Egyptians oppress them."*

CHAPTER 9

Why the Church Covers Up Abuse

Job 19:7 *Behold, I cry out, 'Violence!' but I am not answered; I call for help, but there is no justice.*

Proverbs 25:20 *Whoever sings songs to a heavy heart is like one who takes off a garment on a cold day, and like vinegar on soda.*

Christa Brown's abuser was a Baptist pastor. When she was just a girl, this evil man sexually assaulted her over a long period of time, perverting the words of Scripture in order to seduce her. In her efforts to expose what had happened, she experienced a massive cover up by church leaders in her denomination. Brown recounts how her sufferings were intensified by the refusal of "godly" men, eminent in their circles of influence, to hear her call for justice. In fact, they largely treated her with scorn and contempt.79

Why are victims of all of this abuse we have been learning about *discounted?* Why are they crying "Violence!" calling for help from their fellow Christians and pastors, but not being heard? That such is the case is indisputable. All one need to do is talk to the victims and hear their stories. Anyone who does so will soon realize that largely their stories are "a story," that comes to be all too familiar. The wounded come to their church for rescue, and instead of healing medicine, they find that salt is being poured into their wounds. Why?

Observe once more the usual cascade of events that occurs when a victim comes to the average evangelical, Bible-believing church with her case. This cycle

79 Christa Brown, *This Little Light: Beyond a Baptist Preacher Predator and His Gang* (Cedarburg: Foremost Press, 2009).

is well worth repeating here. I do not want to unnecessarily alienate my fellow pastors in saying these things. I want us all to *read and learn* as I have had to. I confess that I myself have, at times, been guilty of some of the errors in this cycle (i.e., thinking that couples' counseling is the answer). I am ashamed to describe the following process of how we are treating abuse victims. My sense of shame has been growing stronger as I continue to receive real-life, first hand reports of this injustice from genuine, Christian women. I am ashamed that we as conservative, Bible-believing Christians have been and are acting this way to the oppressed. We need to repent.

1. Victim reports abuse to her pastor.
2. Pastor does not believe her claims, or at least believes they are greatly exaggerated. He "knows" her husband to be a genuine Christian man.
3. Pastor minimizes the severity of the abuse. Damage control is frequently the foremost issue in his mind.
4. Pastor indirectly (or not so indirectly!) implies that the victim needs to do better in her role as wife and mother, and as a Christian. He concludes that all such scenarios are a "50/50" blame sharing.
5. Pastor sends the victim home, back to the abuser, usually after praying with her and entrusting the problem to the Lord.
6. Pastor believes he has done his job. But nothing has changed, except perhaps for the worse. The victim tries harder, prays more, but the abuse continues.
7. Pastor decides to do some counseling. He says "I will have a little talk with your husband" or "I am sure that all three of us can sit down and work this all out." Either of these routes only results in further, more intensive abuse of the victim.
8. As time passes, the victim becomes the guilty party in the eyes of the pastor and others. *She* is the one causing the commotion. *She* is pressured by the pastor and others in the church to stop rebelling, to submit to her husband, and stop causing division in the church.
9. After, very often a long, long time (even years), the victim separates from or divorces the abuser. The church has refused to believe her, persistently covered up the abuse, failed to obey the law and report the abuse to the police, and refused to exercise church discipline against the abuser.

10. The final terrible injustice is that the victim must leave the church while the abuser, having successfully duped the pastor and church into believing his victim was the real problem, remains a member in good standing.

Am I being too harsh or overstating the severity of the case? No. And many or perhaps even *most* Christian abuse victims will support us in this conclusion:

> I've been a Christian since I was seven. I was raised in a Christian home and attended Christian schools and college. After 10 years in a marriage where I was abused sexually, mentally and emotionally and where my children were abused emotionally, verbally and even physically by my husband, and after more than a year of professional Christian couples, family and individual counseling, I filed for divorce.
>
> My pastor believed everything I told him about my (now ex) husband. My pastor said after meeting with both of us that my husband had no idea what it meant to be a biblical husband and father. My pastor said that he had no doubt that everything I told him was true and that it was probably worse than I'd told him. My pastor also met with my parents, who attended the same church, were incredibly well respected there, and who verified every thing that I'd said and supported my decision to seek a divorce, 100%.
>
> Then he said that if I didn't withdraw my divorce paperwork that the case would be laid before the elders (twelve men) in the church who would then determine how best to "discipline" me, because abuse does not qualify as a "biblical" basis for divorce. And he further attempted to control me by insinuating that I was jeopardizing my dad's chances to become a deacon in his church.
>
> The church—and pastors—are FAILING. One would think that they might, at some point, stop long enough to consider whose side they are coming down on when it comes to abuse... I left. I will not be part of any organization where women and children are not safe, and I will never stop staying things out loud, ever, ever again. (Elizabeth, abuse victim)

Hurrah, Elizabeth! Christians have not heeded God's command to bring justice and protection to the helpless and oppressed:

> ***Deuteronomy 27:19*** *"'Cursed be anyone who perverts the justice due to the sojourner, the fatherless, and the widow.' And all the people shall say, 'Amen.'*

Isaiah 1:16-17 *Wash yourselves; make yourselves clean; remove the evil of your deeds from before my eyes; cease to do evil, learn to do good; seek justice, correct oppression; bring justice to the fatherless, plead the widow's cause.*

The Cover Up

Watergate. Once, that was just the name of an office complex in Washington, D.C. But after five men were apprehended burglarizing it in 1972, Watergate took on an entirely new meaning with the equivalency of "Waterloo." When we hear the name "Watergate," we immediately think of "cover up."

With troubling frequency, cover up is the reaction of the Christian church to abuse within its ranks. Whether it is sexual abuse of a child or abuse of a wife by a husband who is a "fine Christian man", the "first-responders" (normally the pastor or a board member) tend toward minimizing the severity of the thing and try to smooth it over with superficial treatment. This is not always the case. I know of a few pastors who have acted nobly and wisely in such circumstances. But we are probably not exaggerating to say that when the report is made, a right, immediate, and just response is exceptional.

The dynamic behind the cover up is something that most Christians do not want to even consider, but consider it we must. I propose that the injustice dealt to abuse victims is often due to the sobering fact that the victim is dealing with people who are not Christians at all; people who do not know Christ and are not regenerate. How else, for example, can we explain the atrocious wickedness Christa Brown was subjected to when she reported her rape by a youth minister to her church and to her denomination's head office? I highly recommend reading her account of this madness in her book This Little Light (C. Brown, 2009) as a wakeup call to us all.

Matthew 5:6 *"Blessed are those who hunger and thirst for righteousness, for they shall be satisfied."*

If one quality in every real Christian is this hunger and thirst for righteousness, how then is it possible for a Christian to pervert justice and to oppose righteousness as these men did in Brown's case? The thing is impossible. To such men, we must say no less than, *"Woe to you, scribes, Pharisees, hypocrites!"* Does that seem too harsh? Then consider that Brown's denomination knowingly permitted her rapist to continue as a children's minister for years! Are Jesus' own words for the false religious leaders of His day not just as appropriate for men whose deeds emit a very similar "fragrance"? (Incidentally, we should note that her denomination was *not* the Roman Catholic Church, but a very large evangelical one).

To explain how a local church can become what the Reformed confessions of faith call "A Synagogue of Satan" (Revelation 2:9) would require another book. We will just mention here that the evangelical church's adoption of what is commonly called "easy-believism" is one explanation. This thinking denies the biblical truth that a Christian is a new creation in Christ and therefore *will* evidence a changed life that includes repentance and increasing holiness of life. Many Christians have been taught that a person can be truly regenerate *yet never obey Christ.* Another reason a church can deteriorate into Satan's household is a logical result of this easy-believism, namely, the failure and refusal to practice biblical church discipline. Read the second and third chapters of the Book of Revelation and hear Christ's commandments to His church, then ask yourself if the average local evangelical congregation is characterized by obedience to such commands.

Any Christian who is even an average student of their Bible should not be surprised that it is quite possible for pastors, professing Christians, and entire local churches to be counterfeit. Scripture warns us over and over again that there are wolves in sheep's clothing (Mathew 7:15; Acts 20:29), that Satan can appear as an angel of light and his servants as sons of righteousness (2 Cor 11). We are told to "test the spirits" because many false prophets have gone out (1 John 4). Somehow, we just don't seem to want to believe it is "as bad as all that." Are we greater than our Teacher? He has told us otherwise.

But what of cases in which the pastor and his church *are* truly Christians? They know Christ. They long to serve Him and see people groping in the darkness of sin come to Christ to be set free. They are the genuine article, and yet, they render injustice to abuse victims. Why? What are the reasons they react to reports of abuse with minimization of the seriousness of it and with a desire to cover it up?

Before we examine some possible explanations for cover up, let me describe for you what a typical initial reaction to an abuse report looks and *feels* like, and then we will explore the possible reasons for these responses. While this scenario involves *sexual abuse*, the same dynamics will be observed in cases of domestic violence abuse when it is reported to the church. Indeed, many domestic violence abuse cases involve sexual abuse as well.

Dark Days for Carlton Community Church[80]

Carlton Community Church has an average Sunday attendance of about 100 people. Pastor Garrison has been at the church for 12 years and has worked hard, along with the elders, to faithfully teach and disciple the congregation. The people of CCC are close, many of them having been in the church for ten or more years. The children are particularly close because most of the families home school and cooperate in some activities and classes.

One Thursday afternoon, Pastor Garrison received a call from one of his flock, Mrs. Grey (Angie). She asked if she and her husband could come and meet with the Pastor that evening. At the meeting, the Greys informed Pastor Garrison that their seven-year old son, Clay, had been inappropriately touched by one of their adult friends, Jack Smith, while Clay was staying at the Smith's house. They only learned about it the day before when Clay told his mother about it. Actually, Clay had only indirectly reported the incident to his mother. As he was telling her about the good time he had when Mr. Smith was teaching him to wrestle, he described how Mr. Smith had showed him how to grab an opponent's crotch. As the Greys understood their son to say, this was not the first time this had happened. They decided to talk to Pastor Garrison for advice and had not yet discussed the matter with Jack or Jack's wife (Melinda). The Pastor told them he was very sorry such a thing had happened and that he would look into it and report back to them. This was the first incident of its kind that had occurred in Pastor Garrison's experience, and it was very unsettling to him.

Pastor Garrison had known the Greys and the Smiths for many years. In fact, he considered these two families to be his friends and strong supporters of CCC. Both families were also well thought of by the rest of the congregation, and were very active in the church. As he drove over to the Smith's house and walked up to the front door, as he had so many times before, Pastor Garrison had no idea of the severe trial that was just beginning to unfold for himself and his entire congregation.

80 Carlton Community Church is a fictitious name. The scenario is a fictitious one, though constructed from the study of numbers of sexual abuse cases.

Jack acted surprised when Pastor Garrison explained why he was there. He said that yes, he had wrestled with Clay, and had done so before. The boy enjoyed it and seemed interested in learning some new moves. Could he have touched Clay inappropriately while wrestling? Jack answered that he supposed that was a possibility, but if it had, it had been completely unintentional.

Thanking the Smith's and confident that he had obtained a reasonable and harmless explanation, Pastor Garrison now headed over to the Grey's home to smooth this whole thing out. His anxiety was considerably relieved and he thanked the Lord for what he anticipated was going to be a happy resolution to the incident.

Resolution did not happen.

At the Grey's home, Pastor Garrison reported Jack's explanation and told them of Jack's desire to meet with them to apologize for his poor judgment. Even the Greys seemed to be relieved, ready to accept Jack's account of the matter, explain it to Clay, and get on with life as usual. They had Clay come into the room where they were speaking so that the Pastor could explain to him that all was well. Before he did, however, he asked Clay if he could tell him directly about Mr. Smith touching him. As Clay told the story, Pastor Garrison's heart began to sink. The boy was confident of his facts, although at his young age he did not fully comprehend the gravity of it all.[81] Clay's description of the events included facts that simply did not square with Jack's "accidental contact" explanation. As the expressions on their faces revealed, the Grey's knew it too. Their relief was short-lived. Angie began to sob as the ugly reality of the thing began to register with each of them.

Pastor Garrison called his church board together and reported all of these facts to them. Everyone was shocked and grieved. Nothing like this had ever happened in their experience and certainly not in their church family. They all knew the Greys and the Smiths very well. What was to be done? Should the police be called? Does touching the genitals through clothing constitute a crime according to the state statutes? Maybe it would not be wise to get the state

81 This is NOT to imply that Clay had not been harmed by the abuse, or that he would not remember it for the rest of his life. He had, and he would. It simply means that a young child normally does not know the full evil of what someone like Jack has done to them. Unfortunately, neither do most Christians!

involved in church affairs? Even the Greys had already said they were not out for vengeance and as far as reporting it to the police, well, perhaps that would prove to be hard on their son.[82] Surely there must be some way of proceeding that would be beneficial to the victim, to the Smiths, and to the church and which would result in the least turmoil for all involved. Everyone went home at least a bit encouraged that the thing could be resolved yet.

Two days later however, Pastor Garrison was not at ease. He knew that as a pastor, he was required by state law to report abuse when it came to his attention, although he was still uncertain if what had happened in this case met that definition. For clarification, he decided that he would write the facts out, no names mentioned, and give his paper to the District Attorney for an opinion. The day after he did so, the DA phoned him and told him that he was legally required to report this to the police immediately. The DA also said that this was in fact a very serious matter and that Jack was grooming Clay to be more vulnerable to future and more serious molestation. Pastor Garrison complied and called the Sheriff's Office. He informed the Greys of his actions and also called the Smiths and advised them to find an attorney.

The next Sunday Pastor Garrison and the church board announced these sad events to the congregation, primarily for the protection of other children in the church. They concluded that all parents had a right to know about what had happened in case there had been any other abuse of other victims. In addition, it would be evident to all that Jack was no longer in attendance at church, as the pastor and board members had informed him that he could no longer be around the victim, and questions would be asked.

Eventually, the following developments occurred as well:

1. The entire Smith family left the church, critical of the way the church leadership dealt with their case.
2. Jack was charged with sexual abuse but, after agreeing to undergo counseling, was placed into a diversion program and ultimately did not incur any criminal record nor was he registered as a sex offender.
3. Several theories and opinions were embraced by various members of

82 Actually many victims and their families have found their experience with the police to be a positive one.

the church. A few believed that Jack should have been permitted to continue in the church as a model of Christian forgiveness. Others concluded that Clay himself would have been better off if the whole thing had been handled less formally – that "too big of a deal" had been made out of it and now Jack and his family were really suffering. The majority of members agreed that the pastor and elders had handled the situation properly.

4. Pastor Garrison noticed that a strange transition occurred over time, namely, that empathy and concern for the victim was replaced in a number of church members by a focus on the welfare of the *perpetrator* rather than that of the victim.
5. Jack and his family ended up in another church where Jack is now serving as an assistant in the children's ministry program. No one from that church ever contacted Pastor Garrison as a reference.
6. The Pastor and church board were criticized by Jack's defense attorney and by Jack's counselor for announcing Jack's crime to the congregation. They maintained the matter should have been kept "confidential" out of respect for Jack's privacy.
7. The Greys, in spite of unjust treatment at the hands of a few, realized that by and large the church stood with them, sought justice for them, and sought to provide a safe environment for them in the church.

This narrative of events came to a more satisfactory end than many such cases, although it is still falls short of what we would like to see happen. The case was reported to the police. The perpetrator was not allowed to continue in the church where the victim would see him, in spite of the charges of some that this was un-Christian. The church for the most part realized that their primary obligation was to the *victim* and his family, and that they needed to be provided with a safe environment in their church, free from the stress of having Jack present there.[83]

83 Interestingly, because the victims requested the prosecutor not to "throw the book" at Jack (which seemed to everyone the "Christian thing to do"), Jack was never actually convicted of a crime. He was put in a diversion program that left him with no record. Further, the court then never dictated any terms of probation such as requiring that he not have contact with the victim. He could have *legally* come back to the church if the church leaders would have permitted it. They did not. He was able however to join another church and volunteer in the children's ministry there.

Like some "alternate conclusion" movies, we could have written this story with some different endings. Endings that are far too common. As Pastor Garrison looks back on it all, he shudders when he thinks how easily this case could have gone in one of the two following ways:

1. Jack and his family are permitted to continue as members in the church. The rationale is that this is the Christ-like, loving thing to do. The expectation would be that the victim's family needs to forgive *and reconcile* with the Smiths. To fail to do so would mean they are guilty of unforgiveness. The end result of this course however would have been that the Greys (victims) would have had to leave the church in order to do what they believed best for their son. Result: gross injustice for the victims and increased trauma to them. Also, the stage is set for Jack to commit further sexual abuse.
2. The entire matter could be covered up, with no police report made, no announcement to the congregation. The argument of the church leaders in this case would be that the church is not bound by the state. Christians must not take each other to court as that brings shame on Christ, and Christians must forgive one another. Besides, what had happened was not that serious really. If the victim's family could not abide by this, they would be the ones who have to leave the church. Result: gross injustice for the victims AND disobedience to the Lord by refusing to obey the civil authorities AND the stage set for further future abuse of children by Jack.

Why Are We Tempted to Cover Up?

If you ever find yourself in a similar situation, especially if you are a pastor or church leader, then you can be sure that the temptation toward and dynamics of "cover up" will confront you. Not only in other people, but in your own mind. Why? What reasons can we think of that explain this desire for the whole convoluted "mess" to just go away? Let's consider a few possibilities.

1. Fear.

When we receive a report of a particularly ugly sin happening in our own church, we are afraid. You will *feel* this fear before you understand it. Nevertheless, fear is operative and *decisions made out of fear are rarely good ones.* Fear tends toward cover up. What are we afraid of?

- Harm to our church (destruction of relationships, scandal reported in the newspapers, loss of unity among members, legal consequences, lawsuits, etc.). All of these things are very real possibilities. Churches and ministries have been destroyed more than once over such things. If things really get out of hand in our church, that will almost certainly affect the income of the church and the minister's stipend.
- Criticism. These kinds of situations are complicated puzzles in many respects. There is no resolution that is going to "make everyone happy." Generally, those handling the reported abuse are going to be attacked and criticized by some people before it is over.
- The criminal justice system. In a real church, we are simply not very familiar with courts and police and prosecutors and jails. Suddenly, we are face to face with them when we report abuse. The abuser, who may well be someone we have known for a long time, may end up with a lengthy prison sentence.

If we are going to think clearly and effect biblical justice for the abuse victim, then we must learn to get control of our fear very early in the process.

> ***2 Timothy 1:7*** *for God gave us a spirit not of fear but of power and love and self-control.*

Dealing justly with an abuse report is costly. It is a situation that calls for us to be strong and courageous in Christ, realizing that He promises to be with us in it all. Many people who profess to be Christians simply are not willing to pay the price. Yet Christ Himself tells us:

> ***Matthew 10:34-36*** *"Do not think that I have come to bring peace to the earth. I have not come to bring peace, but a sword. For I have come to set a man against his father, and a daughter against her mother, and a daughter-in-law against her mother-in-law. And a person's enemies will be those of his own household.*

> ***Luke 14:27-28*** *Whoever does not bear his own cross and come after me cannot be my disciple.* (28*) For which of you, desiring to build a tower, does not first sit down and count the cost, whether he has enough to complete it?*

We have seen that one very common tactic of the abuser is the *gaining of allies.* Through deception, lying and other strategies, he works to sway the victim's family members, friends, fellow church members and others to his side. Victims are quite typically estranged from their circle of relationships and even from their own children and grandchildren. When one of these scenarios is playing itself out in a church, there is going to be a price to pay for those who stand with the victim and seek justice for her. This is still another reason why pastors, church leaders, and individual church members will choose to not hear her cause and will even let her be the one to leave the church. In some cases, churches will formally ex-communicate the victim for "sinfully" divorcing her abuser.

Abusers by nature are seekers of power and control. It is not surprising then that the abuser will be the one who has the most resources: money, influence and position in the church, a career, health, etc., while the victim frequently lacks these assets to help her. Therefore, when we stand with the victim, we stand with the weak, the needy, and the defenseless. We stand against wicked forces in high places. We can do so in Christ's mighty power, but often there is going to be a price to pay for taking up the victim's cause. Many people sense this and pass the victim by. The sad truth is that it is less costly to let the victim suffer injustice than to stand with her and defend her. Less costly, that is, until we all stand before Christ!

Christ does not give us an option. If we would be counted as His disciples, then it is to the victim's cause that we must rally:

> ***Matthew 25:37-40*** *Then the righteous will answer him, saying, 'Lord, when did we see you hungry and feed you, or thirsty and give you drink? And when did we see you a stranger and welcome you, or naked and clothe you? And when did we see you sick or in prison and visit you?' And the King will answer them, 'Truly, I say to you, as you did it to one of the least of these my brothers, you did it to me.'*

Jesus calls us to go to Him *outside the camp and bear the reproach he endured* (Hebrews 13:12-13). If we are ashamed to defend victims and join them in their suffering, then Christ is going to be ashamed of us on that Day. Pursuing justice for the weak and helpless is a mark of a real Christian. Turning one's back on such a person is a mark that an individual, despite their outer appearance, does not belong to Christ at all.

To my fellow pastors, let me say this very directly. If you have an abuser in your church and his victim comes to you for rescue, then you are going to be faced with paying a high price for standing with her. Many times family members and friends will side with the abuser not only against the victim, but against anyone, including a pastor or church member, who defends her. Yes, it could even cost a pastor his job. It could divide the church. But then, isn't that the very kind of thing our King has called us to? Aren't there many churches today that *need* to be divided so that those who are approved by Christ might be evident and His church might be kept holy? (1 Corinthians 11:18-19; 1 John 2:19) Yep

2. Don't Ask, Don't Tell

Abuse is an evil that feeds upon silence, secrecy, and shame. Fear fuels this silence and is what the abuser counts on as he continues to assault his victim.

When Pastor Garrison learned that Jack had molested Clay, the pressure of "don't ask and don't tell" began pressing down upon him and his fellow church leaders, and even upon Clay's parents. Initially, it took the form of the temptation to avoid reporting the matter to the police and to deal with the whole thing "in house." Once the impossibility of this route was realized, it became clear that not only would a police report have to be made, but Jack's abuse would have to be announced to the congregation. "Don't ask and don't tell" was simply not going to be an option. However, the pastor, the church, and even the family of the victim continued to be pressured through critics who persisted in maintaining that they should never "tell." This line of "reasoning" maintained that such openness of the abuse actually served up further damage to Jack, to his family, and even to the victim and her family by unnecessarily shaming them.

In abuse cases involving a criminal charge, we should not be surprised to experience this pressure to secrecy from the abuser's attorney. In some cases, a church may even be threatened with a lawsuit unless they keep the facts quiet. But since, as we are learning, our primary obligation is to seek justice for the victim *and* to protect others from the abuser, we must not take our direction from the abuser via his attorney!

Pressure to "don't ask and don't tell" is expected from the defense attorney, but unfortunately we can also expect to experience it from professing Christians and from both Christian and non-Christian counselors and therapists. Some therapists who work with abusers (including sexual abusers) very often have full restoration and reconciliation of the abuser and the victim as their goal. Those who specifically take on the abuser as a client for therapy frequently seek to put him back into his relationship with his victim, or equip him to have healthy, normal relationships with other children or women. Thus, these caseworkers can have the abuser's welfare as their primary goal.[84] Steven Tracy cautions that offenders can be expert manipulators. They will often ask their victims to forgive them. Tracy maintains that it is generally inappropriate for the abuser to ask the victim for forgiveness. Such a request pressures the victim and portrays the abuser as a kind of "savior" to the victim, putting her in an unfair and harmful position.[85]

While the church is not to be completely unconcerned with helping the abuser, we must first be very clear as to what such 'help' really looks like. Don't ask, don't tell is not help. And of primary importance, we must affirm that our fundamental duty is to help and protect the victim. The church, the body of Christ, is the advocate of the weak and innocent. Of any place or institution on earth, the people of Christ should prove to be the champions of the abuse victim, and victims as well as abusers should have no doubt about this.

We must repeat once more, however, that in most cases of abuse, there is huge doubt about this. If this charge sounds too harsh, I advise you to simply talk to abuse victims and hear their stories about how they were dealt injustice by their local church.

"Don't ask, don't tell" is also supported by distortions of Scripture, or more commonly, by vague, broad "biblical" themes such as love, mercy, forgiveness and so on. Matthew 7:1 for example: "Judge not, that you be not judged" is cited as proof that since we are all sinners just like the abuser, we must not announce his sin because that would be too harsh and judgmental. Matthew takes another Scripture-twisting hit when advocates of "don't ask, don't tell" refer us to chapter 18:

---

84 I have experienced this personally. The court-appointed therapist in a sex abuse case functioned in this manner. He wanted the abuser to be reconciled to the victim. A state corrections worker told me that it is commonly understood that the sex offenders he deals with *must* communicate with their victim at some point in the abuser's therapy, for the benefit of both the abuser and the victim. Also see Carla van Dam, *The Socially Skilled Child Molester*, 117.

85 Steven Tracy, *Mending the Soul: Understanding and Healing Abuse* (Zondervan, 2005), Chapter 10.

Matthew 18:15-17 *"If your brother sins against you, go and tell him his fault, between you and him alone. If he listens to you, you have gained your brother. But if he does not listen, take one or two others along with you, that every charge may be established by the evidence of two or three witnesses. If he refuses to listen to them, tell it to the church. And if he refuses to listen even to the church, let him be to you as a Gentile and a tax collector."*

Of all Scriptures, this is the one that I have heard cited the most often by people who ally themselves with the perpetrator either naively or purposefully, or who are abusers themselves and want to maintain a climate of secrecy and cover up. Matthew 18 does *not* apply to cases of abuse. Christians seem to have a simplistic concept that God's single prescription for dealing with sin in the church is Matthew 18! This is like prescribing two aspirin for every ailment a doctor sees in his patients! Consider these Scriptures:

1 Corinthians 5:1-5 *It is actually reported that there is sexual immorality among you, and of a kind that is not tolerated even among pagans, for a man has his father's wife. And you are arrogant! Ought you not rather to mourn? Let him who has done this be removed from among you. For although absent in body, I am present in spirit; and as if present, I have already pronounced judgment on the one who did such a thing. When you are assembled in the name of the Lord Jesus and my spirit is present, with the power of our Lord Jesus, you are to deliver this man to Satan for the destruction of the flesh, so that his spirit may be saved in the day of the Lord.*

1 Timothy 1:20 *among whom are Hymenaeus and Alexander, whom I have handed over to Satan that they may learn not to blaspheme.*

2 Timothy 4:10 *For Demas, in love with this present world, has deserted me and gone to Thessalonica.... [Notice here that Paul names names. No Matthew 18 procedure. He just announces Demas' sin].*

2 Timothy 4:14 *Alexander the coppersmith did me great harm; the Lord will repay him according to his deeds.*

Titus 3:10-11 As for a person who stirs up division, after warning him once and then twice, have nothing more to do with him, knowing that such a person is warped and sinful; he is self-condemned.

Romans 16:17-18 *I appeal to you, brothers, to watch out for those who* *cause divisions and create obstacles contrary to the doctrine that you have been taught; avoid them. For such persons do not serve our Lord Christ, but their own appetites, and by smooth talk and flattery they deceive the hearts of the naive.*

2 Timothy 3:2-5 *For people will be lovers of self, lovers of money, proud, arrogant, abusive, disobedient to their parents, ungrateful, unholy, (3) heartless, unappeasable, slanderous, without self-control, brutal, not loving good, (4) treacherous, reckless, swollen with conceit, lovers of pleasure rather than lovers of God, (5) having the appearance of godliness, but denying its power. Avoid such people.*

We could continue, citing numbers of other such texts as well. But even these few make it quite apparent that God is not in the business of "respecting the privacy" of abusers, nor of keeping evil in the church a secret. As His Word plainly teaches us, when it comes to evil men (and women), we are to name names and announce their wickedness from the rooftops. Nowhere does the Bible promote "don't ask, don't tell." We must *ask* and *tell*; and we must take consequential action. Put them out of the church when their lack of repentance demonstrates their true character. Deliver them over to Satan. Have nothing to do with them. Claiming that Matthew 18 binds us to private confrontation of the abuser, or insisting that every issue be handled "one-on-one" behind the closed door of the pastor's office, is absolutely antithetical to the Word of God. And yet, this bad theology is embraced in the majority of evangelical churches (as evidenced by their reluctance to practice biblical church discipline).

Appeals to "confessional confidentiality" are also used to argue for a "don't ask, don't tell" approach to abuse. Many will insist that *anything* told to a pastor or counselor is confidential. But even the civil authorities understand that crimes cannot be shielded under a cloak of clergy or counselor privilege. Pastors and counselors are required by law now in most, if not all, states to report certain kinds of abuse to the police, and failure to do so is a criminal offense. The reader might do well to give some thought to why such laws have been necessary. We need to make it very clear to anyone that we counsel that we can make no absolute promise to keep everything we are told confidential. There are certain matters that the law and common morality demand be reported. Just as we ought to protect our children from sexual abuse by teaching them that *some secrets shouldn't be kept secret*, we need to teach ourselves and our congregations the same thing.

Kroeger and Clark, in their very helpful book *No Place for Abuse: Biblical and Practical Resources to Counteract Domestic Violence*, include a chapter called "Cruel Deceptions & Christian Conceptions." Challenging Christians to take a second and careful look at their theology of "silence," they tell the story of a woman who survived three attempts on her life at the hands of her husband, who was a well-known and respected Christian leader. One of the criticisms she suffered from her own church when she finally was able to divorce him, was the charge that it was completely wrong for her to ever reveal these "details."[86]. This is nothing less than sheer *idolatry* and just as evil as the worship of Baal or Dagon. When man and sin are exalted to such a status, it is no longer Christ who is being worshipped.

Carla van Dam does a wonderful job clarifying that it is alright to talk about people in many contexts. In fact, she has learned that it is fundamentally *because* we don't communicate our concerns about a potential child molester or abuser that serves the abuser's cloak of secrecy quite well. Talking with other people is a source of valuable information, and it is not gossip or slander when our motives are not malicious and our purpose is to share important information. When we tell someone that we had a bad experience with a person in order to protect them from suffering the same pain, we are not guilty of gossip.[87]

3. Fantasy Thinking.

> *"Delight in smooth-sounding platitudes, refusal to face unpleasant facts, desire for popularity and electoral success irrespective of the vital interests of the State, genuine love of peace and pathetic belief that love can be its sole foundation…"*[88] *-Winston Churchill*

Like pre-war England, we cover up in the church because we want to insulate ourselves from real life and its evils. The Bible does not do this. God

86 Kroeger and Nason-Clark, 118-119.

87 Van Dam, 92.

88 Winston Churchill, *The Gathering Storm,* (London: Houghton Mifflin, 1948), Location 1443 Kindle Edition. Churchill's comments here on failures in the British government that led to World War II.

names horrendous sins, including sexual ones. When it comes to evil, Christians are instructed by Christ to be innocent as doves, yet wise as serpents (Matthew 10:16). While we are to take care to be separate from the world, striving to remain unstained by its wickedness, we dare not be naïve about it. And yet we are. Christians, and in particular, conservative, Bible-believing Christians who truly desire to live for Christ, easily adopt a magical, fantastical worldview in which prayer sprinkles pixie dust and tinsel, removing anything that is "yucky." As their world narrows to the realm of their own protected, safe Christian community, they can grow blind to daily experience of most people. This can be particularly true for people who have been brought up in Christian homes and never exposed to the raw, rough world. Such second generation believers can be incredibly naïve to the realities of evil conduct. Such people go from Christian high school to Christian college, then on to Christian seminary to be trained as pastors, then into the church. And that is a sure formula for dangerous credulity.

And then, suddenly, it strikes them. A victim comes forward from within their own community – one of their own – with stories about horrible evils perpetrated against them by another one of their own. How can it be? This isn't supposed to happen here! "Out there, perhaps, but not among us." This victim describes it:

> I've known abuse for much of my life. Sometimes witnessed, often experienced, it's been one of the defining constants in who I am. What's been normal for me, however, seems to be something that the church at large wishes to ignore. When confronted by stories they'd rather wish weren't true, their thinking almost seems to be 'if we ignore it, it didn't happen.' Sadly, this kind of denial-thinking doesn't make it fiction, but only makes it worse, especially for the one ignored, the one who, most likely, was also the one abused.
>
> We don't want to believe that abuse happens within our churches. These sacred areas are supposed to be set aside and offered up unto God for His bidding, His doing, His will. He who has called us and set us aside for Himself would surely protect, guide and defend His own, wouldn't He? How then, are we to believe that, within the very homes that we believe hallowed by Him, abuse often lurks: hungering for violence to body and mind, destroying what ought to be loved and protected, masquerading as peace all the while acting to kill? The reality is, just as God's Word warns us,

> all that seems to have been hallowed by God, hasn't actually been. There are many people who claim to know Him, who call Him their own, who are, in fact, children of the devil. These sons of perdition are there to do their father's will but their father isn't the God of heaven. He is the prince of the earth, of darkness, of evil masquerading as good.

Still another manner in which fantasy-thinking leads to further injustice toward the victim, is that of the church regarding her as "leper." This same abuse victim goes on to relate how a church elder refused her offer of a book about abuse, claiming that it would not tell him anything that he did not already know:

> That the elder wouldn't study this subject is very telling... and also typical in far too many churches. It's almost like a woman (or family) who has suffered abuse is a leper and others believe it can be caught. She must go "outside the camp" lest she infect others. Plus, it seems to be perceived to be shameful to even admit that there is a problem among us (rather than shameful to refuse to confront a problem... which is where the real shame ought to lie).

Try to imagine yourself as the abuse victim who goes to her pastor for help, and then hears him say something like this:

> I have no doubt that everything you are telling me about your husband is true. However, I want you to drop the divorce proceedings and enter into "biblical counseling" with me. This kind of counseling is what your marriage needs, not the books that you want me to read. Besides, there are only two biblical reasons for divorce and the emotional abuse in your marriage is not one of them. If you continue with the divorce, the church is going to have to discipline you.

It will not take much effort to realize that fantasy-thinking about ourselves and our church communities *is incredibly dangerous.* Our fantasy thinking is a chief reason that an abuser can continue in his evil *among us.* He knows that the prevailing climate in his church is one of denial that anyone here in this place could ever be guilty of such things. We are, it must be said, ignorant of Christ's Word, and too arrogant to admit it.

Fantasy-thinking also explains, at least in part, the typical dead silence that can be "heard" in a church when the topic of abuse is addressed from the pulpit or in a class. The lead balloon feeling when one talks about it. The blank facial affect that sweeps over our listener. Such talk threatens the beloved fantasy. It implies that the Wizard of the Emerald City is just some guy from Kansas, and Toto should just put the curtain back as it was.

In reality however acknowledging that sin (abuse) can indeed hide and masquerade among us is not a denial of the reality of Christ and His church! It is an affirmation of the very things the Bible tells us about the battle in which every Christian is engaged. When we rally around the abuse victim and confront her abuser, we are being Jesus. When we deny that anything like such an evil could possibly be among us, when we push her away as a "leper," we are being…well, let the reader complete the sentence.

> Why, just look at these beautiful, happy children here in our church. There is no way in the world that there could be any abuse happening here. (Church member)

4. The Trauma of the Thing

Closely connected with fantasy-thinking as an explanation for our bent toward cover up is a phenomenon we might call *trauma.* When we are confronted with something ugly and terrible, our head "sets to spinning." The thing somehow doesn't seem real. Carla Van Dam writes about this. She notes that the reaction to "emotionally difficult news" is typically one of shock and disbelief. Reception of such information often results in, as she calls it, an "ostrich-head-in-the-sand" response as the recipient reacts with denial designed to shield oneself against grief and consequences.[89]

When I was a very young college student I was a reserve police officer, in a sleepy, rural college town. A car ran a stop sign in front of me and I proceeded to stop the driver. He wasn't having any of it however and the chase was on. Tragically, several miles north of town, he failed to realize that the road came to a T-intersection. At an incredibly high speed, probably 130 mph, he "launched" himself and his passenger into a freshly harvested wheat field. When I arrived, there was a surreal scene. Sirens were still blaring and lights flashing as other intercepting police and fire vehicles converged. And off in the distance through a huge dust cloud, flames became visible. The car, or what remained of it, was burning out of control, and then the stubble field ignited. The engine had been

89 Van Dam, 86-87.

thrown many feet away from the car and the occupants were nowhere to be seen. Finally, we found one of them and could only hold his head up in some attempt to comfort him as he took his last spasmodic gasps. Only later did we realize that there had been a second occupant as well. After the fire had been extinguished by the fire department, a burned body lay out in the field. I had never seen or smelled such a thing before.[90]

What happens to us when we experience such a traumatic thing totally foreign to our experience and our world? Well the answer is, *denial,* the shock renders us unable to compute and process all our sensory input, our thoughts and our feelings. The subject of post traumatic stress disorder is closely related to all of this.

In their excellent book, *Honeymoon and Hell: A Memoir of Abuse*, Sarah Braun and Bridget Flynn address denial, explaining how it operated in one of them. What they observe can be applied to *us* when a victim reveals her abuse to us. They note that denial is a powerful response in us when we are faced with a horrible thing. Denial works to dilute it. To minimize it. Our minds work to suppress the sickening nature of what has been placed in front of us. We make excuses for the perpetrator that tend toward making him less wicked than he really is. Denial blames the abuser's actions on someone or something else in his background, making him out to be a kind of victim himself. Through these excuses, we try to understand that he is just not a basically evil person, but a struggling and hurt one. After all, since we could never see ourselves abusing someone out of a motivation of pure evil, then surely no one else could. Fundamentally we are all really the same, right?[91]

As it is with fear, so it is with denial. Decisions motivated by denial are neither good nor just. Nothing good will come from them. This can be a particularly dangerous trap for abuse victims. They have suffered trauma. Incredible trauma

90 When I tell this story, which I actually don't very often, I always try to remember to give thanks to Christ for preserving me. Only two minutes before this chase began, another reserve officer had come to the station to ride along with me on patrol. He couldn't sleep. He grew up in the area and it was his warning as we neared the T-intersection that saved me from doing the very same thing the other car had, which would have certainly killed us both as well. Adrenaline and tunnel-vision are dangerous things.

91 Braun, Location 334-344, Kindle Edition.

through sometimes unspeakable acts of terrorism. For these people the hearing about a report of abuse, or hearing a speaker lecture on the subject and describe it can produce a special type of re-trauma as it triggers memories in them. How many people sitting in a church audience for example, will have these memories spark to life when the subject of abuse is addressed? What will their reaction be? Avoidance. Shutting down. It would be wise for a speaker to preface his or her lecture with some remarks addressing this.

We could no doubt list more explanations for the tendency of churches to try to cover up abuse. Certainly *ignorance* of the very nature and tactics of abuse is an extremely common cause. When we fail to understand a thing, we cannot deal with it properly. Until the gravity and destructiveness of abuse is comprehended, we will tend to minimize it and dismiss it. Add *arrogance* to the equation and the conspiracy of silence finds even more fertile ground to flourish among us. When we are ignorant of the essence of abuse and its wickedly cunning deceptions, yet tell ourselves that because we are Christians and read our Bibles we certainly are equipped to handle anything – we add more fertilizer to the soil in which abuse thrives.

Do the Right Things

We cannot encourage the reader enough to learn and embrace the following guidelines *before abuse is reported to you.* These points are the result of hard lessons learned firsthand in the school of "hard knocks" by genuine Christians who have been through the fire. Some of these points will be re-visited in chapter 11, along with a number of other actions you can take to help the victim.

1. Believe the victim.[92] Acknowledge your tendency toward *fear* and *denial* and refuse to permit your decisions to be colored by them. This may require a "let's just slow down a bit and take a deep breath" on your part. Resist the temptation of thinking this can be handled quickly and simply. Consider consulting with professionals who have expertise in

92 We are not promoting blind acceptance of every allegation of abuse. But the truth is that in most cases those who report abuse are *speaking with honesty.* Consider what we have learned about the nature of abuse to this point. The effects of the thing actually hinder the victim from coming forward. For a victim to speak out requires much courage for many reasons, one of which is the shame she feels about telling anyone what has been happening. Our problem is not that we are believing too many victims and doing injustice to falsely accuse people, but quite the opposite.

the kind of abuse that has been disclosed, and bear in mind that secular professionals are often more knowledgeable about these things than Christians are.[93]

2. Do not be respecters of persons. We must not act in favoritism regardless of who the abuser is.
3. Understand that abuse of any kind is *serious.*
4. Embrace the conviction that your purpose is to effect justice and protection *for the victim* as a priority. Ministry to the perpetrator must remain secondary to this. In cases of sexual abuse, the reality is that the perpetrator and very often his family as well *cannot* continue in your church. In domestic violence abuse cases, the abuser will need to cease from fellowship in your church, especially if the victim decides to separate from him. This does not mean, however, "passing him off" to another unsuspecting church!
5. Report to the police immediately. Do not look for loopholes to excuse non-reporting. Do not consider the civil authorities to be your enemy.
6. Let the justice system deal with the perpetrator as with anyone else. Do not ask for mercy or special treatment. Bancroft believes that diversion programs are a failure.[94]
7. Protect the victims from people's accusations. Warn church members not to increase the suffering of the victim through false allegations or distortions of forgiveness and reconciliation.
8. Do not cover up. Announce the abuse to your congregation.
9. Don't try to please everyone. It is impossible. Accept the fact that whatever you do is going to bring criticism and may well cost you relationships. Seek to effect biblical justice and then "let the chips fall" where they may. I received wise counsel many years ago from a police sergeant I worked for. I had been called to a store where a shoplifter was detained. It turned out that the thief was a high-ranking police official with another nearby department. I called the sergeant and asked what to do and his answer was, "Jeff, just do your job. We will never criticize you for doing your job, no matter who you arrest." And I did. If people

93 We can wholeheartedly commend the ministry of Steven Tracy, *Mending the Soul.* You can find him on the web.

94 Bancroft, lecture delivered in Tillamook, Oregon 2010.

want to sweep abuse under the rug and they end up leaving your church when you refuse to do so, the church will be smaller in numbers, but stronger in godliness.

10. Touch on abuse regularly from the pulpit if you are a pastor. Address the subject in study groups. Pray publicly for victims and survivors. This will work to prepare and protect your congregation and will greatly increase the odds that a victim will be dealt with justly in your church.

May this victim's experience never be that of a victim in your church:

One day I will have to tell you the story of how my church dealt with me when I reported my husband's years of abuse to my pastor. It will take chapters to tell. After trying to do what was right for over five years, working under the authority and accountability of my church, I finally realized that they just wanted me and my problem to go away. And that is what, in the end, I had to do. Go away. My ex-husband continues to try to control me and seek revenge against me by using the court system and our own children as weapons against me. Yet he remains a member of my old church while I am outside the camp and largely regarded as the real cause of the whole mess. He was never prosecuted nor did he serve a single day in jail for his crimes.

Exodus 22:22-24 You shall not mistreat any widow or fatherless child. (23) If you do mistreat them, and they cry out to me, I will surely hear their cry, and my wrath will burn, and I will kill you with the sword, and your wives shall become widows and your children fatherless.

CHAPTER 10

Common Distortions of Scripture that Promote Abuse

Matthew 15:1-3 *Then Pharisees and scribes came to Jesus from Jerusalem and said, "Why do your disciples break the tradition of the elders? For they do not wash their hands when they eat." He answered them, "And why do you break the commandment of God for the sake of your tradition?*

"My pastor and his wife kept sending me back to my abuser-husband with instructions to 'love that man to Jesus.' But the terror only worsened. When I finally left him, my church condemned me." (Abuse Victim)

"God has called you to suffering. Be thankful that you have not yet 'resisted unto blood.'" ("Helpful" advice from a Christian friend)

"The Lord will protect you and teach you in the midst of the difficult time. Of course, pray for your husband, submit to him in every way you can, encourage him to seek advice and counsel from other biblically-knowledgeable men—and do everything you can to heal the problems that cause him to be angry or abusive." (John MacArthur, Jr.)[95]

What do you think about this kind of counsel? Hopefully, after reading to this point, you are beginning to see not only the erroneous thinking it is based upon, but also the terrible damage it does to a victim. *Telling a victim these kinds*

95 John MacArthur, "Answering Key Questions About the Family," Grace to You Website, http://www.gty.org/resources/positions/p00/answering-the-key-questions-about-the-family

of things could literally get her killed. Many of the "Bible truths" Christians cling to and apply in abuse cases are, in fact, nothing but what the Bible would call *"the traditions of men."* Just like the Pharisees, we can be guilty of trumping the truth and authority of God's Word with our own connived traditions.

In this chapter, we are going to examine three areas in which man-made tradition is very commonly being taught as authoritative Scripture. These traditions continue to do much grievous harm to victims and empower the wicked. They need to be exposed and rejected under the light of true Scripture.

Distortions of Forgiveness and Reconciliation

> *"Pastor, I have a real concern to share with you. Pam is considering divorcing her husband. She says he is abusive, and we know that he did commit adultery several times some years back. But we are all sinners, including Pam. Surely she has some blame in their marriage troubles too. Jesus calls every Christian to forgive those who sin against us and to then reconcile their relationship with that person. A wife must always forgive her husband and work to reconcile and preserve her marriage. God says that he hates divorce and that if a person divorces and remarries, it is adultery. I have heard that you think divorce is permissible, but it isn't. I want to know what you are going to tell Pam."* (Church member to her Pastor)

> *"Pastor, it just is not right! Oh, I know that sexual abuse is a very serious sin, but we all sin. That is why God tells us to forgive one another and reconcile our relationships. If Jerry's victim (Sharon) could just understand, Jesus is great enough to help her forgive Jerry. She says she has forgiven him, but she refuses to speak to him or have any kind of relationship with him, so I don't believe her. And poor Jerry, he is really hurting. True forgiveness always includes reconciliation and restored relationship. That is what the gospel is all about, right? I think that you need to confront Sharon and show her that she is allowing a root of bitterness in her heart."* ("Concerned" church member)

People like these two church members have embraced tradition rather than truth. They cling to a twisted concept of the Bible's real teachings about forgiveness and reconciliation, and in their misguided zeal they do great harm to victims. Before we compare some of these traditions with biblical truth, let's pin down our definitions. Just what do we mean when we say *forgiveness*, or *reconciliation*, or *repentance*?

Forgiveness is a decision made by the wronged party not to demand payment of the debt owed to him by the offender. The victim determines not to pursue vengeance. Forgiveness always includes the first of the following three agreements, *but does not necessarily include the second or third:*

1. Decision by the wronged party to not pursue vengeance against the offender.
2. Decision by the wronged party to set aside certain consequential sanctions of the wrong.
3. Decision by the wronged party to reconcile their relationship with the offender.

It is vital for us to understand that forgiveness *does not mean* the offender must be "let off the hook" in regard to the consequences of his abuse. A victim can forgive her abuser in the sense of vowing not to seek personal vengeance against him. (We specify *personal* vengeance because it is still proper for a victim to implore God to effect His holy vengeance upon an unrepentant abuser. This is demonstrated by the imprecatory Psalms).[96] Forgiving her abuser does not negate the victim's right to insist upon certain consequential sanctions such as:

Prosecution and sentencing for his crimes.
Dissolution of the marriage.
Treatment and counseling.
Church discipline.

Consider this example from the life of King David:

2 Samuel 12:10-14 *Now therefore the sword shall never depart from your house, because you have despised me and have taken the wife of Uriah the Hittite to be your wife.' Thus says the LORD, 'Behold, I will raise up evil against you out of your own house. And I will take your wives before your eyes and give them to your neighbor, and he shall lie with your wives in the*

96 Imprecatory Psalms are those Psalms in which the Psalmist implores God to bring justice and righteous vengeance upon his enemies. The Apostle Paul uses imprecation in Galatians chapter 1 when he expresses his desire that those who distort the gospel be "anathema" (cursed by God). Examples of imprecatory Psalms are Psalms 7, 35, 55, 58, 59, 69, 79, 109,137 and 139:19-24.

sight of this sun. For you did it secretly, but I will do this thing before all Israel and before the sun.'" David said to Nathan, "I have sinned against the LORD." And Nathan said to David, "The LORD also has put away your sin; you shall not die. Nevertheless, because by this deed you have utterly scorned the LORD, the child who is born to you shall die."

Here we see God implementing the first aspect of forgiveness (dismissal of vengeance) in regard to King David after his sin against Uriah the Hittite (adultery, murder). The Lord forgave David so that David did not "die" – and still there were a large number of painful consequences left in place. Could the Lord have dismissed these consequences as well? Yes. Did He? No. His justice still required these things from David, and they worked to David's good as well as providing justice to Uriah's house. David was King, God's King. The people of Israel needed to know that no one is above God's Law.

Reconciliation is the reestablishment of prior relationship. In Christ, sinners are reconciled to God. Our former fellowship with Him, lost in the Fall, is restored (and even improved upon). Not only is there *peace*, but *relationship* as a result of reconciliation. You see this in the following verse:

Romans 5:10 *For if while we were enemies we were reconciled to God by the death of his Son, much more, now that we are reconciled, shall we be saved by his life.*

But reconciliation is not an essential element of forgiveness when we are considering relationships between human beings. Forgiveness can be effected (agreement to not pursue vengeance) without reconciliation. In abuse cases, wisdom does not require nor even advise reconciliation. Although the Christian exercises love and does good to his enemy, enemies are still just that: *enemies.* The abuse victim, therefore, is not required to reconcile with her abuser. Forgiveness without reconciliation is still forgiveness. Notice that the following Scripture says nothing about trusting an enemy in a relationship:

Luke 6:27-28 *But I say to you who hear, Love your enemies, do good to those who hate you, bless those who curse you, pray for those who abuse you.*

What kind of person is Jesus speaking of? Our enemy. An enemy who hates us. An enemy who curses and abuses us. There is no relationship here. But if we come across this enemy bleeding on the highway, we are going to do good to him

and call an ambulance. That is love. We will pray for his recovery
Lord might show him mercy and bring him to faith in Christ. But none of
requires that we live with him! In fact, doing good to an abuser and loving him most often means just the opposite. Yielding to his evil control or caving in to his demand that the victim move back in with him, is not good nor is it love.

What about a repentant offender? Doesn't *repentance* obligate the victim to reconcile? Let's define our term:

Repentance is unconditional acknowledgment by the offender of his crime/ sin, confessing his guilt without blaming anyone else. True repentance shoulders the entire responsibility for the sin repented of and agrees that the offender is fully deserving of just punishment. Real repentance at least begins to feel the pain and grief caused by the sin and will always evidence a change in behavior. Classic examples of true repentance in Scripture are David, and the Prodigal:

> ***Psalm 51:2-4*** *Wash me thoroughly from my iniquity, and cleanse me from my sin! For I know my transgressions, and my sin is ever before me. Against you, you only, have I sinned and done what is evil in your sight, so that you may be justified in your words and blameless in your judgment.*
>
> *Luke 15:21 And the son said to him, 'Father, I have sinned against heaven and before you. I am no longer worthy to be called your son.'*

True repentance is very rare. In fact, it is a gift from God (2 Timothy 2:25). In dealing with abusers, it is very important that we understand what repentance looks like *and what it does not look like.* Repentance does not use the language of blame or qualification. It does not insist upon conditions. Abusers who tell their victim that they are sorry and that they are changing and if only the victim could do _____, then they could do better, are *not* repentant. There is no room for excuses in true repentance.[97]

Truly repentant people don't focus on their desire for forgiveness. That's a continuation of self-centeredness. Instead, they express a genuine

97 By it [repentance], a sinner, out of the sight and sense not only of the danger, but also of the filthiness and odiousness of his sins, as contrary to the holy nature, and righteous law of God; and upon the apprehension of His mercy in Christ to such as are penitent, so grieves for, and hates his sins, as to turn from them all unto God, purposing and endeavouring to walk with Him in all the ways of His commandments. (Westminster Confession of Faith)

> willingness to bear and focus on the pain they have caused.... Genuine repentance contains no "buts"![98]

> "My husband is putting more pressure on me to 'make things better between us.' I tried once again to tell him how he has hurt me and the children. As always, he simply will not own his sin. He threw it all back at me by saying, 'If you want to put all of the blame on me, go ahead. I'm an easy target.'" [Abuse victim]

Let's return to our question then: When there is genuine repentance, isn't the victim bound to not only forgive, but to reconcile the relationship? Many Christians insist upon this, but to do so is wrong and foolish. Ultimately, all who are genuinely repentant will experience not only full forgiveness in Christ, but full reconciliation with Christ and with all of His people. But temporally, in this life, the consequences of sin do not just vaporize, and the loss of a relationship is often one of those consequences in cases of abuse.

As you compare the following traditions vs. truths, think about them in relation to God's practice of forgiveness and reconciliation. Which column, tradition or truth, best describes what we find in Scripture?

TRADITION	TRUTH
God forgives everyone.	God does not forgive everyone. (2 Thess. 1:5-9)
No matter how many times my abuser sins against me, I must forgive him AND dismiss any demands upon him AND reconcile with him.	Repeating a sin evidences a lack of repentance, making it unwise if not impossible to dismiss consequences and reconcile. (Acts 26:19-20)
Forgiveness must always include reconciliation or it is not real forgiveness.	We can forgive, but we are not required to reconcile relationship in every case. (1 Cor. 7:15)
We must always love our abuser and this means that we can only desire good for him.	It is right to pray that God would strike down the wicked man and deliver his victims. (Rev. 6:10)

98 Jeff Olson, *When Words Hurt: Verbal Abuse in Marriage* (Grand Rapids: RBC Ministries, 2002), 29. Note: Olson maintains that a person who divorces their abuser is not free to remarry. We reject this conclusion.

Forgiveness of consequences is unconditional, requiring nothing on the part of the offender.	Forgiveness of consequences is conditional, in that it is not possible if certain conditions are not met by the offender. (Matt. 3:7-8)
Forgiveness of consequences is always to be total, never requiring any payment of debt by the offender.	Forgiveness of consequences may be granted in part, while still requiring other portions of the debt to be paid. (i.e., a criminal sentence; Luke 23:40-43)
Forgiveness of consequences AND reconciliation must be immediate.	Forgiveness of consequences and a reconciled relationship require time, since repentance must be proven to be authentic. (Luke 6:45; Genesis 42-45)

Traditions like these are based upon an erroneous interpretation of individual Scriptures, a far too common interpretive error that fails to consider all the Bible's teaching on a given subject. Unbiblical traditions can also continue to "live" when we approach Scripture with our own prior opinions and merely search for texts to prove our fallacies. In regard to forgiveness, verses such as the following are often cited in support of what we have had passed down to us, rather than what we have actually derived from God's Word:

> ***Matthew 6:14-15*** *For if you forgive others their trespasses, your heavenly Father will also forgive you, but if you do not forgive others their trespasses, neither will your Father forgive your trespasses.*
>
> ***Matthew 18:21-22*** *Then Peter came up and said to him, "Lord, how often will my brother sin against me, and I forgive him? As many as seven times?" Jesus said to him, "I do not say to you seven times, but seventy times seven.*
>
> ***Mark 11:25*** *And whenever you stand praying, forgive, if you have anything against anyone, so that your Father also who is in heaven may forgive you your trespasses."*

And yet, what do we do with the following verses? We cannot simply dismiss them in our study of forgiveness. To do so is to dismiss the very attributes of God!

John 20:23 *If you forgive the sins of any, they are forgiven them; if you withhold forgiveness from any, it is withheld."*

Psalm 3:7 *Arise, O LORD! Save me, O my God! For you strike all my enemies on the cheek; you break the teeth of the wicked.*

Psalm 10:2 *In arrogance the wicked hotly pursue the poor; let them be caught in the schemes that they have devised.*

2 Timothy 4:14-15 *Alexander the coppersmith did me great harm; the Lord will repay him according to his deeds. Beware of him yourself, for he strongly opposed our message.*

Anyone familiar with the Bible at all will realize that we could cite myriads of verses just like these that not only do not speak of forgiveness, but cry out for God's justice against the wicked. One of the causes of the church dealing injustice to abuse victims is that we ignore God's holy justice, His wrath against the wicked, and His zeal to fight for the helpless. As a result, we come to distorted, traditional, saccharine concepts of things like forgiveness, mercy, and reconciliation rather than to a true biblical understanding of the term.

Two more examples of Scriptures that we can expect to be isolated and distorted and then used to the detriment of an abuse victim are these:

Luke 23:34 *And Jesus said, "Father, forgive them, for they know not what they do." And they cast lots to divide his garments.*

Acts 7:60 *And falling to his knees he cried out with a loud voice, "Lord, do not hold this sin against them." And when he had said this, he fell asleep.*

Are we to take statements like these and extrapolate them into all-inclusive, absolute principles meant to define the very essence of all forgiveness? Of course not. And yet this is what so many people do. Christ forgave those who crucified Him. Stephen forgave those who stoned him. Therefore, we are to passively forgive and pray for our abusers in all cases and endure more abuse at their hands. To make such a comprehensive conclusion is to dismiss a mountain of other Scripture that addresses the topic of forgiveness and how we relate to our enemies. Consider 2 Timothy 4:14-15 again. Did the Apostle Paul pray that the I d not hold Alexander's sin against him? No! He prayed that the Lord y Alexander on the Day of judgment!

Is forgiveness like some "blanket re-set button"? Recently I read an article by a pastor on the subject of God's definition of forgiveness. The definition he proposed is that forgiveness is a four-fold promise:[99]

- I will not dwell on this incident.
- I will not bring up this incident again.
- I will not talk to anyone about this incident.
- I will not let this incident hinder my personal relationship with the offender.

While the author acknowledges that forgiveness does not necessarily eliminate all of the temporal consequences of the sin, he does go seriously astray in the last three of these promises. All we need do is apply this definition to the Apostle Paul's statement about Alexander the coppersmith:

Has Paul forgiven Alexander?	Yes, in the sense that he leaves vengeance up to the Lord.
Does Paul promise never to bring this incident up again?	No. He is bringing it up again in telling Timothy about it.
Does Paul re-establish a personal relationship with Alexander?	No way! And he tells Timothy not to either.

Now, apply this pastor's faulty definition of forgiveness to an abuse case, and imagine pressing the victim to promise to never bring up the abuser's evil again, to never talk about what her abuser has done to her with anyone, *and that she must promise to reconcile her personal relationship with the abuser!* You can see how terribly ridiculous such demands would be.[100] And yet, these are the very kinds of things that pastors, churches, and individual Christians are laying upon victims. I do not necessarily classify such people with the Pharisees and scribes, but certainly there is some correlation to their thinking in what Jesus said about them:

> ***Matthew 23:4*** *They tie up heavy burdens, hard to bear, and lay them on people's shoulders, but they themselves are not willing to move them with their finger.*

99 You can find the very same four-fold definition of forgiveness in *The Peacemaker: A Biblical Guide to Resolving Personal Conflict*, by Ken Sande (Baker Book House, 1991).

100 I am not denying that in some cases where the offender is genuinely repentant, the victim may choose to exercise the other three elements of this pastor's definition. But they cannot be included as fundamental ingredients of the essence of forgiveness.

If you understand the evil, devastating nature of abuse, you will not be able to hear or read these kinds of distortions about forgiveness without sensing the temperature of your blood rising!

> This is a recipe that could send victims of abuse 'round the bend. How can you recover form abuse unless you think about all the incidents and patterns, allowing your feelings and thoughts and remembrances to swell, surge, subside, resurge, and recalibrate, until your poor brain can make some sense of it all by joining the dots, processing the iconic images, venting the emotions (with safe people), and figuring out what you want to do to avoid such trauma in the future?
>
> Many victim/survivors I know have tried to follow that kind of recipe (distorted forgiveness). They end up living somewhat tight, self-constructed lives, stuffing their feelings, blocking their history, being Job's counselors to other survivors, and always in danger of being re-triggered into fear or anxiety by relatively insignificant events that remind their subconscious of the big trauma they've tried to suppress.[101]

The abuse victim rightly possesses a desire for justice and vindication and rescue. When she calls for help, she does not need to hear us remind her of the love of God, nor about how God works everything together for her good, nor how she needs to forgive and reconcile with an evil man (just "forgive and forget"). Rather, she needs to hear that God hates the evil that has been perpetrated against her and how God is ready to rise up and deliver her and strike down the one who has enslaved her. She needs to hear her fellow Christians in her church tell her these things, and then hear them say, "We are going to stand with you against this evil as well. We are going to protect and shield you."

> *We should pray that our enemies be converted and become our friends, and if not, that their doing and designing be bound to fail and have no success and that their persons perish rather than the Gospel and the Kingdom of Christ.* -Martin Luther

Exercise

Listen to the following question from a woman, directed to her church leaders, and then to the answer she is given. Do you think that their answer is a proper application of Matthew 18:21-22 (70 times 7)? –

101 Personal correspondence with Barbara Roberts, 2012.

"My husband has committed adultery numerous times during our marriage. He professes to be a Christian, and after each adulterous episode he has asked me to forgive him. But then he will go do it again. What should I do?"

Answer:

"Keep forgiving him and always be ready to reconcile with him. Jesus said we are to forgive seventy times seven and even though this is difficult, you are not permitted to divorce him."

What do you think? Is this really what Christ would have us tell victims? Is this husband really repenting?

Distortions of Headship and Submission

Still another caustic substance Christians often pour into the wounds of abuse victims results from distortions of the biblical doctrine of marriage and specifically that aspect of marriage concerning the God-given roles of husbands and wives. Often abusive men who masquerade as Christians take what they hear taught in sermons and classes and pervert those teachings to an evil purpose. Pastors and Christians must always remember:

> Abusive men adopt the façade of Christianity and go to church because they know that this is fertile ground for finding a woman who will submit to them, or to be able to practice their abuse under the guise of "headship." Women who refuse to submit to unbiblical power and control are often labeled as rebellious and sinful and may even be chastised by the church. Also, there are many genuine Christian women who truly and zealously desire to give themselves to a truly godly marriage, to be godly wives and mothers, and they are willing to go to great lengths to achieve these things. These women are noble, but they are also ripe for the deceit of the abuser who is quite willing to use his distortions of Scripture to enslave them. (Abuse victim)

After studying the subject of abuse and domestic violence, I realized that although I had accurately taught what the Bible says about the roles of husbands and wives on several occasions, I concluded that I had still erred. Namely, I had not spent adequate time emphasizing *what these things do not mean.* Why the omission on my part? Because I did not realize that there could well be an abusive man listening to what I said, ready to use my words to justify his evil. I hope that I have taken at least beginning steps to correct this deficiency. In the future, when I teach on marriage and marriage roles, I will always be certain that I describe the abuse of God's Word by an abuser so specifically and accurately that any such man will squirm in the pew, realizing that I am describing *him*.

As with the subjects of forgiveness and reconciliation, it is simply not possible to give a full exposition of the pertinent Scriptures about marriage in this present book. What we can do is list some of the common distortions that claim their support from such texts as Genesis 2:21ff; Ephesians 5:21ff; 1 Peter 3:1-7 and 1 Corinthians 11:1-16. As you read these lies, be certain to note the truth that immediately follows. Abuse victims advise me that simply reading the lies triggers unpleasant emotions, so if you are a victim of abuse, please be aware of this:

- *The atmosphere of the home is determined by the wife. She is the one who determines the mood of her husband.* Truth: The atmosphere of the home is a shared responsibility of both husband and wife. In fact, a positive, healthy atmosphere can be destroyed by the abuser himself, and no matter how hard his wife might try, she cannot remove the stench of his abuse, especially since he continues to emit it daily!
- *A wife has no rights unless she is submissive to her husband. A wife is guiltier before God for not submitting to her husband than a husband is for not loving his wife.* Truth: Every human being has rights which are given to them by God. Because God has actually placed more responsibility upon the husband/father, an abusive man's guilt is surely more repugnant to God.
- *A wife can heal her husband of his abuse by being a better and more submissive wife.*[102] Truth: There is nothing that a wife, or anyone, can do to fix an abuser. His repentance is his own responsibility that only he can exercise.
- *A good marriage requires one thing: a woman who truly desires to obey God. If she will do this, she will have a good marriage even if her husband is not a good man.* Truth: A marriage is a covenant between a man and a woman.

102 The first three teachings in this list can be found in a terrible book by Jack Hyles called *Woman the Completer*, 1981. It can be found online. I pity any woman who is trying to follow Hyles' teachings. A similarly dangerous source of teaching is found in Debi Pearl's *Created to Be His Help Meet* (No Greater Joy Ministries). *Me? Obey Him?* by Elizabeth Rice Handford is still another example. Ultra-fundamentalist groups like these enable abusers and oppress their victims.

A good marriage requires both husband and wife to fulfill their vows to one another. A good marriage requires two people. A bad marriage only requires one.

- *If a husband is being abusive, it is because his wife is not obeying and honoring him sufficiently.* Truth: If a husband is being abusive, it is because he is an abuser. Try all she might, the wife will never fix his abusiveness.
- *A wife is to obey her husband without exception or qualification.* Truth: God never allocates absolute authority to anyone except Christ. No government, no parent, no husband has absolute authority. When the abuser orders his wife to do something contrary to the will of God, his wife is fully justified in refusing to do what he says.

Some people believe that the biblical model of marriage is of husband and wife each submitting to one another (Ephesians 5:21) with leadership and authority arising from their individual gifts and abilities. That view is known as the egalitarian view. Others hold the "complementarian" view which argues that while Ephesians 5:21 instructs all Christians to practice submission, the *examples* of submission are given in Ephesians 5:22-6:9.

- Wife to her husband – Husband love his wife.
- Children to parents – Fathers do not provoke to wrath.
- Slaves to masters – Masters give up threatening.

Whatever position people take on this controversy, we must be very clear what it does not mean! If Peter and the apostles could say to the Jewish leaders, *"we must obey God rather than men,"* then why would we think that God requires a woman to submit to the ungodly demands of an abusive husband? Would anyone actually teach (sadly, some professing Christians do!) that it is God's will for a woman to submit herself to being raped and sodomized by her husband? Is she to concede to lying for him by covering up his abuse? Certainly not! No human being has absolute authority. That is possessed by God alone.

Therefore, any man who is justifying the wicked abuse of his wife by citing his God-given "headship," is a tyrant who has made himself an enemy of God. His wife is not obligated to submit to him. When Tom demands respect and obedience from his wife, Elizabeth, citing Scripture as support, he is abusing his wife. Implicit in his demands is that she, as a godly wife, must keep her mouth shut and never, ever question his decisions or challenge his behavior.

Men like Tom often run to 1 Peter 3? Doesn't Peter instruct women married to sinful men to submit to them?

> ***1 Peter 3:1-2*** *Likewise, wives, be subject to your own husbands, so that even if some do not obey the word, they may be won without a word by the conduct of their wives, when they see your respectful and pure conduct.*

If you will look back in the context of this passage (which we should always do, especially when a text begins with a word such as "likewise"), you will find that the "word" to which some husbands are not obeying is "the good news that was preached to you." In other words, Peter is addressing Christian wives of unsaved husbands. He is not addressing a situation in which a husband claims to be a Christian but is actively sinning and unrepentant. Certainly this verse is not some blanket command that a wife is required by God to submit herself to an abusive man.

Indeed, a wife might show respectful and pure conduct by resisting her husband's *disrespectful* and *impure* conduct.

A respectful and pure wife might refuse to comply with or enable her husband's abusive, dishonest or criminal conduct. This will make it harder for him to get away with his sin.

A respectful and pure wife might refuse to remain in a situation where she will be exposed to abuse, thus minimizing her husband's opportunities to sin against her.

A respectful and pure wife might disclose and expose her husband's abusive conduct to those in lawful authority. By doing so she will be helping the State and the Church in their God-ordained task of disciplining the wicked and restraining sin.

> *1 Peter 3:12 For the eyes of the Lord are on the righteous, and his ears are open to their prayer. But the face of the Lord is against those who do evil."*

Insistence that the Marriage be Preserved at All Costs; Distortions about Divorce

"The teaching of the church has compounded much of this hurt rather than alleviating it. Victims of continuing abuse have been told that they must stay married, and if they do get divorced, they have been told that they cannot remarry until their former partner has died. And sometimes those who have divorced and remarried are told by their church that they must now divorce their new spouse because in God's eyes they are still married to the person who abused or neglected them. Thus the church makes them a victim for a second time." (Instone-Brewer 2003, Location 1795)

You cannot truly be a follower of Christ and at the same time reject the biblical model of "one-man, one-woman marriage" which is entered into with the intention that it last for life. Jesus was far too clear on His position to permit this kind of "waffling." This has been God's plan from the beginning. It is an order of creation not to be altered. Therefore, divorce is not God's perfect will for any marriage. But then, enter *sin.*

One of the irritants Christians often apply to the abuse victim's wounds is the assumption that God would have every marriage preserved at all costs.[103] This notion, coupled with the fantasy that "with just a little hard work we can put this thing back together," has worked to enable hosts of abusers, and to intensify the suffering of their victims. Listen to the following Scripture:

> ***Mark 2:23-28*** *One Sabbath he was going through the grainfields, and as they made their way, his disciples began to pluck heads of grain. And the Pharisees were saying to him, "Look, why are they doing what is not lawful on the Sabbath?" And he said to them, "Have you never read what David did, when he was in need and was hungry, he and those who were with him: how he entered the house of God, in the time of Abiathar the high priest, and ate the bread of the Presence, which it is not lawful for any but the priests to eat, and also gave it to those who were with him?" And he said to them, "The Sabbath was made for man, not man for the Sabbath. So the Son of Man is lord even of the Sabbath."*

In Matthew's parallel account, we also have this statement recorded:

> ***Matthew 12:7*** *And if you had known what this means, 'I desire mercy, and not sacrifice,' you would not have condemned the guiltless.*

Christians, like these critics of Jesus, often embrace a traditional view of marriage that is just that – *tradition.* I do not mean the one-man, one-woman

103 In a later chapter we are going to deal with this subject of divorce in more detail. In particular we will be arguing that God does in fact permit divorce for abuse, and rejecting the teaching that divorce is never permissible (a teaching that seems to be experiencing some new life in the evangelical church today).

for life model that is normally intended when the term "traditional" is applied to marriage. The tradition in this case rather is the notion that *man is made for marriage, not marriage for man.* As the Pharisees had inverted God's order for the Sabbath's value and purpose, so Christians do the same in regard to marriage. This means that when an abuse victim comes to her pastor to reveal what her abuser is doing, *the welfare of the victim is made subservient to the institution of marriage.* But marriage was made for man! Marriage is a gift created by God for men and women to enjoy, not an ordinance to which people are to be enslaved at all costs.

What God desires, in the application of His Law, is *mercy.* Yes, the Sabbath is to be observed, but *it is for man's sake,* so that he might rest and refresh himself and enjoy God. The same is true for marriage. Therefore to insist that an abuse victim remain in her marriage "no matter what," is to do what Jesus forbids: *condemnation of the guiltless.* And this is precisely what this book takes as a major thesis, namely, that the evangelical church has been condemning victims of abuse and withholding mercy from them.

Just as the Pharisees' teachings about the Sabbath exceeded God's Word and purpose and placed a huge burden upon people which they were never intended to have to bear, so it is with marriage in the teaching of many conservative, evangelical churches. The end result is sadly common – the guiltless victim is condemned for separating from and/or divorcing her abuser.

When man enslaves people to distortions of things God has instituted for man's good (like the Sabbath and marriage), Christ would have us set those people free! It was not God's blessing of the Sabbath rest that Jesus opposed, but the twisted perversion of it imposed upon people by the Jewish leaders. In the same way, it is not the blessing of marriage as created by God for our blessing that we oppose but the wicked, twisted thing it becomes in the hands of evil people. Consider this statement:

> When we speak of ending a relationship that an abuser might call "marriage," it is not marriage that we are ending, but a distorted, evil, enslaving instrument that ceased to be a marriage long ago at the hands of the abuser.

The guilt, therefore, for destroying a marriage does not lie with the victim, but with the abuser. As we will see later (chapter 15), when the victim departs, she is merely acknowledging what is a fact: that there is no marriage. The abusive spouse has actually never been a husband, but an "anti-husband."[104]

Janelle's Diary:

We move on in the next chapter to a more encouraging topic: *how to help the victim.* This is an exciting subject, because it turns out that there are many things we can do to help victims heal and escape this enslavement. First, however, let's hear from Janelle again. Understand that we do not claim that Janelle's experience with her pastors is the same with every abuse victim who seeks help from her church. However, the following scenario is far more common than most Christians might realize:

> 12/11 I went to the church today and tried to talk to my Pastor about John. It was awful... just awful. He greeted me and asked me what I needed. When I told Pastor Stanley I needed to talk to him about John, he told me that probably wouldn't be a good idea and if I had a problem with my husband, I should go home and talk to him about it. I told him I had tried. I asked... begged... for just a few minutes of his time which he finally grudgingly gave me. I told him that things have never been good between us. He said, "You mean you are unhappy and need to try harder?" I told him, "No, that's not it at all. John is cruel towards me and the children. He hurts us." He demanded I explain "hurts us." I told him he curses us, abuses us verbally and, in some ways, even physically. He stared at me and didn't speak for a moment. Finally he said, "Abuse? Really? Why would you say that?"
>
> I then tried then to tell him about the book on abuse I'd found several months ago and how it opened my eyes and about the others I'd read since then. I told him about John's determination to "discipline" me as his wife and about his yelling, throwing fits over the slightest thing and even shoving and pushing us, how he broke things and the threats he had made. After rushing to get that out, the Pastor sat back in his chair and frowned. "How submissive to John are you? If he is feeling the need to discipline you it must be because you aren't being obedient in your role as his wife. Isn't that possible? You're failing him and he is taking it out on you." I was shocked

104 Credits to Ida Mae for the term "anti-husband." See her at Thoroughly Christian Divorce, a wordpress.com blog.

and I couldn't answer. Then I started crying and said, "No, it isn't like that at all."

"Listen, Janelle, I know John. He's a good man, a good provider and I believe he's a good husband and father. If you two are having problems, you are welcome to come together to see me and we'll set up some couple's counseling. I'm sorry you are unhappy, but you need to understand that being unhappy is no cause for divorce or separation. It is, however, a warning bell that you yourself need to get your heart in line with God's Word and make sure you are doing everything God calls you to do. That's how you, as a wife, can please God: by being obedient to your own husband."

So, this is it? I submit more? I deal with being screamed at and having my children screamed at? With being threatened? Is that truly how I can please God?

3/12 I've worked on my relationship with John. I have tried to be more submissive, more obedient. But no matter how hard I try, John always tells me that "If only you were more obedient, I could be a better husband." His idea of obedience means I don't have a say-so in anything. I feel like a slave. John even calls me his slave sometimes. I can't deal with this much longer. I can't handle my housework and raising the children and everything else I have to do with all of the demands that John has lately put on me. The more I've tried to obey him, the more he wants to punish me for failing to. He slapped me last night because I was late getting his supper on the table. He commanded me to go to the bedroom and he told me he was going to punish me and then, he slapped me. Is this pleasing to God?

3/16 I went back to the church today and tried once again to talk to the Pastor. I felt like I was going to explode inside and I just needed to be heard... be really listened to. It didn't happen. This time he put me off to the assistant Pastor. I had to start all over in my explanation of what is going on. Pastor Gillis listened to me but then, when I couldn't finish for crying, he stopped me and said, "Listen, Janelle. It seems you are overwrought. If John is doing all the things you say he is, then, yes, there is an issue and it needs to be dealt with. It isn't, however, truly abuse. He sounds as if he has an anger issue. No, he shouldn't have slapped you, but you stood there and let him, did you not? That means you allowed him to do so... so it's more like a game than anything else. If he is making too many demands on your schedule then it's either because he doesn't realize he is doing so or he's trying very, very hard to help you do what you are apparently having problems doing on your own. That just means he loves you. If you want me to talk to you together then I will, but I think if you go home and spend some time in prayer and in study of God's Word, you will find you can work much of this out by repenting of your own sins. If you stop frustrating him, he'll be able to focus on what he needs to do rather than having to focus on helping you do what you ought to do. If you care about making things better for your children... as you claim you do... then you will work first on being a better wife."

Psalm 86:12-17 *I give thanks to you, O Lord my God, with my whole heart, and I will glorify your name forever. For great is your steadfast love toward me; you have delivered my soul from the depths of Sheol. O God, insolent men have risen up against me; a band of ruthless men seeks my life, and they do not set you before them. But you, O Lord, are a God merciful and gracious, slow to anger and abounding in steadfast love and faithfulness. Turn to me and be gracious to me; give your strength to your servant, and save the son of your maidservant. Show me a sign of your favor, that those who hate me may see and be put to shame because you, LORD, have helped me and comforted me.*

CHAPTER 11

Helping Instead of Hurting

Matthew 9:36-38 *When he saw the crowds, he had compassion for them, because they were harassed and helpless, like sheep without a shepherd. Then he said to his disciples, "The harvest is plentiful, but the laborers are few; therefore pray earnestly to the Lord of the harvest to send out laborers into his harvest."*

"The day that I found the sermon series (on domestic violence and abuse) had been preceded by a deluge of many days of his anger and acting up. He was just awful towards me and the children. I had been praying, asking God to open my eyes, to help me, to show me what to do. I felt so trapped. That day I got up very, very early and started searching the internet for anything I could find. After reading what articles I could find, I moved into looking for sermons (not really expecting to find anything). That's when God led me to go to Sermon Audio and I found the series. I listened to them as fast as I could; it was like a man dying of thirst who finally finds water." [Abuse Survivor who found our sermon series on Sermon Audio]

In my nearly thirty years of pastoral ministry, I have never experienced any more appreciative or enthusiastic response to anything I have done than what I have experienced in this ministry to victims of abuse. I wish that I had a church filled with Christians who had come through this kind of suffering. It would be a dynamic and fearless bunch that intensely loved Christ, having been refined by Him in fire.

Having learned what we have to this point, we must ask ourselves: *"Am I ready to help these people to freedom, and how do I go about doing it?"* You will have to answer the first part for yourself. As to the second, I can help you! This chapter is at least a good introduction in ministering to the victims of abuse and learning how to help them when they come to you with their almost unbelievable tales that turn out not to be "tales" but truth. I emphasize that *this is only an introduction*, and I highly encourage you to read and learn more.

Before we get into specifics, let me show you an excellent biblical model for helping and healing these people. You know it as the story of the Good Samaritan:

> ***Luke 10:30-37*** *Jesus replied, "A man was going down from Jerusalem to Jericho, and he fell among robbers, who stripped him and beat him and departed, leaving him half dead. Now by chance a priest was going down that road, and when he saw him he passed by on the other side. So likewise a Levite, when he came to the place and saw him, passed by on the other side. But a Samaritan, as he journeyed, came to where he was, and when he saw him, he had compassion. He went to him and bound up his wounds, pouring on oil and wine. Then he set him on his own animal and brought him to an inn and took care of him. And the next day he took out two denarii and gave them to the innkeeper, saying, 'Take care of him, and whatever more you spend, I will repay you when I come back.' Which of these three, do you think, proved to be a neighbor to the man who fell among the robbers?" He said, "The one who showed him mercy." And Jesus said to him, "You go, and do likewise."*

The parable really teaches itself, doesn't it? Here you have a victim, beaten and robbed by evil men. Help appears to be on the way in the form of two of his own nation's religious leaders. But what do they do? They treat him as a leper, passing him by on "the other side." (You can make the application to the treatment given abuse victims by our churches yourself). Then along comes this one who has gone down in history as the Good Samaritan. This man who should have hated the Jewish victim instead:

- Showed him compassion
- Didn't despise him for having been attacked by robbers
- Met the man's immediate needs
- Dealt with his wounds
- Provided food, care and shelter for him, and, was willing to help for the "long haul"

With the background of the first ten chapters of this book, these points should be beautiful to you. This is how to help an abuse victim. *You*, the Christian, must be the Good Samaritan to these people. We have been the priest and the Levite far, far too long, and it is time to repent of it. The work is messy. What do you think the Samaritan's fellow countrymen thought of what he did? I suspect he was mocked for helping a Jew. It may well have cost him greatly. But what do you suppose the Jewish victim said to the Good Samaritan when he returned to the inn sometime later?

Are *you* willing? Would you listen to her story with compassion, and listen again and yet again as she chooses to tell you more? Would you refrain from giving knee-jerk advice? Would you dig into your pockets to help a victim? Would you give her a place to stay and help to get the assistance she needs? Would your church? Would you be prepared to learn and comply with basic safety guidelines for helping victim-survivors? I say again, it is a messy business. The abuser will hate you for it! And don't expect lots of help from others, not even from many who profess to be Christians.

> ***James 2:15-16*** *If a brother or sister is poorly clothed and lacking in daily food, and one of you says to them, "Go in peace, be warmed and filled," without giving them the things needed for the body, what good is that?*

Now Go, and Show Mercy

Alright, you are still reading! I assume that means you are ready to step up and obey Christ! Let's get to it. How do you help an abuse victim?

Believe her. I have found that victims experience incredible relief, if not disbelief, when they hear me say, "If you are telling the truth, I will know it because I know what abuse is, how it thinks and how it acts. And I *will* believe you, no matter who your abuser is or what kind of a façade he is wearing." This is the one thing that victims have told me was of the greatest help to them initially. It is not surprising, since most of them have been disregarded many times before they come to us. *Believe her.* Pastors, let your congregations know that you will believe victims who come to you. This is *not* going to open up a landslide of false accusations![105]

105 Of all the victims who have come to me to tell their story, there have only been two who I doubted. Genuine abuse victims are actually often hesitant to leave their abuser. They are confused by his lies. If anything, they have erred in sticking with him so long,

Take her side. In many marriage counseling cases or in dealing with interpersonal conflicts, pastors and counselors try to remain relatively neutral, directing correction or suggestions to one party, then to the other. The assumption is that both parties in the conflict need to make concessions and correct themselves, compromising where necessary, striving harder to better understand the other. *Cases of abuse cannot and must not be dealt with from such a perspective.* Unfortunately they often are, and therein lies disaster. Abusers should bear the guilt and blame. The abuser is the culprit. In cases of abuse, there is a perpetrator who is guilty, and a victim who is innocent. A right and a wrong. Unless you understand the nature and mentality of abuse, you will not realize this and you will place blame and responsibility on the victim. In fact, since abusers are often very good at deceiving us, you may take *the wrong side* and deem the victim to be the real problem. If you fail here, all of your counsel to her will be wrong.

With a reasonable study of the nature and tactics of abuse, you should be able to recognize when you are dealing with an abuser and victim. Once you realize this, *you can confidently side with the victim.* You will not be rendering injustice to the perpetrator as you begin to call him to account for his evil. This confidence is absolutely vital for anyone counseling the victim of abuse, and certainly in dealing with the abuser himself. Understand, of course, that neither the abuser nor his deceived allies will like this approach.

Think about it. Knowing what we do about the abuser and the reason he is what he is and why he does what he does, is there anything the victim could change in her words or behavior that would change her tormentor? What if she worked harder at "being a better wife" (whatever that would mean), or tried to be more understanding of him, or kept the children quieter at certain times? Would he suddenly transform into a kind, loving husband? Of course not! The guilt and responsibility rest entirely with him. The root of the abusive mentality is in *his* mind. So take the victim's side and stand with her. There is no place for neutrality in these cases. Neutrality, in fact, takes the side of the abuser. There is nothing neutral about it.

---

not in looking for a quick way to "dump the bum." The two that I doubted were very focused upon themselves, even more so than they evidenced concern for their children. Furthermore, once we become familiar with the mentality and tactics of abuse, we can recognize the real thing as a victim tells us her story. Someone "crying wolf" who is just looking to use abuse as an excuse to do what she wants is not going to tell a story that rings true to the abuser mentality we have come to recognize.

> ...when the traumatic events are of human design, those witness are caught in the conflict between victim and perpetrator. It is morally impossible to remain neutral in this conflict. The bystander is forced to take sides. It is very tempting to take the side of the perpetrator. All the perpetrator asks is that the bystander do nothing. He appeals to the universal desire to see, hear, and speak no evil.[106]

As the following Scripture shows, abusers hate the innocent for the same reason Cain hated Abel, *simply because they are righteous!*

> ***1 John 3:12-13*** *We should not be like Cain, who was of the evil one and murdered his brother. And why did he murder him? Because his own deeds were evil and his brother's righteous. Do not be surprised, brothers, that the world hates you.*

Understand that victims fall into a spectrum or a range in regard to their realization of what is actually happening to them. She may come to you and not even use the word "abuse." Or, she may have already done considerable reading and study on the subject. You are going to have to diagnose where she is and help her accordingly.

Address the concrete, practical needs she has. SAFETY is imperative, so don't take it for granted that she is safe. If she feels fear then she is probably not safe. What kinds of threats or assaults has her abuser made against her? Are there guns in the house? Has the level of abuse been escalating? Do not assume that just because her abuser is a member of your church and someone you thought you knew, that he certainly could never actually physically harm her. "Nice" guys kill their wives and children all the time. If she has left the marriage, do not assume she is safe; she may be experiencing post-separation abuse.

Call the POLICE if necessary. I almost said, call the police if she has been physically assaulted because that is what the law in most states requires. However, I would recommend calling the police even if no actual physical assault has occurred, but the victim is in fear of her safety and needs to relocate. If she is going to return home, do NOT tell the abuser that she came to talk with you. You may need to recommend some protective shelter at this point for her and the children, and I would recommend working with your community women's

---

106 Judith Herman, *Trauma and Recovery* (New York: Basic Books, 1997), 7.

crisis center on this point. We can learn quite a lot from them.[107] Community women's resource centers have safe houses or shelters for women who are in fear for their safety.

Do not make the mistakes we have already exposed in the first part of this book. Understand the nature of the beastly thing the victim is up against, act accordingly and resist the temptation to minimize, to cover up, or to yield to your own fear. Resolve that you and your church leadership are going to seek justice for the victim no matter what the cost to you. Avoid thoughtless remarks that commonly come to our minds in settings like this. For instance, don't act surprised or shocked and say something like, "Wow! I have never heard anything like that before! This just blows me away! I've always thought he is such a wonderful guy." Do not yield to the thinking that somehow the real truth must be someplace between what she is telling me and what her abuser says about it, because it just can't be true that one person in the marriage is totally at fault. Do not recommend some kind of mediation meeting between abuser and victim, and do not employ couples' counseling. When Elizabeth reported that her abusive husband had assaulted her daughter, she related the incident as follows:

> He followed my daughter into her room and insisted that she leave it. She said no, that she was trying to calm down after he had been screaming at her earlier. Screaming at her, he crossed the room to her, grabbed her by both arms, dragged her across the room, and threw her into the wall.

Elizabeth has told more than one Christian man this story. Each one has responded, "Well, what did she do first?" Don't be like those Christian men. Don't assume that the victim "had it coming" due to their having provoked the abuse.

Emphasize the justice of God to her instead of launching into a sermonette on the love and mercy of God and how He is putting this on her for her own good. Do NOT tell her at this point she needs to forgive her abuser, and certainly do not tell her she needs to work toward reconciliation with him. Let me emphasize this by showing you how foolish I was at this very point once. After a child was abused, I went to the father and, thinking (actually, not thinking much at all, which was

107 Safety planning for abuse victims is a subject of its own. Many women's resource centers provide training in this important area, equipping people to "red flags" that signal high risk abuse. Pastors and church members well to obtain such training. Also see www.notunderbondage.com/ esstheriskavictimisfacing.htm

the problem), I hit him with "I hope you can forgive the perpetrator." Not only did it do no good, it worked against good. On top of that, when victims appear to not take this talk of forgiveness and reconciliation very well, they become targets for accusations that they are entertaining bitterness. How "noble" I felt in all of this preaching about mercy and forgiveness. But *it* was salt in the wound. I was pathetic. We say again: ignorance and arrogance are a bad combination.

What we need to tell the victim early on is that what has happened to them is wicked and evil in God's sight, and that God is against wicked men who do this. It is vital that you explicitly blame and condemn the conduct of the abuser. If you say something general to a victim, like: "What is happening shouldn't be happening," *you* might be thinking in your head "What's being done to this woman is sinful," but *the victim* is likely to hear it as "What's happening in this marriage is sinful – and lady, you have helped to make it happen!" Or she might hear it as "Lady, you shouldn't be telling me this! You should be dealing with your husband by loving him more, not complaining about him behind his back!" The victim's default thinking is "It's my fault," because the abuser (and often the church) has brainwashed her to believe she is to blame. To overcome this default assumption in the traumatized mind of the victim, the person trying to help her must affirm unequivocally and repeatedly that the abuser bears *all* the blame, and she is not responsible at all for the trouble in the relationship.

After making it clear that God is against the sin of abuse and the sole blame lies with the perpetrator, we then need to assure her that God is actively for her, and we are for her too. We are against the evil man. Believing her and assuring her of your shared indignation against the evil she is suffering will do more to heal her than just about anything else (as long as we back up our words with action!). I recommend even reading or praying through one of the imprecatory Psalms with her. If she is not a Christian, you will have the opportunity later to introduce her to Christ. I suggest that in this early encounter with her, you not overwhelm her. I realize others will differ with me on this point and I respect their opinion. But this is mine. In fact, in doing these first five things you *are* beginning to introduce her to Jesus already.

Expose it for what it is. Because you are reading this book and hopefully have been motivated to read the other books that I have recommended, you can now tell her with confidence:

"What is happening to you is called abuse. It is a very deceptive and confusing thing to be subjected to and it does serious damage even if it does not involve physical assaults. What your husband/abuser is doing to you proceeds from his mentality: his profound sense that he is entitled to have power and control over you. He feels entirely justified in using the various tactics against you that he does to enforce that power and control, and I can help you learn the names of those tactics because you are by no means the first person to suffer in this way. You are not at fault. There is nothing you can do to change him because it is his problem and not yours. One of his tactics is to convince you that you are the problem and put all kinds of false guilt upon you. What he is doing is evil and we stand ready to help you."

We really *can* enable her to know the schemes of her abuser. It is not impossible, although he seems so unpredictable and chaotic in many ways, as the following illustration demonstrates:

Gina is in a very abusive marriage to Ken, who is widely reputed to be an exceptional Christian man. But Gina is still largely in denial about her situation. Her sister, Jenna, has been studying the subject of abuse lately in an effort to help Gina and recently she asked Gina if Ken ever blamed or minimized or changed facts (Jenna was listing some of the typical tactics of abusers that her reading was teaching her about). Gina became very irate and snapped back at Jenna, accusing her of obviously having talked to Gina's children. How else could Jenna know exactly how Ken behaves! In fact, Jenna had obtained her information elsewhere and had not discussed the matter with their children at all. Her description rang familiar simply because the thinking and tactics of the abuser are familiar.

When the victim begins to realize that it is possible to sort out the fundamentals of her abuser's beliefs and attitudes, and why he does the things he does, she is going to experience a new power and freedom.

Provide her with resources such as books, counseling, and a sermon series on abuse and encourage her to begin to educate herself about what has been happening to her. You could provide her with a copy of this book, or of Bancroft's book, and perhaps *The Verbally Abusive Relationship* by Patricia Evans. As she learns the truth about how her abuser thinks, why he does what he does, and the effects his abuse are having on her and her children, she will experience even more freedom and the ability to make good choices about her future. [See the recommended reading list at the end of this book for further resources.]

Expect trouble. Understand that when you begin to oppose, expose or leave the abuser, his abuse will very likely increase. Listen to this example from an abuse victim:

> Finally, the Lord was gracious to me and opened my eyes. I demanded he stop treating me as he did. He is a very weak man emotionally and, because I was now stronger and sure of myself and my stance theologically, he unwillingly complied. Still he would get angry that I wasn't "being obedient any more" or that "you're no longer submissive to me" and "aren't a good wife" and say things like, "One day I'm just going to have to take you in hand and punish you for all of this." He'd sulk, pout and refuse to talk to me, or he'd pitch a fit and get mad at everyone because he was mad at me. Looking back, when I demanded a stop to the madness, that's when he escalated his ill-treatment towards all of us verbally and emotionally. That's also when he went into overdrive in telling the children how "mean Mama is" or "she mistreats me" or "she doesn't care about your schooling like I do." That's also when he started encouraging our daughter to dress "sexy" or "sensually." He just had to misbehave in some way.

We must realize, and so does the victim, that one of the most (if not *the* most) dangerous times for her is when she sets out to leave her abuser. Many of the women who are seriously injured or killed by their abuser are either in the process of leaving or have left. I encourage you to do further reading on abuse. You will learn that there are certain factors that can help you and the victim assess the risk of danger she is in. These factors include such things as:

Perpetrator Risk Factors

- Use of a weapon in past abuse.
- Access to weapons.
- History of harming or threatening to harm the victim.
- Threatening to kill the victim, the children, or other family members or pets.
- History of suicide threats.
- Stalking the victim.
- Sexual assault of the victim, including coerced sex.
- History of violating orders of protection.
- Drug and/or alcohol abuse.

- Controlling behaviors.
- If the perpetrator is currently unemployed.
- History of or current mental health issues.
- History of violent behavior.

Victim Risk Factors

- Is the victim pregnant or has she just given birth?
- Depression or mental health issues
- Drug and/or alcohol abuse.
- Has the victim ever felt suicidal or attempted suicide?

The degree of the victim's isolation.

Relationship Risk Factors

- Has the victim separated from the abuser?
- Has the abuse been escalating in frequency or severity?
- Are there financial difficulties?

This list is certainly not exhaustive, but it does give the reader an indication of how much we need to learn in just this one aspect of abuse – assessing the risk of danger to the victim.

The Cycle

Additional study of abuse will educate you about what is commonly called the "cycle of abuse." There are varying descriptions of this cycle, some more detailed than others, but it is widely recognized that this cycle is real, and that it goes something like this:

- **"Normal" Phase:** While nothing is ever "normal" in an abusive relationship, there are periods when it *seems* to be so. The abuser may be quite nice and pleasant in what is also often called the "honeymoon period." Even during this time, however, the abuser's mentality is the same and he is using this period of apparent peace against his victim. It serves to give her false hope that things are better now, to convince her that she is to blame, that he really does love her, and so on. It is no honeymoon at all! It is part of the abuse cycle and is just another form of abuse motivated by the same lust for power and control. Barbara Roberts calls it the "buy-back" phase:

I prefer to call that period the "buy-back" stage. Buy-back directly names what the abuser is doing: trying to buy back the affection and loyalty of the one he has hurt. It captures the manipulative aspect of what's going on. While a victim (especially in the early years of the abuse) may feel "honeymoon" feelings at those times, she's being conned. It's a travesty of a true honeymoon.[108]

- **The Buildup Phase:** The cycle of abuse is like some electric device that just needs some time to re-charge itself before it delivers another jolt. The abuser begins to see that his victim needs "to be taught" who is in charge. He interprets things she says or does as challenges to his power and begins to think about how he is going to deliver his next jolt of abuse to bring her back into subjection.
- **The Setup:** At this point, the abuser is like a rogue national dictator who is "just looking for an excuse" to strike. In fact, he looks for ways to set his victim up by creating some "incident." He might use his tactic of changing the rules to do this. No matter how the victim tries to please him, she will fail because he has no desire for peace.
- **The Abuse:** Whatever form or tactic is his choice, the abuser now launches his attack to remind the victim that he is in charge, that she exists only to serve him, that she is really nothing, and that his rage is entirely her fault.
- **Pity and Excuses:** Abusers at this stage often put on displays of guilt and remorse accompanied by excusing and blaming. Such a person can appear to be absolutely broken and contrite, promising that such a thing will never happen again. He expresses his love for the victim in what appears at first to be a very genuine way. BUT, all of these displays of repentance are always accompanied with some form of excuse and blame directed toward others, away from the abuser. He is working to garner pity from the victim and his actions simply strengthen the traumatic bond between him and her.

And then it is destined to cycle back to the beginning, to the normal phase, only to repeat itself over and over again. Normal never lasts. Say that to yourself another 100 times! Normal never lasts! Normal is not normal! Normal is manipulation in disguise. In every phase of this abuse cycle, abuse is operating! Some of the worst damage is done to victims during the "normal" stage because it is s(

108 Personal correspondence with Barbara Roberts, 2012

Helping in the Long Term

These points are just the beginning. The process of a victim getting free from her abuser is quite often a long one. It can even be a period of years as we will see in a later chapter that addresses the abuser's use of the children and the court system to carry on his campaign of terror after separation or divorce. We must be committed to provide continuing support to victims for the long haul. One church I know about made sure members were present with the victim at every one of the subsequent court sessions. Here are some basic details about long-term advocacy. The list is by no means comprehensive:

- Safety and security needs. Most states offer victim protection programs through the secretary of state. There are address-protection programs. Also, the social security administration offers changes of social security card numbers under some conditions. Most of these services are offered through the domestic violence shelters and assist women with relocating and building their new lives and identities. For example, in my home state of Oregon, the Department of Justice administers an Address Confidentiality Program (ACP). This is a free mail forwarding service which provides victims with a substitute address to be used in place of their actual address. The substitute address can be used on the victim's driver's license, for the reception of child support, for delivery of mail, and for enrolling their children in school.
- Counseling and Therapy needs. From our earlier discussion of the effects of abuse on victims, we should expect that the victim and her children may well need some extended trauma counseling to help them overcome the damage done. You and your church can be a big part of this. Remember that abuse works its evil by tearing down the victim's sense of humanity. It causes distortions in how she thinks about herself and others – and about God. Victims wear all kinds of blame and false guilt. These effects are to be expected in anyone who has undergone a prolonged program of terrorism, which is really what abuse is.

Here is an example, written by an abuse victim, of just how foggy the victim's thinking can become and how the deceptions of the abuser need to be almost constantly countered with truth. Her words are a perfect example of the benefit of putting good resources on abuse into her hands:

> I got out my favorite book on abuse a couple of days ago and began re-reading some of it. The section that describes the kinds of angry men is interesting to me. My older children and I read it together today and discussed it. They were just nodding and kept saying, "Yep, there he is, and there, and there...." It's sad for them, I think, but also good that they have the ability to realize that what their father is doing isn't just unkind or rude or something, but to understand that what he does is actually abusive. For so many years, I bought into the lie, "A good wife doesn't do this, think that, say whatever...." so I wouldn't let myself say he was abusive (even although, at times, I thought it). I wanted the relationship to be good and several books that I got my hands on (like *Me? Obey Him?*) turned out to be chock-full of dangerous theology and bad advice. Until I realized this, I just kept trying to point out the good in their dad to them and to others. That went on until five years ago and then it couldn't be denied any longer, because the older the children got, the worse he acted.

Victims should also receive counseling that is designed to help them learn more about themselves and how to detect abusers so that they are less likely to become victimized again. Henry Cloud and John Townsend address this subject in part two of their book *Safe People*.[109] We all need to be regularly reminded how charming an abusive person can be in order to snare a victim into a relationship. "His inordinately attentive, charming, and tempting behavior cannot be considered anything more than bait."[110]

The Psalmist knew this all too well from hard experience: "His speech was smooth as butter, yet war was in his heart; his words were softer than oil, yet they were drawn swords." Psalms 55:21

Another abuse victim relates the following experience from her life as a warning to others:

> My ex married me so that he would have a better chance at gaining custody of his children from his previous marriage. He considers the children his property and demands every minute of visitation he has been granted by the courts. If the boys had something planned with friends or church, they could only go if I traded days with their father. He would only allow them to

109 Henry Cloud and John Townsend, *Safe People* (Grand Rapids: Zondervan, 1995), 83.
110 Braun, Location 771, Kindle Edition.

do things on my time with them. He also said my oldest son could not get a job until he turned 18 and it didn't interfere with visitation. My ex-husband also seems to play the same scenario with women, in that he portrays himself as a wonderful godly man with horrible, crazy, ungodly wives who have left him even though he wanted to stay married.

- Economic, Medical, and Legal Needs. Victims quite frequently have very few assets. Abusers like to keep their victims in economic deprivation for purposes of control. We have also learned that many if not most abuse victims suffer from various physical ailments, often due to the terrible stress they have lived in. If the victim lacks job skills, she may need assistance in obtaining further education to enable her to be more employable. Abusers are not typically generous and forthcoming with child support when their victim leaves them. Recently I heard that one abusive man told his children that although he had the ability to help them, he couldn't do it because he would be helping their mother as well and this he refused to do. Victims also quite often are going to need a good attorney who is versed in domestic violence and abuse. Such lawyers are not always easy to find.
- Spiritual help. Whether the victim is a Christian or not, as we help victims we have a remarkable opportunity to turn their eyes to Christ as their ultimate Helper. Of the victims who have contacted and corresponded with me, the strongest and healthiest ones are those who obviously have a living, vibrant relationship with Christ. One wrote the following as she told me her story:

> I remember that it was in these very hopeless and fearful times of my husband's terrible raging that the Lord came to me. I was not a Christian, but I began reading the Bible during the night until I fell asleep. Through His Word, Christ came to me, comforted me and revealed Himself to me. It was also Christ, through His Word, that freed me to eventually leave my husband regardless of the opposite counsel and even some condemnation that I received from my church and friends.

Obviously, if a church, a pastor, or fellow Christian is going to effectively help a victim spiritually, then we need to have our thinking straight in respect to what God's Word really says about the abuser, about abuse, about the victim, and about related subjects such as divorce, forgiveness, and reconciliation. As long as we embrace man-made traditions rather than Scripture, we are not only going to fail to help victims, but we will do them serious harm instead.

- Check Your Own Motives. It is one thing to genuinely do what you can to rescue a victim from her abuser. It is quite another to *need to be a rescuer.* The first is noble, the second is really quite selfish and it can exist in you far more easily than you might realize. Ultimately, we cannot "fix" anyone. Only Christ can do that. We can help them, and we can point them to Christ. But the victim has to be the one who makes her own decisions. Bancroft makes a very good point when he warns that victims of abuse have long been told what to think and what to do *by their abuser.*[111] As a result, they might even have problems thinking for themselves and making decisions. But this is all the more reason for us to provide them with help and information, but leave the final decisions to them. Some of those decisions will not necessarily be the ones you would desire, but we must be willing to permit people to make mistakes and learn from those mistakes.

  We must guard ourselves against the common temptation to become "rescuers." The rescuer swoops into the crisis, confident he can resolve every problem for the victim. He begins to not only offer advice, but tells her what she should do. To avoid this error, we will do well to ask questions rather than make statements. Instead of "You need to leave him right now," ask "Have you considered leaving your husband …Have you left him before? … How did that turn out? … What reasons might you have for leaving?" This enables her to think and give her own answers for herself, something she has not been given the chance to do by her abuser. We must be different. Help her to think, but do not tell her what to think.

When Victims Ally With the Abuser

Allow me another couple of police stories. In the late 1970's I was on patrol on Sandy Boulevard in Northeast Portland. In the car directly in front of me I

111 Bancroft, *Why Does He Do That?,* Location 260, Kindle Edition.

saw the driver, a man, steering with one hand while using the other to beat the woman in the passenger seat. Well, being the sharp and observant officer that I was, I pulled the car over. I had the man step out of the car, obtained his license to identify him, and then handcuffed him and put him in my car. The hero to the rescue, right? *Wrong!* The woman began screaming at me, demanding that I let him go. She insisted that they were just having a "discussion" and he hadn't hurt her. In those days, the victim had to sign a criminal complaint against the perpetrator or the police could do nothing, at least in a misdemeanor case like this one. I hated to do it, but I had to release the man from custody and let them drive on (with a careless driving citation of course).

The next month, I was patrolling the same area and received a call to a residence. It seemed that someone wanted to report an assault. When I walked in, I saw a young man and, in the living room, that same woman who had been beaten by the driver. Only this time, the side of her face was swelled out to a horrific extent, all black and blue. Yes, the very same boyfriend had done it to her. But she still would not press charges, and she still shouted angrily at me to just leave her alone. The young man was her son, and he had called us. Again, there was nothing we could do.

Fast-forward now to the early 1980's when I received a call one night to a domestic disturbance. Accompanied by several other officers, I walked up to the front door of the residence and was met by a hefty looking man, semi-intoxicated, who demanded to know why we were there. A woman stood just behind him. I explained that someone had called us to report a disturbance. His wife's eyes looked rather like "yes-it-was-me-but-don't-tell-him." The fellow put his hand on my chest and said angrily, "Leave my property, you aren't coming into my house."

Now, I don't know how things work in the present day, but back then we police had a kind of unwritten code that the old-timers passed down to us: *don't ever let anyone lay a hand on you.* We represented the law, and we expected the law to be respected. So when the man put his hand on my chest, I pushed him away, hard. Actually, harder than I thought, because he toppled backwards, stumbled, and down to the floor he went. We all rushed in and held him there and as we did, another officer said, "Hey, this revolver fell out of his back pocket when he tipped over!" Sure enough, the guy had met us at the door with a .44-magnum in his belt. Off to jail he went.

Once more, heroes to the rescue? Once again, no! As we led him away to take him to jail, his wife followed us and screamed and yelled the entire time that we had to let him go, that she did not want him to be arrested, and that she was going to sue us.

The victims in these two cases were no doubt acting out of fear—fear of their abuser. Each woman wanted their man to think that she was on his side because she knows there will be hell itself to pay when he gets out. You may encounter some of the same fear in a victim whom you have contact with. After learning more about abuse, you may see things that cause you to suspect that a man is abusing his wife, and you may try to help. She may side with him against you. For a number of reasons, she may not want exposure of what is going on behind the scenes. If not fear, it may be embarrassment or the loss of social standing. She may realize that the truth would threaten other benefits that she is receiving from her relationship with the abuser. Whatever the reason, your assistance is not going to be welcomed.

There is a third common dynamic which I have seen functioning when a victim allies with her abuser, and it is a particularly deceptive device of the abuser. I emphasize that this is *common.* I encounter frequently as I speak with abusers and their victims. The abuser will scan the horizons of his victim's situation, watching for scenarios in which he can be her hero and come to her rescue. Often the abuser will be the one who fabricates the situation, setting up his entry as the knight in shining armor. The thing can take many different forms, but at its heart it is the same strategy: to make the abuser appear to be the victim's rescuer from some third party or situation. Like a fireman who torches off buildings so he can come screaming down the street with lights and siren, so it is in these cases with the abuser and it often works quite effectively. The victim is won over to her hero's side. In fact, however, the whole thing is a sham. This strategy is often effective in alienating the victim from those who are truly attempting to help and rescue her. The victim, under all of the pressures of abuse, easily forgets that all of her suffering is ultimately caused by her abuser.

Really, in such cases there is not much you can do, especially if there is no physical injury. In contrast to the 1970's and '80's, there are now much better tools for law enforcement to use in arresting the abuser even if the victim refuses to prosecute. Still, the victim is the real key to exposing and opposing abusers and until she is ready to take that step, it is quite difficult to help her. Don't be naïve. You will not be regarded favorably in many of these cases. In some, you might even end up being seen as the villain! But the Lord has a way of bringing hidden things to light, especially when those things are hiding in His Church! And perhaps your role is simply to be the first step in the process by which God is leading a victim from captivity to freedom.

> ***Psalm 10:10-14*** *The helpless are crushed, sink down, and fall by his might.* (11*) He says in his heart, "God has forgotten, he has hidden his face, he will never see it." Arise, O LORD; O God, lift up your hand; forget not the afflicted. Why does the wicked renounce God and say in his heart, "You will not call to account"? But you do see, for you note mischief and vexation, that you may take it into your hands; to you the helpless commits himself; you have been the helper of the fatherless.*

CHAPTER 12

It's Not Over Yet: How Abuse Continues After Separation

"Now he had not run far from his own door when his wife and children, perceiving it, began to cry after him to return; but the man put his fingers in his ears, and ran on crying, Life! Life! Eternal life! So he looked not behind him, but fled towards the middle of the plain. The neighbors also came out to see him run, and as he ran, some mocked, others threatened, and some cried after him to return; and among those that did so, there were two that were resolved to fetch him back by force. The name of the one was Obstinate and the name of the other Pliable. Now by this time the man was got a good distance from them; but, however, they were resolved to pursue him, which they did, and in a little time they overtook him. Then said the man, "Neighbors, why have you come?" They said, "To persuade you to go back with us." But he said, "That can by no means be: you dwell," said he, "in the city of Destruction, the place also where I was born: I see it to be so; and dying there, sooner or later, you will sink lower than the grave, into a place that burns with fire and brimstone: be content, good neighbors, and go along with me."
-Christian, *The Pilgrim's Progress*, by John Bunyan[112]

With Friends Like These...?

When the abuse victim leaves her abuser, a difficult road still lies ahead. As was the experience of Bunyan's character, Christian, so it will be with her. New

112 John Bunyan, *The Pilgrim's Progress From This World to That Which is to Come* (Theographa Publications, Digital Edition), Location 244, Kindle Edition.

pressures will be brought upon her from different directions, but all with the common goal of pressuring her to return and to maintain the status quo. The old state of affairs has many benefits for numbers of people in her life: family members, church members, and friends. Not only do such people not want to have their own world "rocked" by the victim severing the relationship with her abuser, but remember that abusers work with deceitful skill to recruit allies from among these groups. Victims who leave will receive unjust criticism and blame. Some of their closest relationships are often lost. Some of the arrows launched at them include statements like these:

- I just don't understand how she could just leave the poor guy like that.
- Well, you can leave him if you want, I guess. But don't expect me to take any sides in this. After all, there are always two sides to any disagreement (to *not* take a side, the side of justice, is to in fact take the side of the abuser).
- You *say* that's what happened, but what did you do to cause it… if it happened at all?
- Now she's got him! Poor guy. She's a woman who has to have it all her own way—or else.
- She just won't let sleeping dogs lie! Sure, he was unfaithful to her (well, yeah, more than once), but that was years ago and it just isn't right that she keeps throwing it in his face. Christians are supposed to forgive and forget.
- She says she is a Christian, but if she were, she would never divorce him. She should know that God hates divorce and if she remarries she will be committing adultery.[113]

As we have already learned, an extremely common scenario the victim faces when she leaves her abuser is that she is ostracized by her family, friends, and even her church. It is my conclusion that people who blame the victim do so not only out of ignorance or because they have been deceived by the abuser, but because people are just plain selfish. We tend to forget about the victim and focus upon what all of this disruption means for us. *We* now have to stand on one side or the other. *We* will experience the wrath of the abuser if we stand with the victim. *We* might lose a job, or some other financial benefit that stems from

113 Also see "Unhelpful Comments by Well-Meaning People", by Barbara Roberts, www.notunderbondage.com/resources/UnhelpfulComments.html

our relationship with the abuser. *We* might have to reevaluate our well-worn theological traditions, or our rose-colored view of the world. In other words, most people simply are not willing to pay the price of doing justice. It is easier to blame the victim. And in cases where the abuser is guilty of a criminal offense (sexual abuse, assault, etc.) this means he may well go to prison. This is highly unpleasant for many people and often they really just want the victim and her complaints to go away.

But this is just the beginning of the victim's post-departure suffering.

The Courts and the Children as Weapons

Because the abuser is all about his entitlement to power and control over persons who are "his property," his post-separation attacks are rather predictable. Probably his favorite scheme is the use of the children as a weapon against their mother. He has been doing this all along, but now through the court system he can really intensify his attacks.

Typically, abusers do not seek custody or visitation rights out of any sense of love for their children. If the abuser really loved his children, he would not have abused their mother in the first place. No, it is not about love; it is about power and control. It is about winning. For these reasons, abusers will carry on the battle over a long period of years if necessary.

When family courts get involved, all kinds of other mechanisms come into play that often add to the suffering of the victim and her children. The victim needs to have help finding an attorney to be her advocate who is familiar with domestic violence cases and in particular who is wise to the mentality and tactics of the abuser. Such attorneys are not always easy to find.

Here are some typical experiences of post-separation abuse victims:

- The abuser fights against paying child support. His mentality simply cannot accept that his victim has any right to *his* money.
- Even after child support terms are set, the abuser will often file additional court motions to try to minimize these payments, or will play the system to reduce his payments in such a way that the survivor has to expend enormous time and energy trying to get the payments properly restored.
- Abusers will use visitation to try to alienate the children from the victim.

He might feign crying to elicit pity from the children, or he may tell them lies about their mother. He may disclose to the children things about the mother's private life which she had told him in confidence during the marriage, things which will make the children dislike or distrust their mother. And he might use the children as messengers to deliver unpleasant messages or orders to their mother, thus making the child feel like meat in the sandwich.

- The victim may face burdensome legal fees, inhibiting her ability to provide for herself and her children. Very often abusers represent themselves in court and thereby pursue litigation indefinitely without great cost to themselves.
- Victims might find themselves very limited in their ability to put geographical distance between themselves and their abuser because of visitation requirements set by the courts.
- Children who find themselves healing because of the peace resulting from being away from the abuser will regress in their recovery after spending a weekend with the abuser due to court-ordered visitation. After visitation children lose sleep and sometimes miss school because they are so distressed by the manipulations and activities of the abuser. The mother and children live on a perpetual roller coaster, she mopping up the children's distress when they return from visitation, things settling down to relative calm, only to have the next ordered visitation cast them into a turmoil once more. True recovery cannot take place under these circumstances, though it is still preferable to living in-house with the abuser full-time.
- A case manager might be assigned to oversee the divorce and custody issues. Case managers have broad authority and may not always render justice to the victim and her children.
- Courts and therapists often assume that the children need relationships with both parents and therefore are going to be hesitant to prohibit the abuser from having any contact with them. Abusers play this assumption of the professionals to their own advantage.

I cannot adequately describe for you the discouragement and weariness post-separation abuse victims have expressed to me that results from the seemingly never-ending court actions initiated by the abuser. "Is this ever going to end?" "I just don't know how much more of this I can endure. We just get to a point of thinking it is over now, and here comes another court action." This adds all kinds of uncertainty and insecurity to the victim's world (and to her children's). Will they have to move again? Will they have to spend more time with dad even though they don't want to? Maybe he will take them away from the victim entirely? Often, these court actions come with some new and frivolous accusation against the victim, so she feels as if she is always on trial.

One of the most common tactics an abuser uses in the court process is called the claim of *parental alienation*. This is a kind of self-fulfilling prophecy tactic. When the children tell therapists or courts that they do not want to spend time with the abuser, it will be argued that this is evidence of the victim alienating them against him. The assumption is that a child will *want* to spend time with his father, and therefore the other parent must be guilty of alienating the child against him. In one case, the children were forced to go to a visitation center to spend time with their father. Once there, they refused to see him. Their actions were immediately interpreted as proof that their mother had turned them against him.

However, many of these parental alienation claims can be easily disproved if the courts and case managers would simply take the effort to verify some facts. Children who have been subjected to the abuser's rages and accusations and the rest of his evil arsenal, frequently begin to calm down and experience healing once the abuser is gone and the victim is able to provide them with a stable, safe, loving environment. Symptoms, both emotional and physical, tend to start to disappear. Then, after just a weekend visit with the abuser, those symptoms recur. *It is a fallacy that children are always better off having a relationship with both parents.*

The Restraining Order Experience

Post-separation victims are likely to be confronted very soon with the decision of whether or not to obtain a restraining order (also known as an order of protection). This is an order of the court served upon the abuser which limits his contact with the victim, often forbidding any contact whether physical or verbal or even what is called "third-party" contact. That is, the abuser is prohibited from using someone as a "go-between" to deliver messages to the victim. We all must be careful not to be duped into functioning as such third-parties by the abuser.

In many or most states, temporary restraining orders can be obtained very quickly, but are then subject to review within a short period of time. The person upon whom the order is served can appeal the order. The victim is then required to come to court and substantiate her basis for the order by explaining why she has reason to fear his future conduct. The judge can then either dismiss the order to issue a permanent one ("permanent" meaning for a longer, stated period of time such as one year). If the abuser violates the terms of the order, he is subject to arrest and criminal penalties.

The effectiveness of restraining orders is subject to some debate. For a fuller discussion of this debate, see Gavin de Becker's *The Gift of Fear* in which he emphasizes that these orders are not always advisable and may actually incite the abuser further. One victim told me that she decided in her case that a restraining order would only make her abuser dangerously more angry. However, when she decided not to obtain the order, she was criticized by her friends and family who then suspected her of exaggerating her claims of abuse. After all, their reasoning went, if it was as serious as she claimed, surely she would not hesitate to get the order. In the end, a restraining order may restrain the least dangerous abuser and yet have a "fuel on the fire" effect on the most dangerous. And after all, paper isn't bulletproof.

Stalking Orders

Post-separation abusers may also stalk the victim as a tactic to control and punish. Stalking stems from the mentality of power and control and is strengthened by the abuser's notion that the victim and children are his owned property. There are different kinds of stalkers, the domestic abuser being one.[114]

In domestic violence/abuse cases, stalkers may continue their abuse by stalking in some of the following ways:

- Delivering written or verbal messages, often using "code" or cryptic language which can later be easily denied to mean any kind of threat.
- Secretly entering the victim's home and moving items around or leaving some subtle signal that he has been there.

114 J. Reid Meloy, ed., *The Psychology of Stalking: Clinical and Forensic Perspectives* (San Diego: Academic Press, 1998). Chapter seven by Walker and Meloy is devoted to stalking and domestic violence.

- Driving past or parking near the victim's home, in order to intimidate.
- Following the victim to work or school; waiting outside the place where the victim is.
- Just "happening" to be eating at the same restaurant the where the victim is eating.
- Excessive filing of court motions.
- Spying on the victim's friends or family.
- Making unwanted phone calls, voice-mail messages, emails and texts.
- Delivering unwanted gifts.
- Hacking into the victim's email or cell phone calls; monitoring her internet activity in general.
- Leaving messages on computer social forums such as Facebook (Note: Facebook-style forums are frequently used by abusers to assist in stalking their victims).
- Making threats against the victim to her friends.
- Posting embarrassing or damaging material on the internet to compromise the victim, or threatening to do so in order to blackmail her so she will not report his illegal activities to the police.
- Monitoring or tracking the victim's mileage, her mail, or her financial transactions.
- Recruiting the children to report the victim's activities to the abuser.

Stalking is a crime in which a person pursues another person for a period of time in such a way as to make the person being pursued have a reasonable sense of fear. There are usually three elements required by the law for stalking to be committed: 1) A *pattern* of behavior exercised upon another person that is not desired, 2) This pattern of behavior expresses a threat, 3) The person pursued is put in reasonable fear.[115] If the victim can demonstrate that the required elements of stalking have occurred, the court may issue an anti-stalking order. The abuser may oppose this action in court to argue that he has not been stalking the victim and that such an order is not justified. It is very stressful for a victim to be required to argue against her abuser in the courtroom in these hearings. I have personally witnessed an abuse victim being cross-examined by her abuser who was acting as his own attorney. This is all the more reason why we must provide support to an abuse survivor long after she has left her abuser.

115 Ibid., 2.

A Post-Separation Story

An abuse victim, separated from her ex-husband/abuser for a number of years, has suffered greatly from his continued abuse. His tactics have included filing repeated court motions that have cost her many thousands of dollars; money that could have been used for the benefit of her children. In addition, she has experienced the following tactics:

- He will claim to have genuinely changed because now he says he has really become a Christian. Nothing changes.
- He successfully won her old friends and church over to his side, against her.
- He will send emails or phone her, even at very late hours.
- He likes to use the pity card, pleading and weeping for her to take him back.
- He claims to be consumed with care and love for her.
- At every opportunity, he will try to obtain information about her from their children.
- When he doesn't hear her say what he wants, he rages.
- He tells the children lies about her during visitation and will talk this way to them for hours.
- He uses cryptic and indirect, easily deniable threats such as mentioning that he has just purchased a new pistol.
- He lays false guilt and accusations on her at every opportunity.
- He tries to sabotage her business and her efforts to pursue more education.

This remarkable woman has exhibited ongoing strength, remaining faithful in her walk with Christ, in spite of these years and years of this kind of terrorism. Though she experiences some dark valleys, she is quick to tell how the Lord has faithfully sustained her through it all.

A Challenge to Christ's Church

> ***Psalm 72:11-14*** *May all kings fall down before him, all nations serve him! For he delivers the needy when he calls, the poor and him who has no helper. He has pity on the weak and the needy, and saves the lives of the needy. From oppression and violence he redeems their life, and precious is their blood in his sight.*

I need to add one more detail that supports the thesis of this book, *A Cry for Justice,* namely, that as a whole, this lady's church did not support her and in fact has cast her off and embraced the wicked man. She anxiously waits for the day when her children are all of legal age and all of them will then finally be free of this man. But today, at the very moment that I write these words, *he* remains in his church while *she* had to leave.

Are you beginning to feel a rising sense of righteous anger at all of this? Are you asking yourself what you and your church might be able to do to effect justice for such people? If you are really a Christian, I cannot understand how it could be otherwise. Let me encourage you with this scenario – an alternate ending, you might say –

Mary has separated from her abusive husband. He is a man who has raged at her for years, all the while pretending to be a pious, godly man. When Mary went to her pastor and told him what had been going on in her home for over ten years, the pastor believed her and told her that he and her church family were going to stand with her over the long haul and see her through this.

That was seven years ago. Oh, her ex-husband still pulls all of the tactics listed above, and it has been no easy road for Mary and her children. But the support of her church family has made all the difference in the world. Her abuser was never able to deceive them – they saw right through his tactics because they listened to their pastor teach them about this evil and they were willing to read the books that were provided to them. Yes, there were a few who wanted nothing to do with it, but they left some years back. Mary has <u>never</u> had to go to a court hearing without at least several people from her church sitting right behind her. Oh, and did we mention that the church actually exercised church discipline against her ex-husband? Mary is in the church. He is not.

The church enabled Mary to install a security system and security lights in her home. They paid for quality locks on all the doors and windows. Husband and wife teams help her with yard and house maintenance. The men may do heavy work outside or repairs on the house, while the women help Mary with spring cleaning, baking, or just sit and chat with her over coffee. This protects Mary from any allegations of impropriety, while helping the church families keep in touch with her needs and feelings. Other folks from the church who are adept at technology have helped her re-configure all of her online systems (phone, internet) so that she is protected from electronic stalking.

Because of all of this support and atmosphere of truth and justice, Mary's children are handling the whole thing very well. Yes, they have to spend every other weekend with their father and yes, he tries all of his tactics on them too. But they know what he is up to and sooner or later, *he* will know that they know!

This is the answer to a cry for justice*!* Will you and your church be a part of it?

Psalm 10:1-2 *Why, O LORD, do you stand far away? Why do you hide yourself in times of trouble? In arrogance the wicked hotly pursue the poor; let them be caught in the schemes that they have devised.*

CHAPTER 13

Dealing With Abusers

1 John 3:10 *By this it is evident who are the children of God, and who are the children of the devil: whoever does not practice righteousness is not of God, nor is the one who does not love his brother.*

"I warned my pastor that my husband, Gary, would attempt to deceive him and the entire church by using one of his favorite tactics, a ploy I like to call 'bait and hook.' I had seen Gary do this many times with counselors and our friends that he wanted to recruit to his side against me. Gary would cast out the 'bait' by readily admitting to not having been a good husband or father. He even admitted in surprising detail some of the abuse he had committed against me and the children. He seemed humble and sincere and was very convincing. But he was neither humble nor sincere. What he was doing was giving just enough 'true confessions' to them so that they would be convinced he was truly serious now about repenting and wanting to change. Then, when I didn't buy it, Gary would set the hook and he would have them on his side. "See, this is what I mean. I am really trying to change. I am changing. But she just won't let the past lie. Until she starts believing me and helping me, how is our marriage ever going to get better?' I would look like the culprit and they all would be set against me." (Abuse victim)

There are some hard, cold rules we must adhere to in dealing with abusers. Here are a few of them:

1. Question everything. Even "facts" he states with absolute confidence.
2. Believe nothing without corroboration.

3. Assume he is attempting to deceive you.
4. Accept nothing less than full, unqualified repentance.
5. Do not pity him, no matter how emotional he might be.
6. Accept no excuses.
7. Do not let him blame others.

Believing these things is difficult for normal people whose minds do not work the way the abuser's mind does. But we must discipline ourselves to do it.

Let me illustrate this with another story from my police days. I had taken a report of a man and woman stealing a gallon of very expensive weed control chemical from a local farm store. After stealing it, they returned it the next day for a cash refund, claiming they had forgotten the receipt. The store manager told me that he would not be surprised if they had done this elsewhere, so I proceeded to contact other similar stores in the tri-county area, asking them if this sounded familiar. It did. This couple had been to every single one of the stores I called in the last three months. They were raking in the money.

I had a description of them and of their car, but nothing else. One afternoon not many days later, incredibly I happened upon them. This was a large municipal area and the probability of this happening was extremely slim, but there they were. I stopped them, arrested them (they had some gallons of the chemical in their car) and took them to the station for further questioning and processing.

Now, I had a choice. I could book them into jail, or I could issue them citations to appear in court and release them. The male suspect proceeded to put on a masterful act, complete with tears, about their hard luck and how they were just trying to put food on the table for their children. Can you believe it? I hate to admit it, but I felt sorry for them, cited them, and released them. In spite of their promises to break off from crime, they were caught doing the very same thing a few days later. My pity for them had sucked me in.

In dealing with an abuser, we must be *hard.* Not mean. But hard. We must continually be reminding ourselves that such a person's mindset is quite different from ours and that abusers are very capable of lying and deceiving, acting and weeping, showing what sounds like unshakable logic – and doing it all with no pangs of conscience. Martha Stout has concluded that the tactic of eliciting *pity* from others is one of the surest signs of a sociopath when it occurs in a person who also demonstrates a habitual pattern of antisocial (abusive) behavior.[116]

If you do not believe this is necessary, or if you just don't see yourself being able to deal with anyone in this manner, then you are not a person who is qualified to counsel with the abuser. He will only use you to continue his abuse. As Anne Pike notes, the abusive, conscienceless person employs and uses 'friends' who are people lacking true emotional maturity themselves and therefore will work to protect him from any consequences of his abuse.[117]

Is He a Christian?

> "*I think that he really is sorry he's messed up his life so much but the sorrow has more to do with the way it is affecting him than it does with the way it's affecting/has affected us. He is reading his Bible, going to church and praying but it just doesn't seem to be connecting in any way. It's like he's looking for something that he can't find.*" (Wife of an abuser who says he is a Christian)

As I have read books about abuse, written by Christian authors, I have noticed a number of times that they assume, or at least give the impression, that the abuser may be a real Christian. In other words, some people maintain that a Christian, a genuinely regenerated, new creation in Christ, can still be one of the villains which this book is about. The answer to this question—can a Christian be an abuser?—will have profound implications regarding how we deal with such a person. Who is it that you are dealing with? A saint who is still struggling with his old sinful flesh, but is fundamentally a child of God in his real person? Or are we dealing with an individual whose entire profession of Christ is a sham and façade? It is a vital question to answer before we can proceed with him. Consider, for example, the case of Thomas:

> Thomas was a real puzzle to his wife, his children, and his Pastor. He was a church member and no one in the church doubted that he had a genuine relationship with Christ. Everyone had heard him pray prayers that were "right on" and he had a very good knowledge of Scripture, often answering questions in Bible study groups. Thomas was a key member of the church.

116 Stout, 107.
117 Pike, 52.

Now, most everyone who knew Thomas also realized that he had some personality "glitches" that could drive people a bit crazy sometimes. Pastor Williams knew about this and had even experienced it himself in his many years of association with Thomas. But no one is perfect and patience seemed to be the most appropriate way to relate to Thomas. After all, he had so many positive qualities too, and the Bible does say that love covers a multitude of sins. And this is the very thing Pastor Williams told the several church members who had come to him over the years with complaints about how Thomas had treated them.

It wasn't totally surprising then when one day Thomas' wife, Sadie, came to see the Pastor. She expressed some rather intense frustrations regarding her husband, describing some of the things Thomas had done to her and the children over the 12 years of their marriage. Oh, there was nothing criminal at all – nothing like that, she said. But Thomas had long-standing patterns of doing things like:

- Making himself the center of attention.
- Being "checked out" and unconcerned about the welfare of the rest of the family.
- Disregarding the law.
- Distancing himself from her after an argument, avoiding her for as long as a week, without seeming to be bothered by the unresolved conflict at all.
- Blaming everyone but himself.

Thomas had been married previously, and until now, Sadie believed that what Thomas had given as the reason for that marriage ending in divorce was true. Namely, that his ex-wife was a totally selfish person who was a flirt with men and who never gave Thomas the respect God says a husband deserves. Sadie asked Pastor Williams for help.

Now, imagine that you are Pastor Williams. How are you going to deal with Thomas? As a Christian who is plagued by some sins that are the result of some self-defensive mechanisms he developed over the years? Perhaps the explanation for his problem behavior in the present stems from some unresolved trauma in his past, or from issues in the child-rearing style of his parents? This scenario is possible, right? After all, Christians are certainly not perfect, not in this life anyway. Or, will you deal with him as an unsaved man, as a human being who is still alienated from Christ and whose profession of Christ is a false one?

Pastor Williams didn't hesitate in his decision. He actually did not really even consider the second possibility, but rather immediately embraced the assumption that Thomas was in fact a real Christian who was struggling with some strongholds of sin in his life. It would be Pastor Williams' job to help Thomas see that the sinful behaviors his wife had described stemmed from wrong thinking about who Thomas really was in Christ.

Pastor Williams employed this theory and tried to help Thomas for five years. There was no change. The marriage ended in divorce. What had gone wrong? Why had nothing happened for the better? It is vital that we find out.

What Does the Bible Say?

> ***2 Corinthians 7:10*** *For godly grief produces a repentance that leads to salvation without regret, whereas worldly grief produces death.*

I am going to just "put it out there" right up front. Here is what I conclude the Bible says, and I believe that it says it quite clearly:

> While every Christian can certainly hurt, mistreat, or be insensitive to another person, and more frequently than we think, it is impossible for a Christian to be what we have defined as an abuser in this book. That is to say, Scripture makes it plain that a person whose very mentality and habitual practice is that of entitlement, power, control, and justification, does not know Christ, nor does Christ know him.

And this is where Pastor Williams went wrong. Even after years of work, Thomas persisted in unrepentance. He continued to practice the very things his wife had complained about, and in fact it became evident over that time that Thomas was regularly guilty of a number of other abusive patterns. Nothing changed. Regardless of all of the pastor's work in trying to show Thomas that his issues were due to the residual erroneous thought patterns in him, Thomas did not change, except for the worse. Why? Because Thomas is, in fact, unchanged in heart and soul and mind. He is not a Christian.[118] No one was addressing *the real Thomas.*

Why, then, did everyone assume that Thomas was a Christian? The answer is not that difficult to see now – Thomas put on a really convincing façade of Christianity. And most of the time, this is the "Thomas" that Pastor Williams and the rest of the church had contact with. It was natural for them to assume that the Thomas they knew was the real Thomas – the nice, no-not-perfect, Christian man who struggled with sin like every Christian does. And that is how they related to him.

But the rest of Thomas' life revealed a totally different state of affairs. Thomas *habitually* served himself. Thomas was a user of people, a man who considered himself superior to others and entitled to their service. His tactics revealed this, though you had to look below the surface to see it. Listen to what God has to say about all of this:

> ***1 John 2:3-4*** *And by this we know that we have come to know him, if we keep his commandments. Whoever says "I know him" but does not keep his commandments is a liar, and the truth is not in him…*
>
> ***1 John 2:9-11*** *Whoever says he is in the light and hates his brother is still in darkness. Whoever loves his brother abides in the light, and in him there is no cause for stumbling. But whoever hates his brother is in the darkness and walks in the darkness, and does not know where he is going, because the darkness has blinded his eyes.*
>
> ***1 John 4:20-21*** *If anyone says, "I love God," and hates his brother, he is a liar; for he who does not love his brother whom he has seen cannot love God whom he has not seen. And this commandment we have from him: whoever loves God must also love his brother.*

---

118 I refer the reader once again to two of George Simon's excellent books, *In Sheep's Clothing* and *Character Disturbance.* Also, Robert Hare's book, *Without Conscience* is excellent. Both of these men argue that the attempt to explain the sociopath/psychopath (people without a conscience) in terms of what Simon calls "neurotic" over-active, guilt-producing conscience, is not only futile but damaging. There are, they maintain, people who are simply *bad.* People who have no conscience. Dealing with them requires entirely different methods. Sarah Braun and Bridget Flynn give further excellent descriptions of the same conclusions, *Honeymoon and Hell: A Memoir of Abuse.* All are listed in the bibliography of this book.

1 John 5:18 *We know that everyone who has been born of God does not keep on sinning, but he who was born of God protects him, and the evil one does not touch him. [The present tense of the Greek verb means "to continue to sin as a habit; to be characterized by being sinful].*

Romans 8:7-9 *For the mind that is set on the flesh is hostile to God, for it does not submit to God's law; indeed, it cannot. Those who are in the flesh cannot please God. You, however, are not in the flesh but in the Spirit, if in fact the Spirit of God dwells in you. Anyone who does not have the Spirit of Christ does not belong to him.*

Do we need to go on? It would not be difficult to continue citing verses like this for quite some time. What does the Bible say? It says that when Christ saves us, He gives us a new heart. It says that He makes us a new creation. Our entire mindset and mentality is changed from hatred for and hostility toward God, to one that loves God, loves His Word, and loves those who belong to Christ.

Therefore, we must necessarily conclude that an abuser simply cannot be a Christian, no matter how convincing his masquerade of Christianity might be. His very mindset remains unchanged, as his perseverance in his abuse demonstrates. In contrast, a Christian will come to repentance, as did King David when confronted by Nathan the prophet. Jesus stated the unbreakable principle:

Luke 6:43-46 *For no good tree bears bad fruit, nor again does a bad tree bear good fruit, for each tree is known by its own fruit. For figs are not gathered from thorn bushes, nor are grapes picked from a bramble bush. The good person out of the good treasure of his heart produces good, and the evil person out of his evil treasure produces evil, for out of the abundance of the heart his mouth speaks. Why do you call me 'Lord, Lord,' and not do what I tell you?*

It is a serious error then to treat an abuser as if he is a real Christian. We need to carefully qualify our words when we speak about such topics as: "the tragedy of abuse in the Christian family or "Christians who abuse" lest we give the impression that we believe a "good" tree can produce "bad" fruit season after season after season. Sarah Braun describes this error that she once embraced and which kept her enslaved:

> I believed this resulted in his having issues that included fear of intimacy, low self-esteem and improper expression of his pent up feelings. The remedy included my love, understanding and forgiveness. It matters little what I might have imagined his greater pain to be.... There was always something that explained away his awful behavior and cast it in a sympathetic light. Certainly his abusiveness was not his true intent or representative of his true character or nature.[119]

But it *was* his true intent and it did indeed represent his true character, as she eventually came to realize.

Ultimately, the issue comes down to, yes, theology. Doctrine. These words are simply synonyms for what we believe to be true according to Scripture. And there is no more vital a question demanding a clear answer than, who is a Christian? I believe that many churches and Christians today are giving a wrong answer to it. They maintain that a Christian is simply: 1) A person who believes in Jesus Christ, and 2) Whose sins are forgiven and who is therefore on his way to heaven. These things are certainly true. A Christian *does* believe in Jesus Christ (but so does the devil). A Christian *is* a person whose sins are forgiven and who will end in heaven, but he is also much more than that. A Christian is:

- A new creature, a new man (2 Corinthians 5:17; Ephesians 2:1ff).
- A son of God (Galatians 4:4ff).
- A person upon whose heart God has written His moral Law (Hebrews 8:10-11).
- A person who has been taught by the Spirit of Jesus (Ephesians 4:20ff).

And certainly we could continue listing many more characteristics which are true of every Christian. They are true because salvation in Christ entails far more than just forgiveness of sins and a place in heaven (which in themselves are marvelous!). Salvation in Christ effects a radical change in the very essence of our personhood so that we are no longer the person we used to be. Once an enemy of God, we are now His child who loves Him. Once haters of His Law, it is now written on our hearts so that we love it. Understanding these things will revolutionize how we diagnose and deal with a person who is defined by the abuser mentality and practice. Any church that embraces a theology of "just pray this sinner's prayer and you will be a Christian" is setting itself up to be a hiding

119 Braun, Location 116-123, Kindle Edition.

place for the abuser. The abuser, as we define him in this book, is not a Christian, and we must deal with him with that understanding.

Here are some poignant words from a woman who was the victim of terrible abuse at the hands of a man who professed to be a Christian:

> Sitting in many a church pew, serving on many a committee, supposedly leading within many a home, are these workers of darkness: the classic raging, ravenous wolves in harmless sheep's clothing. And they will do almost anything to keep from being found out.

The agenda they promote isn't God's, as they want us to believe. Their agenda is that of self-promotion, self-preservation, self-aggrandizement. In classic "the world is my oyster" style, these abusers of home, family and, often, the church, believe that what they want is theirs for the taking, theirs for the using, theirs, even, for the destroying should they so wish. And wish for this they do, for to destroy people who wish only to love them or to trust them, seems to be one of the ultimate acts of achievement for them. That and, of course, hiding all evidence of the act from others. This they are quite good at, quite good at, indeed. They are, in fact, so good at hiding their desire to control and destroy from others that, should the occasion arise in which they are accused of an act of destruction or abuse, they easily laugh, shrug it off, and leave both their accuser and all who are observing, shaking their heads and wondering if what they thought was real, ever actually happened at all.

Does this all sound too harsh, even for an unsaved person? Once again, we must compare our opinions with what God has to say in Scripture:

> ***Romans 3:10-18*** *...as it is written: "None is righteous, no, not one; no one understands; no one seeks for God. All have turned aside; together they have become worthless; no one does good, not even one. Their throat is an open grave; they use their tongues to deceive. The venom of asps is under their lips. Their mouth is full of curses and bitterness. Their feet are swift to shed blood; in their paths are ruin and misery, and the way of peace they have not known. There is no fear of God before their eyes."*

Some More Traits to Watch For

Now that I speak "Abuser," I am free to recognize the deceitful, accusing rants for what they are.

I used those words to answer an abuse victim's question. "How did you know? Why can't I see these people? What is wrong with me?" Her blindness wasn't really that there was something wrong with her. It stems from what is wrong with the abuser. He is the master of façade. He is a liar and con by nature. But once we learn his language, and it is remarkably consistent in its nature, we can identify him. Despite how charming a "Christian" abuser is capable of presenting himself, study of his mentality and tactics will ultimately enable you to identify him (or her) more easily than you might think. Let me list and briefly discuss a few of the things that commonly express themselves in the abuser's thinking, words, and actions that are observable indicators of the abuser mentality. Some we have mentioned already, but a bit of repetition certainly will not hurt.

1. The abuser often uses **unbelievable exaggerations** but makes them believable with remarkable certainty. For example, in his efforts to convince us that his wife/victim is to blame and that *he* is the victim, he may invent "facts" that are simply bizarre. However, his ability to do so with such conscienceless conviction makes us conclude that it all must be true. "She is a real tramp. I have caught her more than once in a bar trying to pick up a guy." That statement is totally contrary to what you know about her, but the way he presents the claim is so convincing. "Surely no one could actually say something like that if it weren't true, could they?" we ask ourselves.
2. You may find yourself faced with some story he claims took place, yet you have absolutely no recollection of the event. Still, he is so certain and so confident in his demeanor that you begin to doubt your own memory. He is **distorting reality** and **rewriting history** for his own purposes.
3. Not being bothered by **inconsistencies in his statements** is yet another common characteristic identifier. Abusers will, without hesitation, present contradictory facts and do so quite convincingly. Their stories evolve as necessary and if they meet some objection in us to the logic of what they are saying, they can simply change the storyline. Once more however, the listener has difficulty *not* believing them because of the confidence and unblinking certainty with which they speak. Many times these inconsistencies are present because the abuser is lying and therefore he has no *true story* in his memory that would keep his facts

straight.[120] With this in mind, we will remember to press the abuser for more details, and we will often find that he cannot provide any. If we detect any variation in his story from one telling to the next, we will make a mental and perhaps even a written note about it, so we can confront him with the discrepancies as appropriate.

4. Abusers often **act like experts** on the subjects they speak about, but when questioned further, it becomes evident that their knowledge is actually quite superficial, though they still will not admit it. For churches, at least in part, we should be wary of the individual who, even on his first visit, expounds about some theological point in a manner that presents him as an expert. In our church, we have learned that a first-time visitor who readily and at some length "tells us what he thinks" during the Sunday school class is someone we might well want to be careful of.
5. The abuser **uses our own conscience against us**. When he is confronted with the facts about what he did to a victim, he skillfully manipulates what we are saying so that we find ourselves feeling that perhaps we have been too harsh or judgmental of him. We wonder if we owe him an apology and need to retract the charge. When you start feeling like this, you are probably talking to a genuine abuser, and you need to "get your head back on straight" by recounting the facts that you know to be true rather than listening to his words, no matter how confidently he speaks them.
6. Be on guard for signs that the individual has a mentality that includes a **double standard**. This means that he will condemn his victim for something and then, even in the very next sentence, reveal that he does the very same thing. It is what the Apostle Paul wrote to the Romans about:

   Romans 2:1 *Therefore you have no excuse, O man, every one of you who judges. For in passing judgment on another you condemn yourself, because you, the judge, practice the very same things.*

   But the abuser doesn't see it this way. His wife is a horrible, selfish spendthrift because she spent $50 at the grocery store on food, but his purchase of coke, candy, alcohol, cigarettes, lottery tickets is quite alright.
7. Watch for indicators of **immaturity**. Like a baby, the abuser often screams when his wants are not met, or throws a tantrum when

120 Anne Pike, *Danger Has a Face*. Pike gives many examples throughout her book of this same phenomenon.

confronted, or displays rank selfishness. He is not concerned with the needs of others (though remember, if Christianity is his façade, he can feign such concern very convincingly).

8. Repeatedly, abuse victims tell me that their abusers are into **pornography**. I am not entirely certain yet why this is true, but it is a very common trait of such a person. Perhaps it reveals the male abuser's disdain for women, or makes him feel superior to his victim as pornography portrays women in a subservient, demeaning manner, thus serving to confirm his own ideas about what women are for. Also, by lusting and getting orgasms from porn, he obtains pleasure that temporarily quenches the thirst of his godless soul. And just like alcohol, drugs, or gambling, it's addictive. Once hooked, the addict needs increasingly more degrading and perverted images in order to obtain the same degree of excitement. Several abuse victims have related to me that eventually their abuser became impotent.
9. Consistent refusal to understand and consider **another person's point of view**, especially that of his victim. The abuser's lack of empathy or remorse is a void where there should be motivation to step into another person's shoes. If your efforts to show him how his victim sees a situation are met with excuses and devaluing of her opinions, you are probably talking to an abuser.
10. Evidence of **shamelessness** is still another sign of an abusive mentality. If there have been actions committed against a victim that would evoke shame and disgust in normal people, but do not do so in the person you are dealing with, this also is an indicator of an abusive mentality. A shameless mindset will act as if nothing serious has happened, as did Judas when he shamelessly kissed Jesus.
11. As we have learned, the abuser **demands forgiveness and seeks pity**. He may terribly abuse his victim, and then weep and wail, insisting on her forgiveness and pity because he is so miserable and sorry. He may threaten or attempt suicide (especially if she's recently left him) to evoke our pity. We need to constantly be scanning the abuser's words and actions that betray his expectation of being forgiven. This is a certain sign that he is in no way really repentant.
12. Watch for displays of **unusually compelling charm**. This "con" trait is a familiar one in an abuser. In connection with this false charm, you may

also see **manipulation and mind game tactics**. We must be able to spot these and refuse to be drawn into them.

13. How does he **relate to the law and social norms**? Many abusers violate rules and regulations without any pain of conscience. Because they see themselves as superior, they are above the law as they choose and justified in breaking it. The abuser who wears a "Christian" mask may well cite various Scriptures in an attempt to justify his illegal acts. He enjoys breaking laws and rules because then he has an opportunity to fight and, if he can win, he will show everyone that he is indeed above the law.

Suggested Analytical Questions

The abusive mentality can be revealed if we put it under the light of effective "test questions." This presumes, of course, that we are already familiar with the abusive mentality and its tactics. Consider these analytical questions for instance. Some are designed for use with a person who claims to be a Christian, while others can be used in any case. Listen very carefully for accompanying "incidental" comments. These may provide the real answers you need. The questions can be easily modified for use with a female abuser:

- Can you define your relationship with Christ? (Not necessarily *when* he was saved, but how Christ has changed him -- or how he says he has changed).
- Can you explain to me your understanding of your obligations in your home and how you live this out among your wife and children? (By asking for concrete examples, his lack of godly husbanding ought to show up if he can't provide them).
- How do you serve those who are under your authority?
- What are your wife's obligations to you?
- What are your views of marital obedience/submission? Do you consider your wife obedient to you? Please explain.
- How are you laying down your life for your wife as Christ laid down His life for the church?
- How are you raising your children in the nurture and the admonition of the Lord? What does that even mean?
- What are the kinds of things that get you upset? What happens when you

get upset? How does your wife feel when you get upset? How does your wife get you upset?

- When you are at fault in an argument, what do you do? How do you handle things when the argument is over? Do you think that your wife handles arguments correctly?
- What does repentance mean? How do you show repentance when you have failed as a man, as a husband, as a father?
- How often can we commit the same sin or same type of sin and still call ourselves a Christian?
- How does your Christianity affect your view of ... (Lying, pornography, obeying the law, adultery, etc.)
- What does forgiveness mean? If you have been sinned against, what is your reaction? When you sin against someone (through word or deed), what is their obligation to forgive?
- Does your wife have complaints about you? Do you think they are true and fair?
- Why are you here speaking with me?
- Tell me about women. What do they want from men? What is their role in a marriage?
- Does God command your wife to obey you?
- What would cause a man to hit his wife?
- What could your wife do to make your marriage better?
- Does your wife always think clearly?
- Does your wife ever misunderstand your motives? Can you give me an example?
- How should children show respect to their father?
- What methods of discipline are proper for a father to use on his children?
- Since the Bible says that fathers are to discipline their children, and that a husband is the head of his wife, isn't there a basis then for a husband to discipline his wife? If so, what methods of discipline might he use?
- Is it right for a wife to spend money without first discussing it with her husband?
- How many friends should a wife have besides her husband? Do you think that a wife's women friends can cause problems in her marriage? How?
- Have you been married before? Could you tell me why those marriages ended? What kind of women were your previous wives? How would your previous wife explain the ending of that marriage?

As you study abuse and become more familiar with it, you will be able to design these kinds of questions that will reveal the underlying mentality and the tactics of abuse. When the abuser is revealed for what he is, you can know with certainty which side you need to stand for – *the victim's!*

Knowing that we are dealing with an abuser, what next? Scripture gives us a plain answer, but one which many Christians and churches in our day seem to refuse to believe – the biblical application of church discipline.

Church Discipline and the Abuser

The Church of Jesus Christ possesses one of the most powerful and effective tools to use against abuse, perhaps even the most effective. Ironically, this tool is gathering dust in most churches, left unused for many years. Oh, you will find it referred to in just about every evangelical church's bylaws, but rarely is it actually put into play. This tool is, of course, church discipline. Let's refresh our memories:

> ***Matthew 18:15-19*** *"If your brother sins against you, go and tell him his fault, between you and him alone. If he listens to you, you have gained your brother. But if he does not listen, take one or two others along with you, that every charge may be established by the evidence of two or three witnesses. If he refuses to listen to them, tell it to the church. And if he refuses to listen even to the church, let him be to you as a Gentile and a tax collector. Truly, I say to you, whatever you bind on earth shall be bound in heaven, and whatever you loose on earth shall be loosed in heaven. Again I say to you, if two of you agree on earth about anything they ask, it will be done for them by my Father in heaven.*
>
> ***Romans 16:17-18*** *I appeal to you, brothers, to watch out for those who cause divisions and create obstacles contrary to the doctrine that you have been taught; avoid them. For such persons do not serve our Lord Christ, but their own appetites, and by smooth talk and flattery they deceive the hearts of the naive.*
>
> ***1 Corinthians 5:1-5*** *It is actually reported that there is sexual immorality among you, and of a kind that is not tolerated even among pagans, for a man has his father's wife. And you are arrogant! Ought you not rather to mourn?*

Let him who has done this be removed from among you. For though absent in body, I am present in spirit; and as if present, I have already pronounced judgment on the one who did such a thing. When you are assembled in the name of the Lord Jesus and my spirit is present, with the power of our Lord Jesus, you are to deliver this man to Satan for the destruction of the flesh, so that his spirit may be saved in the day of the Lord.

1 Corinthians 5:11-13 *But now I am writing to you not to associate with anyone who bears the name of brother if he is guilty of sexual immorality or greed, or is an idolater, reviler, drunkard, or swindler, not even to eat with such a one. For what have I to do with judging outsiders? Is it not those inside the church whom you are to judge? God judges those outside. "Purge the evil person from among you.*

2 Thessalonians 3:6 *Now we command you, brothers, in the name of our Lord Jesus Christ, that you keep away from any brother who is walking in idleness and not in accord with the tradition that you received from us.*

Titus 3:10-11 *As for a person who stirs up division, after warning him once and then twice, have nothing more to do with him, knowing that such a person is warped and sinful; he is self-condemned.*

2 Timothy 3:1-7 *But understand this, that in the last days there will come times of difficulty. (2) For people will be lovers of self, lovers of money, proud, arrogant, abusive, disobedient to their parents, ungrateful, unholy, (3) heartless, unappeasable, slanderous, without self-control, brutal, not loving good, (4) treacherous, reckless, swollen with conceit, lovers of pleasure rather than lovers of God, (5) having the appearance of godliness, but denying its power. Avoid such people. (6) For among them are those who creep into households and capture weak women, burdened with sins and led astray by various passions, (7) always learning and never able to arrive at a knowledge of the truth. [We include this passage because it describes one way abusers operate, hiding behind a cloak of godliness. The text also tells us, avoid such people.]*

Revelation 2:20 *But I have this against you, that you tolerate that woman Jezebel, who calls herself a prophetess and is teaching and seducing my servants to practice sexual immorality and to eat food sacrificed to idols.*

There are many more Scriptures like these, but this will suffice. Surely no one will try to argue that the abuser does not require the discipline of the church! By Christ's own authority, the church is to confront sin, insist upon repentance from that sin, and put the unrepentant man out of the church. Being put out of the church (excommunication) is a declaration that such a person is choosing to live in disobedience to Christ and therefore cannot be in the body of Christ. He is to be put out into the world to live where Satan rules. This is for the protection of Christ's flock and as a means to work repentance in the offender, as in the Prodigal Son did when he came to his senses in the pig pen. And yet:

> I told my pastor about Brad's abuse five years ago. After hours and hours of counseling with the pastor, Brad is still unchanged. And yet, he is still a member of our church. I have asked the pastor many times to announce Brad's sin to the church and if he still will not repent, to put him out of the church. I asked this because I believe that church discipline is a powerful means of Christ to bring hardened sinners like my husband to repentance. And yet, nothing. I am beginning to worry that someday I will be the one who will have to leave the church while Brad is allowed to stay here. Even now the pastor and a couple of elders have implied that I have exaggerated my claims of abuse and that perhaps it would be best for the church's unity if I would just be a better wife and stop talking about this. (Abuse victim)

Why? Why does the church so often refuse to bring Christ's power in church discipline upon the abuser? Let me suggest some reasons:

1. Unbelief. We simply do not believe Christ's promise to accompany us in the process of discipline and through it to bring His own power upon the offender.
2. Disobedience. We know we should discipline, but out of fear or simply not wanting to pay the possible cost of discipline (criticism, splitting the church, etc.) we disobey Christ. It is more comfortable to stand with the abuser in many cases than with the victim.
3. Ignorance. We don't know the evil nature of abuse, and so we minimize it. This ignorance is one of the chief evils that we pray this book might be used by Christ to correct.
4. Being a respecter of persons. We place the "dignity" of the abuser above the rights of the victim and the command of Christ. We don't want to embarrass him by exposing him.

5. And perhaps the most common reason is: our arrogant notion that we can "fix" the abuser ourselves. I trust by now that the reader will understand the impossibility of such a "fix."

But whatever the reason, surely this all cannot please our Lord. If Christ held it against the church at Thyatira for tolerating a wicked, false teacher in their midst, then we know that He holds it against us when we permit the abuser to remain in our ranks.

Let me suggest a principle in connection with church discipline that I believe to be very, very important because every sin is not the same, neither is the form of discipline that is prescribed by the Bible. There are multiple Scriptures that deal with church discipline. Not every sinner is the same. The openly defiant, shameless man at Corinth was to be simply put out of the church at the very next church gathering! The Matthew 18 process is used to deal with more personal, private sins against another person, but even it leads up to excommunication if there is no repentance. In other cases, such as a divisive person (which some abusers can be), a first and second warning is given, then he is to be excluded. Once more, the principle is -- because not every sin and not every sinner are the same, neither is the form of discipline that is applied. Some sins are more odious to the Lord than others. Some sinners are more devious and dangerous than others.

Abuse is a scandalous sin. It is not a private sin between just two people, though it is deceptively hidden in secret most often. In some cases of serious abuse, immediate exclusion from the church (and making a police report) is the proper means of discipline. This provides immediate protection for the victim. In other cases, the church may decide to confront the abuser first and see what his response is. But even if there is apparent repentance, the safety of the victim must have first priority. Abuse is an evil that should not even be named among us and for the glory of Christ's name, we must faithfully apply His discipline to it. Largely to this present time, we have not done so.

Exercise

How would you answer the following question in light of all that you have learned so far about abuse? The question was submitted to us from a real life situation:

The leadership of a large church I am familiar with, say that they never exclude a domestic abuser from the church or make the man's sin public, because if they did that it would frighten off every other victim from disclosing her abuse, and would just send the whole sin of domestic abuse further underground. They say they reprimand the abuser firmly in private, and help the victim into a shelter if she wishes, getting her support from the local domestic violence support service, but they never make the situation public in the church. They say that most abusive men leave the church eventually after being dealt with in this manner, because they realize they cannot win allies in the church leadership.

What do you think? Does this method square with Scripture's instruction regarding how we are to deal with unrepentant sin in the church? Is it really true that public announcement of sin and discipline of the abuser frightens off victims? Haven't we been learning that in fact it is just the other way around – that failing to confront the sin is what discourages and drives the victim away? Just because the abuser eventually leaves, does that mean he is finished trying to gain allies from among the church members?

Confronting the Abuser –Draw Him a Picture

"*You are the man!*" With those stinging and powerful words, the prophet Nathan fearlessly confronted King David's sin. And it worked. David repented and confessed his sin. Prior to all of this however, Nathan did something that contains a crucial lesson for us whenever we confront sin, and particularly when we confront the sin of abuse. Nathan painted a powerful verbal picture of what David had done. Listen to it:

> ***2 Samuel 12:1-7a*** *And the LORD sent Nathan to David. He came to him and said to him, "There were two men in a certain city, the one rich and the other poor. The rich man had very many flocks and herds, but the poor man had nothing but one little ewe lamb, which he had bought. And he brought it up, and it grew up with him and with his children. It used to eat of his morsel and drink from his cup and lie in his arms, and it was like a daughter to him. Now there came a traveler to the rich man, and he was unwilling to take one of his own flock or herd to prepare for the guest who had come to him, but he took the poor man's lamb and prepared it for*

the man who had come to him." Then David's anger was greatly kindled against the man, and he said to Nathan, "As the LORD lives, the man who has done this deserves to die, and he shall restore the lamb fourfold, because he did this thing, and because he had no pity." Nathan said to David, "You are the man!"

Imagine that you are Nathan, and your job is to go confront a man in your church. His wife has come to you and described the abuse she and her children have been enduring for years. Knowing what you know now about such a man's mentality and tactics, how are you going to confront him? If warranted, you might immediately call the police and the fellow may be arrested. If not, his wife may choose to return home and you plan to meet with her husband in a day or two. Or she might stay away from home for a time. However the different scenarios might play out, it is a given that you are going to sit this man down and bring his sin before him. But how to do it? Please note: You need to take great care in planning what his wife should do for her safety once you talk to him and he learns that she has spoken to you. Don't confront the abuser without the victim's permission. And if she is still living with the abuser, make sure she has a safety plan in place. Unless this is what we might call a less severe case in the spectrum of abuse, it is highly probable that she will be the object of his wrath when he returns home. Remember, we are talking about *abuse* here, not a simple annoyance between husband and wife.

Would it not be wise to write out a word portrait of this fellow's sin in advance? You might choose to incorporate the details his wife has told you characterize his abuse, or you may elect to draw your portrait from the things you have learned in this book about the mentality and tactics of abuse. The goal is to put this man's sin before him in as much clarity as possible. (I myself would choose the second alternative so that the man does not immediately realize you are talking about him. Remember, you cannot betray the victim's confidence if she has talked to you, unless she has given you permission to disclose what she's told you).

Now, what should you expect? Lundy Bancroft, as we have mentioned earlier, has found in his abuser therapy groups, abusive men can come crashing down upon another abuser when they hear the other man describing his abuse and then making excuses to justify himself. Really, that is what happened with David!

He was incensed and ready to exact justice upon the man Nathan described. That is, until he heard these ominous words, "*You are the man!*"

This is one of the major reasons why Christians and perhaps pastors in particular, need to become very familiar with the nature and tactics of abuse. We need to know the sin so that we can put it right in front of the eyes of the abuser. This is a vital first step in presenting the gospel of Christ to such a person. Just think of the detailed descriptions found in the Old Testament prophets that do the very same thing: strike the sinful person right "between the eyes" with his sin, and then announce, "You are the man!" May the Spirit of Christ take such words and wield them like a two-edged sword, cutting right into the deepest recesses of the abuser's being!

Listen to this comment from an abuse survivor:

> I think that often pastors preach sermons that are aimed to "strike the sinful person right between the eyes," but because it's being preached to the congregation as a whole, the abusers brush it off thinking it doesn't apply to them, while victims take it far too much to heart, scrutinizing and condemning themselves because of their over-sensitive consciences. Many times I sat beside my husband in church, examining myself scrupulously for every particular sin that the sermon was warning about, while my thick-skinned husband seemed to believe that none of the sermon's warnings applied to him.

Christ's Truth: The Weapon of Our Warfare

> ***2 Corinthians 10:3-5*** *For though we walk in the flesh, we are not waging war according to the flesh. For the weapons of our warfare are not of the flesh but have divine power to destroy strongholds. We destroy arguments and every lofty opinion raised against the knowledge of God, and take every thought captive to obey Christ…*

Strongholds. When we present the gospel of Christ to a person who is still in the grip of sin, we are always going to meet *strongholds.* Heavily reinforced and defended, These strongholds are opposed to the truth of Christ's gospel and hold the abuser in bondage to his sin and corruption. Paul speaks of the same thing in an earlier chapter:

2 Corinthians 4:3-4 *And even if our gospel is veiled, it is veiled only to those who are perishing. In their case the god of this world has blinded the minds of the unbelievers, to keep them from seeing the light of the gospel of the glory of Christ, who is the image of God.*

Consider some of the strongholds in the abuser's mind:

- An incredible sense of entitlement. He deserves to be served. His victims are here on this earth for his pleasure.
- His mission in life is to control others for his own selfish ends.
- He is justified in doing "what has to be done" to achieve his goals.
- His thinking about women is terribly skewed. He sees his wife as a conniving, scheming female out to dominate him, who must be conquered.
- "Truth" is something to be modified for his own purposes.
- He is his own law.

The situation is hopeless. Who or what could ever smash through these thick walls that are set up in the abuser's mind? How can we ever enable a blind person to see? The thing is Satanic by nature; the "god of this world" is actively blinding such a person to the truth about who he is, what his sin really is, and who Christ is. So the madness of abuse goes on. Here is a perfect description of the thing, taken from *The Brothers Karamazof* by Fyodor Dostoevsky:

> Above all, do not lie to yourself. A man who lies to himself and listens to his own lie comes to a point where he does not discern any truth either in himself or anywhere around him, and thus falls into disrespect towards himself and others. Not respecting anyone, he ceases to love, and having no love, he gives himself up to the passions and coarse pleasures, in order to occupy and amuse himself, and in his vices reaches complete bestiality, and it all comes from lying continually to others and to himself.

But Paul says that there is an arsenal of weapons, empowered by God Himself, that can not only scale the walls of these fortresses – but can pulverize them into dust! This arsenal is the Word of God – the Holy Scriptures. The light of truth overcomes darkness, just as a light bulb inevitably lights up a totally dark room. Notice carefully what Paul says *will not work*: weapons of the flesh. No man-made argument or therapy will do the job. There may be some tools fashioned by us that can perhaps to some degree hold the abuser in check. But smash these forts of deception in his very mind? Never.

The weapons of Christ destroy *arguments* and every lofty *opinion* raised against the knowledge of God, taking every such enemy thought captive and bringing it into obedience to Christ.[121] And once again, we see the vital necessity that we become very, very familiar with the mentality and tactics of the abuser. Why? Because if we cannot identify the target, we will never hit it with our weapons! We need to know that the abuser has this huge fortress of entitlement and superiority in his thinking so that we can then destroy it with God's arguments – God's truth. You see the same point made by Paul in his letter to the Ephesians:

> ***Ephesians 6:10-12*** *Finally, be strong in the Lord and in the strength of his might. Put on the whole armor of God, that you may be able to stand against the schemes of the devil. For we do not wrestle against flesh and blood, but against the rulers, against the authorities, against the cosmic powers over this present darkness, against the spiritual forces of evil in the heavenly places.*

After describing the weapons in Christ's armory, Paul points us to the specific *offensive* weapon:

> ***Ephesians 6:16-17*** *In all circumstances take up the shield of faith, with which you can extinguish all the flaming darts of the evil one; and take the helmet of salvation, and the sword of the Spirit, which is the Word of God...*

Our sword is God's mighty, powerful Word which, according to the Apostle to the Hebrews, is able to penetrate right into the middle of these strongholds.

> ***Hebrews 4:12-13*** *For the word of God is living and active, sharper than any two-edged sword, piercing to the division of soul and of spirit, of joints*

121 The problem with Christianity-as-superstition is that people pay no heed to the "destroy *arguments* and every lofty *opinion*" part of that text, and instead mystically imagine that they can cast down the wrong thoughts in the Spirit World. This is so close to Theosophy and Paganism. Many self-styled "prayer warriors" truly believe they are engaging in spiritual warfare every time they use their active imagination in prayer. Other folk do "prayer walks" in the streets of cities, thinking they are tearing down strongholds! Satan must be chortling with laughter! Few Christians actually take the text in its plain literal sense: we must verbally challenge the false beliefs of false believers, refuting the false beliefs with the Word of God! This takes guts, grit and a sharp mind. (From a conversation with Barbara Roberts, 2012)

> *and of marrow, and discerning the thoughts and intentions of the heart. And no creature is hidden from his sight, but all are naked and exposed to the eyes of him to whom we must give account.*

What is the secret of the effectiveness of our weapons? *Exposure.* In essence, God's arsenal is *light* that shines so powerfully into the recesses of even the abuser's unconscious mind, that the lying, enslaving nature of these strongholds is exposed so that the man himself can see them for what they are. And that is when those walls "come tumblin' down." The whole process is empowered by the Spirit of Christ and if He chooses to grant repentance and faith, the captive is set free. The old abusive man dies in Christ and a new creation is raised up. Life as it was is over because Goliath is dead.

Our work with the abuser then is a labor of becoming wise to the psychology of sin. So wise that we can, as we are enabled by Christ, identify, demystify, and expose his tactics and the thinking that lies behind them, and then bring the battering ram of Christ's truth to bear. We must tell the abuser: "This is what you are doing right now, and this is the thinking in your mind that leads you to use this tactic. This is what God says about what you are doing. This is God's truth that needs to replace the lies you have embraced in your mind."

This is what the Scripture means when it tells us to take up the sword of the Spirit, which is the Word of God. And this is the abuser's (and every sinner's) only hope.

> ***Acts 9:1-4, 9*** *But Saul, still breathing threats and murder against the disciples of the Lord, went to the high priest and asked him for letters to the synagogues at Damascus, so that if he found any belonging to the Way, men or women, he might bring them bound to Jerusalem. Now as he went on his way, he approached Damascus, and suddenly a light from heaven flashed around him. And falling to the ground he heard a voice saying to him, "Saul, Saul, why are you persecuting me? ... And for three days he was without sight, and neither ate nor drank.*

Saul of Tarsus died. The Apostle Paul was born.

CHAPTER 14

The Abuser's Quest for Power in the Church

3 John 1:9-10 *I have written something to the church, but Diotrephes, who likes to put himself first, does not acknowledge our authority.*

Ed and Terri welcomed their new pastor with enthusiasm, volunteering to pick him up at the airport and take him to his temporary quarters at another church member's bed and breakfast. This was Pastor Rick Walker's first church after his graduation from Bible College and he was excited, energetic, and ready to bring the gospel to this community. He had dreamed of being a pastor since childhood, and both he and his parents were ecstatic that the Lord had called him to this church.

In three years, Rick would leave this place, discouraged, rejected and wondering if his call to serve Christ as a pastor was just his own imagination. Ed and Terri played a central role in his departure.

At first, Ed and Terri seemed to be not only genuine Christians, but also very mature ones, offering to help Pastor Rick in any way that they could. Ed talked with Rick often and Rick enjoyed their conversations about various Scripture passages and the teachings of numbers of popular and doctrinally sound Christian teachers. Both Ed and Terri professed a zeal for winning the community for Christ. They both served on boards of other Christian organizations as well.

Terri's ministry in the church seemed a bit odd. She taught the youth Sunday School class, but insisted that she do so during the regular worship service. This meant that the young people would never hear Pastor Rick's sermons. Terri said that the youth just cannot relate to adult sermons. But, as Rick thought, a new pastor cannot and should not try to change things overnight, and he was confident that as they worked together Terri would come to accept change.

Ed offered to meet weekly with Pastor Rick for prayer and Bible study. Rick looked forward to these sessions (being a pastor can be a lonely experience) and over time, he began to confide and trust in Ed. Ed seemed more than willing to hear about Rick's personal struggles and to "be there" for him.

And then the attack came.

A little over one year after Rick arrived, Terri publicly attacked him at a congregational meeting. Her youth class was going to begin a new study, and she had talked to Rick about it. She didn't specifically ask him to announce it from the pulpit, but it turns out that she expected it. When that did not happen, Terri's ire flamed. She sarcastically put Rick down in front of everyone for his negligence and proceeded to make the promotion herself.

After that Sunday, Ed and Terri were Rick's enemies. As Rick would later come to realize, they had been his enemies from the very beginning. Their "support" was nothing more than a strategy to control the new pastor; to gain his trust so that he would be their ally in their real mission. Ed and Terri wanted to be first in the church. The next two years of Rick's ministry would be misery and heartache, his efforts and preaching being constantly undermined by these two children of Diotrephes and those they gained as allies to their cause. Those allies included at least half of the church board. Rick was subjected to:

- Accusations that he lacked tact and Christian love in his dealings with people (this stemmed from a phone conversation with Terri which she terminated in anger and hung up on Rick).
- Accusations that Rick did not have a real pastor's heart for people.
- Terri garnering more support from the board and the congregation by using her favorite tactic of "playing the victim." Terri would launch her attacks against Rick, and then revert into the injured, wronged victim mode when Rick tried to correct or answer her. Terri loved to tell others that when she spoke with Rick, she "felt attacked."
- Ed and Terri, in a threatening countenance, told Rick and the board chairman that their previous church had harmed them greatly. So much so, in fact, that they could never trust a church board again. Once, when

the pastor and deacons requested that Ed and Terri sit down together with them and discuss Terri's ministry, they refused to do so and said that if the board insisted upon this, they would leave the church. The board, against the pastor's advice, chose to drop the matter.

- Conflict with Ed and Terri eventually reached such a level of severity the church board requested that a denominational representative come and act as a mediator. Of course, at least three of the four church board members saw the whole thing as a mere conflict between Pastor Rick and Terri, Rick being the primary problem. This lengthy process ended with the mediator siding with Ed and Terri, suggesting that Pastor Rick take some further training in the art of "dealing with difficult people." This "dynamic duo" successfully duped the mediator, just as they had duped Rick when he first arrived.
- After two more public attacks against his ministry style and preaching, Rick resigned from his pastorate. He was depressed, and his health was starting to fail him. Most people in the church were sad to see him leave. Two people, at least in part, understood what had really happened. Everyone else just accepted the fact that pastors move on, "called by the Lord" to another ministry.

Ed and Terri had won. They would be sure to express to the board more clearly this time just what kind of pastor this church needed. Rick, in their opinion, certainly had been one big mistake. To some degree, Rick now wondered that himself. Today, Rick is still unemployed, learning just how difficult it can be for a pastor to find a secular job. As of this writing, Rick is doubtful that he will ever be a pastor again, and wondering sometimes (though he knows it is wrong to question the Lord) about the power and goodness of Christ.

Incidentally, neither Ed nor Terri *were members of the church!* They did not believe in church membership, claiming that it was an unbiblical means of powerful, dominating men controlling others. No matter. Their power and control and their sense of entitlement to that power was sufficient to make most everyone else in the church cower and capitulate.

As I mentioned in the Introduction, I originally planned to entitle this book *In Search of Diotrephes*, because abusers, like Diotrephes, so effectively disguise themselves as "sheep" and hide in the local church. If you are a faithful pastor or church member, the probability that you have met one or both characters in this evil duo is quite high. In Scripture, Diotrephes and Jezebel were both abusers. Today, they still exist within many if not most churches. Masquerading as pious saints, they set themselves up in power and expect the pastor, the elders, and the people to do their bidding, all the while ready to punish any who resist them.

Diotrephes and Jezebel are bullies. They need a David with his slingshot and a full, courageous faith in the power of Christ to bring them down. The purpose of this chapter is to help pastors and Christians who have been or perhaps still are victims of abusers in the church to understand what is happening to them and to learn how to get free. Essentially, I will be applying what we have learned in previous chapters to the victimization of pastors and church members by abusers who choose the church as their arena of operation. For simplicity, I will focus only on the pastor as victim, but the reader can easily apply what we learn to others in the church.

Meet Diotrephes

At the beginning of this book I described how, in the process of studying the abuser and domestic violence, I realized that what I was reading was an accurate description of the mindset and methods of numbers of men and women I have encountered in the church. These are people who have caused great harm to Christ's flock, and in particular, to Christ's under-shepherds – *pastors.* Such people see themselves (as Diotrephes apparently did), as entitled to power and control over the flock, and thus regard their abusive tactics, which they use to gain and maintain power, as fully justified. This is one of the most common reasons pastors have short tenures in many churches. The church I presently pastor had a history of pastoral turnover that averaged about three years in the decades before I came, and that number would be much lower except for the eight year ministry of one man. A high pastoral turnover rate is desirable to the Diotrephes' ability to maintain his control.

Listen again as the Apostle John describes these diabolic characters:

> ***3 John 1:7-10*** *For they have gone out for the sake of the name, accepting nothing from the Gentiles. Therefore we ought to support people like these, that we may be fellow workers for the truth. I have written something to the*

church, but Diotrephes, who likes to put himself first, does not acknowledge our authority. So if I come, I will bring up what he is doing, talking wicked nonsense against us. And not content with that, he refuses to welcome the brothers, and also stops those who want to and puts them out of the church.

"Who likes to put himself first." That brief description perfectly paints a word picture of the abuser in the church. This is what it is all about for him. Notice what Diotrephes did, and continues to do today:

- He opposes genuine servants of Christ.
- He undermines the real work of Christ.
- He exercises an evil power and control over the flock of Christ.
- He slanders Christ's servants.
- He works to isolate Christ's people from genuine servants of Christ.
- He opposes the Word of Christ, not acknowledging the Apostles.
- He drives genuine believers out of the church.
- He is motivated by a craving to be *first.*

Sound familiar? Yet all too often such people are not dealt with as the Lord would have us deal with them. Notice what John says he is going to do about Diotrephes: *"So if I come, I will bring up what he is doing, talking wicked nonsense against us."* John is going to announce and expose! John was fearless and had a strong faith in the Chief Shepherd whom he served. Familiar with the tactics of the enemy, John was able to identify Diotrephes for exactly what he was.

The Worst of the Worst

2 Corinthians 11:20 *For you bear it if someone makes slaves of you, or devours you, or takes advantage of you, or puts on airs, or strikes you in the face.*

It is my conclusion that the Christian church faces the most devious abusers of all. Scripture warns us of this many times, cautioning us to carefully be on guard against wolves in sheep's clothing, to be expecting Satan's emissaries to come wrapped in a façade of righteousness. We are to carefully test teachers and teachings to see if they derive from the Spirit of Christ or not. In many ways then, we need to realize that the *most* deceptive of abusers will select *the church* as their disguise, all the while exercising an incredible intensity of hypocrisy and possessing a conscience that is dead. It is one thing for an abuser to operate in the realm of the non-Christian world, never making any claim to the name of Christ whatsoever, but what level of wickedness is required for a person to do the same under the guise of Christianity? The Apostle John would answer: "It takes the spirit of antichrist" (1 John 4:1-3). The preposition "anti" affixed to this word not only means "against," but it can also mean "instead of." The abuser in the church then is a representative of the "instead-of Christ." The counterfeit. And therefore I repeat my conclusion, *the "Christian" abuser is the worst of the worst.* And the most dangerous.

The Tactics

Essentially, all of the tactics of the abuser which have been described in this book are practiced by the Diotrephes (both men and women) within the local church:

- Blaming, false guilt.
- Re-writing the facts.
- Playing the victim.
- Pitting people against one another.
- Threatening in order to instill fear.
- Morphing the victim's words (and God's Word!).
- Accusing.
- Deceiving with a cloak of excessive charm.
- Gathering allies.
- Particularly targeting the pastor and other genuine believers who are active in the Lord's work. (Sometimes Diotrephes is the pastor himself. An entirely new dynamic of abuse occurs in such a case).

And there are many more. Satan has an impressive array of weapons and schemes, but it is not an infinite arsenal. We *can* become familiar with his tactics and recognize them for what they are, naming them and countering them with the truth.

One of the earliest attacks to be expected from an abuser in the church (if his or her charm doesn't work), is that his ire is raised against anyone who opposes him. You see this described in the case of Diotrephes who would expel his opponents from the church. It's his way or the highway. As soon as he senses that someone (a new pastor, for example) is even questioning his program, he goes into attack mode with the intent of crushing all opposition.

As Anne Pike so accurately notes, the abuser is very jealous of his power and control, and this jealousy impels him to particularly target a "popular" person.[122] In the case of the local church, that target is often the pastor. Diotrephes goes into "search mode" to find vulnerabilities in his victim upon which he can focus his attacks. If the pastor refuses to yield, which most often means a refusal to exalt the abuser, the level of attack will increase. Alternating between his disguise as a kind, caring and empathetic saint, and his real identity, the abuser will work tirelessly to maintain his holy image, and if that means destroying the pastor's ministry or reputation, so be it. This is probably the primary reason that a Diotrephes is able to obtain power over an entire church in the first place. He constantly sends out "vibes" that communicate to everyone what will happen if they oppose him. In other words, he reigns by *fear*.

The abuser in the church further solidifies his power by building a support base. Like a bully on the playground, he has his "associates" beside him whom he controls and manipulates. Sometimes this infection can spread to virtually the entire congregation in a local church. Those who are wise enough to see through the abuser's façade will also become targets. Very often then, in fact normally, a pastor may find himself standing virtually alone. I remember speaking with some church board members regarding a person who was abusive to her husband and who practiced her controlling tactics in the church as well. I told them they needed to stand up to her, confront her with her sin, and call her to repentance. They actually responded to me by saying, "But if we do that, she will divide the church. Besides, this is a small town and the fallout would be just too costly." I think neither the Apostle John nor Christ Himself would commend them for that refusal.

Fear of the abuser, as it spreads through the church, will infect people like a disease until they unwittingly become his allies. The fear instilled in them will make them defensive and suspicious of the victim, eventually even coming to the point of wishing that the victim would just "go away." Sadly, many times this is exactly what happens. The pastor leaves. Diotrephes remains. The children are alienated. Once again, Ann Pike is very perceptive when she writes that abusers make it very costly and difficult for people to support the victim, even if they see what is really happening. They know that they themselves will become a

122 Pike, 30-32.

target if they stand for what is right. Blend in a good dose of confusion and deception about what is really going on and most people will not be able to tell who the abuser is and who the victim is. The whole clash will be written off to a "personality conflict," or "the pastor just tried to change things too quickly." Yes, there certainly can be genuine personality clashes. And new pastors can try to effect change too quickly. But in the scenario of a Diotrephes, neither of these issues is the real problem.

Still another common tactic of the abuser is evidenced in his reaction to newcomers to the church. Eager to quickly project himself to them as the most eminent saint they have ever met, he will zero in on them very quickly. This gives him the appearance of being a real people-lover who delights in exercising biblical hospitality and love. In fact, he is merely working to recruit the new folks to his team, and is often quite successful. To quote Anne Pike once more as she describes the abuser who is a psychopath:

> There are therapists who refuse to treat psychopaths, attorneys who will not take a case if the opposing counsel is a psychopath and teachers who remain silent if they know the parent is vindictive. This causes us to have a limited support structure at a time when we need help the most. This keeps us somewhat isolated and this works to the psychopath's advantage as he can hurt you more easily when you are alone and vulnerable.[123]

But what is Christ's commission to His people? We are to stand against evil no matter what the cost. He calls us to be wise to the schemes of the enemy and to oppose Diotrephes. That is what the Apostle John announced he was going to do. Shepherds do not abandon the flock when the wolf comes because real pastors are not hirelings (John 10). The genuine Christian's desire to obey Christ must overcome all fear. In fact, I would suggest that *it will overcome all fear.* How many local churches persist in letting a Diotrephes rule simply because, dare we say it, *most of the people in the church are not real Christians at all?* Is that too judgmental? Well, listen to our King's own words:

> ***Matthew 10:34-38*** *Do not think that I have come to bring peace to the earth. I have not come to bring peace, but a sword. For I have come to set a man against his father, and a daughter against her mother, and a daughter-*

123 Pike, 59-60.

in-law against her mother-in-law. And a person's enemies will be those of his own household. Whoever loves father or mother more than me is not worthy of me, and whoever loves son or daughter more than me is not worthy of me. And whoever does not take his cross and follow me is not worthy of me.

And here are John's thoughts on the matter. Does this sound like people who refuse to stand up for truth and defend the victim just because they will suffer for doing it?

1 John 4:4-8 *Little children, you are from God and have overcome them, for he who is in you is greater than he who is in the world. They are from the world; therefore they speak from the world, and the world listens to them. We are from God. Whoever knows God listens to us; whoever is not from God does not listen to us. By this we know the Spirit of truth and the spirit of error. Beloved, let us love one another, for love is from God, and whoever loves has been born of God and knows God. Anyone who does not love does not know God, because God is love.*

The Effects of Abuse on the Pastor

Just as the tactics of the abuser in a domestic setting are also used in other environments, such as the church, so the effects of abuse on victims are very much parallel as well. This means that a pastor, for example, can benefit greatly by studying the non-physical, psychological tactics and effects of abuse in particular. He will be enabled to see what injuries he has sustained, wounds that can be significantly hindering his ability to shepherd God's people as effectively as he could be, though he probably has not even been aware of them. Ultimately, if the abuse continues, the pastor may conclude that he was never called by Christ to the pastorate in the first place and give up, deeming himself as a failure and weighed down with false guilt. Here is Pastor Martin Bleby's description of his experience of awakening to the effects of abusive power and control upon him:

"I have felt like that!"

What is it that reduces a grown man, warm in his relationships and acknowledged by others to be experienced and competent in his life's work, to such a threatening state of self-doubt and disablement, in a moment? Why this sense of stress and nameless anxiety, this churning of my stomach?

> How come I now lie awake at night, just from having to think about it? What makes it difficult for me now to perform the simplest tasks, or to face other people with evenness of spirit?
>
> I had experienced this only a few times in my life, each time lasting only a matter of days, but each time quite devastating, and puzzling. Now I was beginning to understand. I was at a training session on 'Power and Trust', run by our church organization. We were going through how it feels to be bullied, where someone with whom you are in a relationship of respect, affection and trust brings undue pressure to bear on you through that relationship, in a way that leaves you feeling disempowered. I recognized it immediately, and it rang bells for me. It was good to realize that it had not been just my own inadequacy and deficiency, but something that happens in relationships when the real power that is there is put to inappropriate use.
>
> I was then able to identify and recognize other situations where this dynamic could be seen to be operating. I determined to find out more about it. In particular, how could this misuse of power arise in the church, and how is it addressed by the Scriptures and the gospel? I attended a conference on "Bullying and Abuse in the Church" where I became more aware of the widespread nature of the misuse of power in relationships, and of the considerable range of ways it was being tackled, not only in the church, but also in the secular society. There I realized that I had not been bullied as such, since the definition requires that this behavior be sustained over a prolonged period of time, but that I had been subjected, and had submitted, to bullying treatment.[124]

I have observed a rather curious phenomenon among pastors: they usually don't want to talk about these things. I am not certain why. Perhaps it is because a pastor is supposed to be a giant of faith or because of some faulty notion that to acknowledge these issues is to admit weakness or failure. Once, when I was a relatively new pastor, I remember writing a letter to the head of our denomination, giving him an honest report of the state of affairs in our church. I included the fact that I was finding the injuries sustained in pastoral ministry to be far more difficult to deal with than those I ever sustained as a police officer.

124 Martin Bleby, "Power in Relationships: Issues of Love and Control," http://www.newcreation.org.au/books/pdf/418_Power_Relations.pdf, 2008, Introduction.

While I was expecting a supportive and understanding reaction I was shocked by his response. Essentially, he said that it is wrong to think about such things and he did not want to hear anymore about it. Either that man was incredibly foolish, or an abuser himself!

What are some signs and symptoms that can suggest that a pastor is the victim of a Diotrephes?

- **A loss of personhood**. Diotrephes has a huge ego, big enough to suck his victim's own personhood into it. A pastor who is dominated and abused will begin to think only of what the abuser wants. A victim's very existence comes to be only for the use of the abuser. Choices, feelings, and other personal qualities and functions lose personal meaning.
- **A mind dominated by the presence of the abuser.** Along with the loss of personal personhood comes a loss of personal thought. If the pastor finds himself being drawn to "what will Diotrephes think?" then these are indicators of unhealthy dominance. Christ's will and Word fade as the mind is overcome by the abuser's will and word. Victims might be shocked if they could track the amount of time each day in which their thoughts are filled with the presence of the abuser.
- **Erosion of his ability to focus his thoughts, prayers, and energies upon the flock.** Abuse victims are dominated by the abuser, just as the abuser desires them to be. Victims are pre-occupied with their abuser out of necessity to guard against their attacks and schemes. This precipitates a nasty, vicious cycle that serves the abuser quite well. People in the congregation begin to wonder why their pastor does not seem to care about them. He doesn't even seem to know the names of the children, nor does he visit them very often. And they are right. A pastor who is being dominated by an abuser simply loses the energy and focus that is necessary to care for his flock. Unfortunately, the real cause and culprit of this failure is rarely understood and the pastor himself is blamed. In fact, *pastors victimized in this manner often do not even realize what is happening to them and they begin to blame themselves for not having more of "a pastor's heart."*
- **A loss of confidence.** A pastor may enter the ministry with great confidence and vision. His faith is strong and he is ready to serve Christ like a Joshua. But gradually, under the power of a Diotrephes, that

confidence fades. Constant criticism, character attacks and accusations take their toll, especially when they are launched from behind the disguise of an eminent "saint." The crazy-making methods we discussed earlier serve to create self-doubt in one's abilities to lead the church.

- **Loss of enthusiasm.** Originally full of zeal, in love with his calling, life under Diotrephes can become an existence of just trying to survive from week to week. Sermon preparation, once the pastor's greatest love, can become an almost impossible chore.
- **A sense of isolation.** As is true with the domestic abuse victim, so it is with the pastor. Loss of self, loss of confidence and enthusiasm work to isolate the victim, serving as more ammunition yet for the abuser's accusations that the pastor "just isn't good with people." Diotrephes' methods work to destroy a victim's willingness to entrust himself to others because it is often Diotrephes himself to whom the pastor first extends that trust, only to have it eventually used against him. Abusers consider confession of personal struggles as a sign of weakness and make careful note of these vulnerable areas for future attack. Jane Middelton-Moz describes how the shaming tactics of the abuser work toward isolation of the victim. As the shaming continues and is internalized by the victim (because there is no one to talk to about it), isolation increases. A person who is shamed into believing that she is uniquely worthless is simply not going to connect in relationships.[125]
- **A burden of guilt and sense of failure.** The abuser is all too happy to permit his victim to bear the blame. Abusers are divisive people in the church; just as they work to turn family members against one another in a domestic setting, so they work their same sorcery in the church family. And they are quite masterful at convincing everyone, including the pastor, that this division and unpleasantness is all his fault.

Confronting Diotrephes

Acts 13:8-10 *But Elymas the magician* (for that is the meaning of his name*) opposed them, seeking to turn the proconsul away from the faith. But Saul, who was also called Paul, filled with the Holy Spirit, looked intently*

125 Jane Middleton-Moz, *Shame and Guilt: The Masters of Disguise* (Deerfield Beach, Florida: Health Communications, Inc., 1990), 282-284.

at him and said, "You son of the devil, you enemy of all righteousness, full of all deceit and villainy, will you not stop making crooked the straight paths of the Lord?

While we would like to be able to strike the modern-day Elymas blind like Paul did, the Lord does not seem to grant us this same ability today![126] We have not been left defenseless by any means, but our ignorance of the enemy and of our own arsenal is defeating us. What can we do to turn the tide? We must know our enemy and we must know our weapons.

1. Know your enemy. In large part, this book is written to familiarize Christ's people with the nature and tactics of our enemy. The character and methods of Diotrephes are so similar to those of the domestic abuser (indeed, Diotrephes is often a domestic abuser as well) that the study of the one reveals the other. The first thing to do then is to set ourselves to the study of this thing we are calling abuse. As you learn, you will be pleasantly surprised, I believe, to realize just how often God's Word speaks to instruct us on this very subject. Somehow we have failed to connect the dots and realize that *this is the very kind of person the Lord has been warning us about all along*. The study of abuse turns out to be the study of the psychology of sin itself.

To know our enemy, *we must first acknowledge his existence*. I finished my seminary education in my mid-forties, later than most pastoral ministry students. I already had a dozen or more years of experience, unlike most of my fellow classmates and I discovered something quite strange during those seminary years. When I would tell the other students stories of my experiences as a pastor, they were frequently dumbfounded. I told them, for instance, of a ring-leader who led ten of his followers into one of my first church's congregational meetings and threatened to lead his party out of the church if his demands were not met. They had never heard anything like that. Or there was the rebellion incident during a worship service after I called the church to repentance from widespread sin. Their jaws dropped. Certainly nothing like this was being taught to them in their seminary classes!

126 However, Diotrephes should take careful note: Christ is still mighty and He is quite capable of dealing with His enemies now as He did then. One thing is certain, the Day is coming when He will deal with His enemies. The Psalmist's admonition to the kings of the earth is an appropriate warning for the abuser of Christ's people: *Kiss the Son, lest he be angry, and you perish in the way, for his wrath is quickly kindled.*

How can it be, in light of the truth that we have in the Scriptures, that the existence of Diotrephes in the local church is a shock to us? Somehow, we don't want to believe it and many churches just don't want to hear about these "negative" things. We seem to believe that if Korah shows up in our church, we should listen carefully to his complaints, reach a compromise of some type, and hug each other! After all we tell ourselves, Korah's problem isn't that he is actually a wicked man, it's that he is a misunderstood man. And we have to admit, we have our own problems too!

Our Lord told us how it would be:

> ***Luke 6:22-23*** *"Blessed are you when people hate you and when they exclude you and revile you and spurn your name as evil, on account of the Son of Man! Rejoice in that day, and leap for joy, for behold, your reward is great in heaven; for so their fathers did to the prophets.*
>
> ***2 Timothy 3:12*** *Indeed, all who desire to live a godly life in Christ Jesus will be persecuted,*

The pastor who does not have a firm grasp on this fact, namely, that the world will treat him exactly like it treated Christ and the Apostle Paul and every other true Christian, is a pastor who is going to be very confused when Diotrephes does his evil work on him. We are not better than our Master! As I look back on my seminary training, I really cannot think of a single course that addressed these facts. It is almost as if speaking of topics like this is "taboo." God does not agree.

The pastoral ministry is rarely "pastoral." It is a battlefield, and that is exactly how Christ pictures it for us in His Word. He said that He told us the truth about how the world is going to hate us in order that when it happens, *we will be kept from falling away.* Apparently, Jesus thought it was pretty important for every Christian and in particular every pastor, to know this before experiencing something like the following story, as told by a pastor:

> A parishioner repeatedly berated me for not living up to his ideals of pastoral leadership. He believed my pastoral leadership should be based on models contrary to my Christian tradition and understanding. When I tried to explain and work with him, he refused to listen, rejected my ideas and put all the onus on me for our church not growing. He refused to believe

that his negativity about me to the parish and his personal ranting against our bishop, former members and some visitors had anything to do with us not growing. While during this nearly two-year long experience, the church welcomed several new members whom I had personally spent time with and encouraged to become members. During this time, the only person he ever brought to a Sunday worship service, he personally told never to come back, allegedly because she might have been attracted to him as a single lady, he was married. At no time was I ever consulted on dealing with any possible improprieties for discipline within the church.

Finally, after going behind my back and demeaning me in personal conversations to over half of the congregation, he demanded I meet with him at his home with two of his friends in order to instruct me on what I must do to live up to his expectations. I refused, but offered to let him provide a list of his complaints in writing after which I would arrange to meet him at the church alone or with his wife. He never came back to the church.

> ***John 16:1-4*** *I have said all these things to you to keep you from falling away. They will put you out of the synagogues. Indeed, the hour is coming when whoever kills you will think he is offering service to God. And they will do these things because they have not known the Father, nor me. But I have said these things to you, that when their hour comes you may remember that I told them to you. I did not say these things to you from the beginning, because I was with you.*

2. Know your weapons. Once we acknowledge the existence of the enemy and familiarize ourselves with his tactics, we are ready to bring our weapons to bear upon him. That is what the Apostle Paul did to Elymas the magician. He turned to him, announced to everyone exactly what Elymas was and what he was doing. That is how we need to handle Diotrephes. I ask again, does that sound too harsh? Well,

> ***Galatians 1:6-9*** *I am astonished that you are so quickly deserting him who called you in the grace of Christ and are turning to a different gospel--not that there is another one, but there are some who trouble you and want to distort the gospel of Christ. But even if we or an angel from heaven should preach to you a gospel contrary to the one we preached to you, let him be accursed. As we have said before, so now I say again: If anyone is preaching to you a gospel contrary to the one you received, let him be accursed.*

Abusers in the church inevitably preach a gospel contrary to the true gospel of Christ. Their message is one of self-exaltation. They are not out to bring glory to Jesus Christ, but to themselves. They are enemies of the souls of our people and must be dealt with as such. Remember who we are talking about. These are people who:

- Have an entitlement mindset, seeing themselves as superior to everyone else.
- Insist upon having power and control over others.
- Justify their abusive tactics used to enforce that power and control.

Diotrephes rejected the true servants of Christ (thus rejecting their message as well), and ex-communicated anyone who tried to defend them. He didn't want bold believers in the church because they would expose him. Why? Because he wanted to be first. That is what we mean by entitlement. He preferred the church to be full of lukewarm, weak, pseudo-Christians because they gave him a stage on which he could strut his stuff. Therefore the abuser really is a wolf in sheep's clothing.

The Apostle Paul spoke of his weapons. We discussed the nature of these weapons in chapter 13 (Cf. 2 Corinthians 10). There is also another important New Testament text that deals with our weapons, also written by Paul:

> ***Ephesians 6:10-18*** *Finally, be strong in the Lord and in the strength of his might. Put on the whole armor of God, that you may be able to stand against the schemes of the devil. For we do not wrestle against flesh and blood, but against the rulers, against the authorities, against the cosmic powers over this present darkness, against the spiritual forces of evil in the heavenly places. Therefore take up the whole armor of God, that you may be able to withstand in the evil day, and having done all, to stand firm. Stand therefore, having fastened on the belt of truth, and having put on the breastplate of righteousness, and, as shoes for your feet, having put on the readiness given by the gospel of peace. In all circumstances take up the shield of faith, with which you can extinguish all the flaming darts of the evil one; and take the helmet of salvation, and the sword of the Spirit, which is the word of God, praying at all times in the Spirit, with all prayer and supplication. To that end keep alert with all perseverance, making supplication for all the saints…*

We cannot deal exhaustively with this passage here, but let's at least look carefully at some of the key points:

1. **The abuser is not harmless**. Behind him are the schemes of Satan himself and his demonic minions. They aren't low-ranking soldiers either. They are rulers, authorities, and powers. Fred, the stalwart "pillar" of the church may look like Fred, but Paul pulls back the veil here and shows us what is energizing him. Abuse is a particularly Satanic evil. It expresses the very defining qualities of Satan: lying, accusing, destroying, and deceiving, as any domestic abuse victim will readily acknowledge.
2. **We are called to *stand* against him.** We are to withstand him. We are to wrestle him. There can be no conscientious objectors or pacifists in this battle. Christ does not give us this option. Every Christian is in the battle. You can be a naked, weaponless soldier, or you can be an armored soldier with weapons at hand! Either way, you are in this battle.
3. **If we are going to do this battle, we must put on God's armor.** Now, think carefully about this for a moment. Just how familiar with the armor of God is the average Christian? Or even the average pastor? If you are a pastor, you have probably even preached on this subject, maybe putting a Roman soldier drawing up on the overhead. And yet, we still fall prey to Diotrephes. Why? I suggest:
    - We don't believe that we really have a Diotrephes among us.
    - We don't think we need this armor, so we don't use it.
    - We have been taught that the armor is something we should don like a garment each morning in our prayer time, so we've been dutifully visualizing the symbolic images of the armor, but we've never understood the reality behind the symbols. We have never really learned what it the armor is, let alone how to use it.

I very much hope that having read to this point, the reader is convinced that there *is* an enemy, that there *is* a battle, and that we seriously need to get a handle on the weapons with which God has provided us. Because we really are not doing very well in this battle! If Satan is truly prowling around us like a roaring lion looking for an easy lunch, why are we still leaving the flock and ourselves unprotected? When I used to walk through the mountains in Alaska, I always took some firepower along. I knew there were both moose (nasty critters they can be!) and grizzly bears. I don't seem to be that smart when it comes to this spiritual warfare, which is every bit as real and far, far more dangerous.

Let's consider a general overview of our arsenal. Notice that the defensive pieces are all assigned to protect our vulnerable parts and to expose and attack those of the enemy:

- Belt of truth.
- Breastplate of righteousness.
- Readiness given by the gospel of peace.
- Shield of faith.
- Helmet of salvation.
- Sword of the Spirit, the Word of God.
- Persevering, alert prayer.

These are not imaginary or mystical items. They are very, very real. And they are *mighty*! They work! In fact, the powers of hell cannot stand against them. He who is in us really is greater than he who is in the world (1 John 4:4).

It would be profitable to take the time, if we could, to carefully relate each one of these armor pieces to the battle against the abuser. But that will have to wait for another time. Let me just summarize in general the nature of the armor and how to put it on and use it. Here is my theory, and I believe it is correct:

> The armor of God is Jesus Christ. He is truth (John 14:6); He is our righteousness (1 Corinthians 1:30); He is the subject of the gospel of peace which we proclaim and thereby overcome the world (1 Corinthians 1:17-18); He is the source of our faith (Eph 2:8ff); He is our salvation (Acts 4:12); and He is the Word of God, the sword of the Spirit (John 1:1ff). To put on the armor of God, we must put on Christ (Romans 3:12-14).

Here are the perfect instructions for putting on the armor: *put on the Lord Jesus Christ*, just as Paul says. They are the very same words the Spirit of Christ used to smash down the fortresses in the mind of Augustine and bring him to repentance and faith:

> ***Romans 13:12-14*** *The night is far gone; the day is at hand. So then let us cast off the works of darkness and put on the armor of light. Let us walk properly as in the daytime, not in orgies and drunkenness, not in sexual immorality and sensuality, not in quarreling and jealousy. But put on the*

Lord Jesus Christ, and make no provision for the flesh, to gratify its desires.

When Diotrephes looks at and hears a pastor who has put on the Lord Jesus Christ, rejected the world and refused to yield to the desires of his sinful flesh, thereby keeping a clear conscience, that abuser *is going down!* Like the devil, he will roar and accuse and lash out, but he cannot stand, just as darkness cannot dispel light.

Final Helps for the Battle

I cannot leave off this chapter without adding a few more points about recognizing and dealing with an abuser in the church who, like Diotrephes, is on a mission to be first. My goal, as I hope the reader understands, is particularly to help the *pastor* who is the target of this evil and who, perhaps, is feeling that he is neither qualified for nor capable of persevering in his ministry. Here are some things I have learned and which have helped me greatly. It took me nearly 30 years to learn them!

- Like all abusers, Diotrephes is quite shallow. He is skilled at creating a façade and convincing us that he has deep theological knowledge and insight. *He does not!* If you press him on a subject, his 'great learning" will break down and turn to nonsense. So we must not be intimidated by some "pillar" of the church who so confidently expounds on his chosen topic. Remember, he is wearing a mask, and masks are only skin-deep, if that.
- Diotrephes is a child in his level of maturity. He is selfish and given to the instability of tantrums. Watch for these telltale qualities in some supposed spiritual "giant" in your church. When he does not get his way, you may well find yourself watching a full-grown man or woman "pitching a fit" as they say down in the South. Genuine, godly men and women simply do not do this.
- Abusers seeking to be "first" in the church target the pastor because they are jealous of the power and control they perceive the pastor to have (which of course, a true undershepherd of Christ does not crave). They will use one or more of the following approaches:
  1. **The Flatterer**. "Oh, pastor, the Lord used you in a mighty way this morning! I have never heard a sermon that powerful. May the blessings of Jesus be upon you!" (Those are the exact words used by such a person to me, by the way). The abuser is using flattery

to put himself off as an eminent saint, *and to draw you into trusting him!* Pastors, including myself, need to realize that *no sermon we will ever preach warrants that kind of praise!* The person is being deceitful and that for an evil purpose. The individual who showered me with this praise abruptly left the church when he was informed that, as a newcomer, he would be interviewed soon by the elders so that we could learn more about him, about his Christian testimony, and about his church background.

2. **The Concerned Citizen.** "Pastor, I just need to speak with you for a moment about a concern that I have." I believe I can accurately say that virtually every time I have ever heard those words, an accusation followed. Feigning a genuine concern for the cause of Christ, the abuser uses this deceptive tactic to launch what is actually a wicked, discouraging accusation. *If you feel a fearful, uneasy knot "in your gut" when someone does this, recognize that you are feeling this way for a valid reason.* I recommend that we tell the person "I think it would be best if you speak to myself and the elders at the same time." Be very careful of the "phone call." When we receive a telephone call, we seem to sense some pressure to immediately answer questions put to us and deal with criticisms or charges made by the caller before we hang up. That is a mistake. *As soon as you feel that 'pang' of fear or sense that you are talking to an unsafe person,* take a deep breath and slow down. Very often your feelings will tip you off before your thoughts will! And, as we have seen, answers given or decisions made out of fear are rarely good ones.
3. **The Setup.** Abusive, entitled individuals often work to "set up" the pastor for criticism. We see this in the tactics of the Pharisees trying to trick Jesus and back Him into a no-win corner. When we see someone doing this, we need to recognize what is happening and understand that we are speaking to a Diotrephes. Set-up scenarios are most often launched in front of other people in the church. Unlike most abuser tactics, which are wrapped in secrecy, this particular maneuver is designed to publicly discredit the pastor. "Now Pastor, I thought that everyone is welcome in Christ's church, isn't that right?" These words, spoken by a person out of evil motive, are really an

attack against the pastor and church for dealing with an unrepentant individual. They are designed to exalt the questioner, to discredit the pastor, and to gain allies. The best way to respond is *to not respond.* By this, I don't mean not saying anything, but rather not permitting yourself to be drawn into a question which is really an accusation. Once more I would recommend telling the person "That is a question that myself and the elders will be happy to respond to. When would you like to meet with all of us?"

4. **The Friend.** As we have learned, abusers are masters of disguise. Sometimes unmasking the abuser takes a very long time. With the knowledge presented in this book, we hope that this time frame will be shortened, but still, sin remains very deceptive. This is probably what Paul was instructing Timothy about:

   1 Timothy 5:22-25 *Do not be hasty in the laying on of hands, nor take part in the sins of others; keep yourself pure....the sins of some men are conspicuous, going before them to judgment, but the sins of others appear later. So also good works are conspicuous, and even those that are not cannot remain hidden.*

   I must admit that I have been far too trusting of people over the years, sometimes naively embracing them as genuine Christian brothers or sisters, only to regret the outcome. I do not enjoy having to think that someone just may be a wolf in sheep's clothing. But this is reality. Remember, as the pastor of your church *you* are going to be sought out by abusers who will try to win you as their adoring ally. So let us beware when someone quickly speaks well of us.

Having carefully considered the nature and mentality of abuse, the tactics of the abuser, and its evil effects on the victim, we are now in a position to deal with a question that is the source of much of the injustice being worked upon victims who ask for our help: Does God permit an abused spouse to divorce their abuser? I approach this subject with "fear and trembling, yet with confidence. As David Instone-Brewer said as he set out to deal with this same question, ".... *we no longer burn heretics – which is fortunate for me, because some of you will conclude that I am one!*"[127]

127 David Instone-Brewer, *Divorce and Remarriage in the Church: Biblical Solutions for Pastoral Realities* (Downers Grove: InterVarsity Press, 2003), Location 181 Kindle Edition.

Psalm 18:16-19 *He sent from on high, he took me; he drew me out of many waters. He rescued me from my strong enemy and from those who hated me, for they were too mighty for me. They confronted me in the day of my calamity, but the LORD was my support. He brought me out into a broad place; he rescued me, because he delighted in me.*

CHAPTER 15

What About Divorce?

I John, in the presence of God and these witnesses, take you Janelle, to be my wedded wife. To have and to hold, from this day forward, for better, for worse, for richer, for poorer, in sickness or in health, to love and to cherish 'till death do us part. And hereto I pledge you my faithfulness.

"Although the corruption of man be such as is apt to study arguments, unduly to put asunder those whom God hath joined together in marriage; yet nothing but adultery, or such willful desertion as can no way be remedied by the Church or civil magistrate, is cause sufficient of dissolving the bond of marriage…". (Westminster Confession of Faith*)*

Abuse is not a biblical cause for divorce. A woman may have to find shelter and protection through her church, but she has not been given the right by God to divorce her abuser. (John MacArthur, Jr., Pastor*)*[128]

"Persons remarried after divorce will forego positions of official leadership at Bethlehem which correspond to the role of elders or deacons (1 Timothy 3:2, 12*)." (John Piper, Pastor)*[129]

---

128 John MacArthur, "Key Questions About the Family, Grace to You Website, http://www.gty.org/resources/positions/p00/answering-the-key-questions-about-the-family.

129 John Piper, "A Statement on Divorce & Remarriage in the Life of Bethlehem Baptist Church," (Desiring God Website,1989), http://www.desiringgod.org/resource-library/articles/a-statement-on-divorce-remarriage-in-the-life-of-bethlehem-baptist-church

"Yes, no, maybe… what was the question again?"

That phrase sums up the dilemma in which the abuse victim finds herself when she seeks to know what God says about divorcing her abuser. Normally, the Christian victim will go to her pastor, read books written on the topic by respected Christian teachers, or ask for the advice of her Christian friends. Unfortunately, she does not hear a clear note, but a chaotic dissonance of opinions. At best she will be confused. At worst, which is sadly very often the case, her burden and suffering are greatly increased by what she is told. Listen to some of the titles of Christian books written on divorce and you will get a hint of the confusion:

- *The Divorce Dilemma: God's Last Word on Lasting Commitment*, by John MacArthur
- *Not Under Bondage: Biblical Divorce for Abuse, Adultery & Desertion*, by Barbara Roberts
- *Marriage, Divorce, and Remarriage in the Bible: A Fresh Look at What the Scripture Teaches*, by Jay E. Adams
- *Divorce and Remarriage: A Permanence View*, by Wingerd, Elliff, Chrisman, and Burchett

The first in this list maintains that divorce is permissible for adultery or for desertion by an unbelieving spouse. God's "last word" according to Pastor MacArthur is that the victim of the evils we have been learning about in this book *is not justified in divorcing her tormentor.* The second says that divorce is permitted for adultery, desertion and abuse – understanding abuse as a kind of desertion. The third book allows divorce for adultery and desertion. It is not clear whether Adams would permit or forbid divorce in cases of abuse, because he does not discuss abuse.

In the fourth book, Jim Elliff and the other elders of Christ Fellowship Church in Kansas City propose and practice what they call the "permanence-view": no divorce, no remarriage for any reason at all as long as one's spouse is still living. They will bring church discipline upon those in their congregation who violate this position.[130] As I scanned the internet for reviews and responses to Elliff's permanence-view, I saw that many were quite favorable, even raving

130 Daryl Wingerd, Jim Ellif, Jim Chrisman, and Steve Burchett , *Divorce and Remarriage: A Permanence View* (Kansas City: Christian Communicators Worldwide, 2009), 6.

about how clear this position has made everything for them. But it is grievous to read this through the eyes of an abuse victim. The permanence-view can only be held by people who are clueless regarding the real nature of abuse, as I hope that the reader of this book can now understand. Permanence-view pastors and Christians may be well-meaning in their zeal for God, but it is zeal without knowledge, and it is working great injustice and harm.[131]

So, which is it? If an abuse victim divorces her abuser, is she a sinner to be excommunicated from the church, handed over to Satan so that she might be taught "not to blaspheme," or does Christ permit her to be free? The issue here is not whether church discipline in general is biblical: it plainly is, as we maintained in the earlier chapter on dealing with the abuser. The question is simply, is divorce of an abuser by his victim *sin*, or is it *right?* As the reader has no doubt already guessed, we maintain that *it is right and that it is justice to tell victims they can be free.*

Lost in the Trees, but Missing the Forest

> ***Matthew 12:7*** *And if you had known what this means, 'I desire mercy, and not sacrifice,' you would not have condemned the guiltless.*

"The trouble with most theologies of divorce is that they aren't sensible. They may give a reasonable account of most of the texts, in a forced way, but their conclusions just aren't practical in the fallen world we inhabit."[132]

---

131 In *The Divorce Myth* (1981), J Carl Laney presents his thesis that divorce is only permitted where the spouses are closely related by kinship. Adultery and desertion (let alone abuse) don't qualify, and divorce and remarriage are adultery because the original marriage is still intact from God's perspective. Remarried divorcees are to be subject to church discipline. In *Jesus and Divorce* (1984), Gordon Wenham and William Heth maintained that divorce is not permitted for adultery and that all remarriage is forbidden. This book is still on sale despite the fact that Heth has changed his mind and accepts divorce for adultery and desertion, and (after *Not Under Bondage* by Roberts changed his mind) he now accepts abuse as a ground for divorce. Heth's commendation on the back cover of *Not Under Bondage* says, "This book removed the scales from my eyes and brought me face to face with the plight of victims of abuse." Typifying how confused the church is about divorce, *Jesus and Divorce* continues to be sold nearly 30 years later, despite the fact that one of its authors has completely disavowed what he originally wrote.

132 Instone-Brewer, *Divorce and Remarriage in the Church: Biblical Solutions for Pastoral Realities*, Location 102 Kindle Edition.

The Pharisees and scribes were, apparently, careful students of the Scriptures. And yet they missed it. They completely missed the greater things, like the fact that the Lord desires *mercy* even more than sacrifice. As a result, these scholars ended up misapplying the Word of God and condemning the innocent. Matthew tells us about it:

> ***Matthew 12:1-7*** *At that time Jesus went through the grain fields on the Sabbath. His disciples were hungry, and they began to pluck heads of grain and to eat. But when the Pharisees saw it, they said to him, "Look, your disciples are doing what is not lawful to do on the Sabbath." He said to them, "Have you not read what David did when he was hungry, and those who were with him: how he entered the house of God and ate the bread of the Presence, which it was not lawful for him to eat nor for those who were with him, but only for the priests? Or have you not read in the Law how on the Sabbath the priests in the temple profane the Sabbath and are guiltless? I tell you, something greater than the temple is here. And if you had known what this means, 'I desire mercy, and not sacrifice,' you would not have condemned the guiltless…"*

Mark adds this great summation in his record of the very same incident:

> ***Mark 2:27-28*** *And he said to them, "The Sabbath was made for man, not man for the Sabbath. So the Son of Man is lord even of the Sabbath."*

I don't know if Bible scholars have a name for the principle that I am about to propose to you. It is similar, I suppose, to what we call "the analogy of Scripture." I will just call it the *"Don't forget the Big Picture"* principle of Bible interpretation, or maybe *"The parts must always agree with the sum."* The Pharisees' detailed interpretations of the Sabbath did not add up to the greater, overarching principle that God desires mercy and that the Sabbath was made for man. As a result, they focused only on sacrifice and ended up reversing the very purpose of the Sabbath. Their practice was the very opposite of God's provision of the Sabbath, which *was given for the good of man.* To the Pharisees, the Sabbath was so exalted that man was made its slave. That which was good and refreshing was made into an oppressive tyrant.

It is my contention that this is the very thing that has happened in the evangelical church in regard to marriage and divorce. Yes, I realize that there are evangelical "libertines" who do not hold diligently enough to the holiness of marriage and are far too liberal in permitting sinful divorce and even other perversions of marriage. But the solution to these evils is not to race to another extreme by maintaining a no-divorce view that essentially contends that *man was made for marriage, not marriage for man.* When we tell abuse victims that God does not permit them to divorce their abuser, and that if they do so and then remarry, they will be guilty of adultery, we are condemning the guiltless and demanding sacrifice rather than extending God's mercy to the weak and helpless: "They tie up heavy burdens, hard to bear, and lay them on people's shoulders, but they themselves are not willing to move them with their finger" (Matthew 23:4). Eugene Peterson's rendition of this verse is very vivid:

> Instead of giving you God's Law as food and drink by which you can banquet on God, they package it in bundles of rules, loading you down like pack animals. They seem to take pleasure in watching you stagger under these loads, and wouldn't think of lifting a finger to help.[133]

When even the most careful and minute examination of Scripture leads us to interpretive positions that are in conflict with God's greater principles, we can be sure that our conclusions are flawed. To prohibit what God allows, is to judge by appearances, rather than with right judgment.

> ***John 7:23-24*** *If on the Sabbath a man receives circumcision, so that the law of Moses may not be broken, are you angry with me because on the Sabbath I made a man's whole body well? Do not judge by appearances, but judge with right judgment."*

This is exactly what is happening in the evangelical church when victims are being told that they must remain with their abuser and suffer his evil. God's greater principles have been forgotten as we minutely dissect the meaning of "*porneia*," or make one statement of Jesus into an absolute rule given to govern every single scenario, when in fact He never intended it to be so. What are some of these forgotten greater principles? They are:

- God desires mercy.
- Marriage was made for man.
- We are to zealously protect and advocate for the poor and helpless.
- We are to defend human life.

133 Scripture taken from The Message. Copyright © 1993, 1994, 1995, 1996, 2000, 2001, 2002. Used by permission of NavPress Publishing Group.

And yet, as I recently discussed with our weekly abuse-victim's support group, the no-divorce-for-abuse position leads to absurd injustices. Think about it. This means that we would tell a woman who has been subjected to domestic terrorism for years, beaten and raped and sodomized by her "husband," whose children have been similarly tormented, that God does not permit her to divorce this tyrant. Yes, she can hide out from him. She can report him to the police. The church, if he is a member, can ex-communicate him. But she cannot divorce him. She is bound. And if she *does* divorce and remarry, she must wear the Scarlet Letter of an adulteress.

Pastor John Piper's no-divorce teaching envelops the abuse victim in an even more cruel bondage. He teaches that because the ultimate purpose of marriage is to display the glory of God and the love of Christ for the church, divorce is never permitted. He maintains that marriage is not mainly about being in love, nor even about staying in love. Rather, it is about modeling God's covenant-keeping love with the church.[134] Through this convolution of logic, Piper insists that a loveless, abusive marriage must persist because it must model covenant-keeping. Covenant-breaking models covenant-keeping! This teaching is going to send an abuse victim into a serious overload of false guilt, and the more serious her resolve is to follow Christ, the greater the guilt will be. Piper tells her that if she separates from or divorces her abuser, she is letting down the evangelical mission of the church by discrediting Christ in the eyes of the world.

I do not take what I am about to say lightly, but I must say it for the welfare of abuse victims: I encourage any victim of abuse who is in a church that binds people in such a manner, to leave that church for her own safety, sanity and health and find a church that does not make the error of going beyond Scripture. It is my conclusion that, even though it may come from a zeal for the Lord, teaching people that God forbids divorce for abuse (as abuse has been defined and presented in this book) is spiritual malpractice. To bring church discipline to bear upon victims is to compound this injustice and I must believe that it is obnoxious in God's sight. Strong words, I know, but consider again what is being done to victims of terrible abuse when they are authoritatively taught by their church, pastors, and Christian friends that God requires them to remain married to their abuser. Would you tell the following woman, who has suffered terribly

134 John Piper, *This Momentary Marriage* (Wheaton: Crossway Books, 2009), Chapter 1.

for nearly thirty years at the hands of her professing Christian husband, "God forbids you to divorce him"?

> It doesn't help that I am feeling so awful I can barely stay up. I still haven't been able to get to a doctor and get my medicine which I've been out of for some time. Ray insisted that I make the last refill last for four months, even though it was a three month supply. I have no clue what his medical insurance is; he doesn't share that with me. If I had a way to just make an appointment myself, I would. Yesterday, when I asked him again, (as I have been asking now for five months) if he had gotten me a doctor's appointment, he told me no, not yet, but added "Honey, you know how hard I am trying to get you one, though. I want you to get better." So I asked him point blank: Have you even called one doctor? His answer: "No."

How many abusers deny their victim medical care in ways just like this, slowly killing them? If you knew that a woman's husband intended to kill her, would you tell her to submit to him and to keep on living with him? Some Christians are doing exactly that.

> I asked my pastor whether he would be telling me I could not divorce my abusive husband if I had come into the office covered in bruises on the outside, instead of just on the inside, and he said "yes." He said that he would never demand that I live with someone who was *hitting* me, but that I would still not have a right to a divorce. For the first time in my 37 years on this planet, I found myself unwilling to agree or comply with my pastor. He said "What do we have to do to get you under control?" And I quietly answered, "You can't." And I left. My abuser was able to continue in the church, presenting himself as a poor victim in need of sympathy. (Elizabeth, abuse victim)

Divorced from the Devil

Jesus Christ effected what we might call the *greatest divorce of all time.* He came to destroy the works of the devil by which we were held in slavery all of our lives, and this is how Christ pulled it off:

> ***Colossians 2:13-15*** *And you, who were dead in your trespasses and the uncircumcision of your flesh, God made alive together with him, having*

forgiven us all our trespasses, by canceling the record of debt that stood against us with its legal demands. This he set aside, nailing it to the cross. He disarmed the rulers and authorities and put them to open shame, by triumphing over them in him.

We were the oppression of Satan and all of those "rulers and authorities." The wedding certificate was the Law which condemned us because under the Law, the wages of sin is death. Sin. Death. There is no other option when a human being's relationship to God is the Law. The Apostle Paul explains it:

Galatians 3:10-14 *For all who rely on works of the law are under a curse; for it is written, "Cursed be everyone who does not abide by all things written in the Book of the Law, and do them."* (11*) Now it is evident that no one is justified before God by the law, for "The righteous shall live by faith." (12) But the law is not of faith, rather "The one who does them shall live by them." (13) Christ redeemed us from the curse of the law by becoming a curse for us--for it is written, "Cursed is everyone who is hanged on a tree"-- (14) so that in Christ Jesus the blessing of Abraham might come to the Gentiles, so that we might receive the promised Spirit through faith.*

Christ canceled this record of debt" which kept us under the old tyrant's power by meeting its holy demands. He ransomed us by dying on the cross, thereby paying the debt that stood against us.[135] *And then He made us His bride.* A new wedding contract was issued, and it is called the New Covenant. This New Covenant does not mean we are free from the Law in the sense that we can sin all we want. No! Rather, in the New Covenant (Hebrews 8), God, by His Spirit, writes His Law on our hearts so that we love it and are enabled to willingly obey it.

This is *divorce and remarriage*. Divorced from our old covenant of death, and re-married to a new marriage of life in Christ. And it is a very, very good thing! Paul reasons in much the same way in Romans 7 –

Romans 7:1-4 *Or do you not know, brothers—for I am speaking to those who know the law—that the law is binding on a person only as long as he lives? For a married woman is bound by law to her husband while he lives, but if her husband dies she is released from the law of marriage. Accordingly, she will be called an adulteress if she lives with another man while her*

135 This debt was paid to God, not to Satan. It is God who is wronged by all sin and it is His Law that condemns the sinner.

husband is alive. But if her husband dies, she is free from that law, and if she marries another man she is not an adulteress. Likewise, my brothers, you also have died to the law through the body of Christ, so that you may belong to another, to him who has been raised from the dead, in order that we may bear fruit for God.

The original contract, you see, is made void by the death of the woman's husband. It is the contract that is the basis for the marriage, in this case, the Law of God. But when there is a death of one spouse, the other is free from that contract. But death is not the only way to void a marriage contract. It is also made void by habitual, unrepentant, hard-hearted breaking of the vows; the terms of the contract. Once voided, it is no longer binding and the innocent spouse can formalize the divorce which has already happened and is free to remarry.

Let's remind ourselves once more what we are telling an abuse victim, and an abuser, when we maintain that the victim cannot divorce her abuser for any reason, or that she cannot divorce him because his actions, though terribly abusive, do not qualify as "biblical" desertion (1 Corinthians 7). Imagine the following victim sitting in front of you, presenting her case:

> I have extreme issues with sensitivity in my neck due to a traffic accident when I was a teenager. I was told that without fairly regular treatment, I would wind up having nerve damage on the right side of my body and getting arthritis in my neck.
>
> My husband always said we couldn't afford to have me see the chiropractor regularly even although most of the cost was covered by insurance. Now, after all of these years, I have no real curvature in my neck and there is nerve damage, including some degree of hearing loss in the right ear, arthritis and other issues such as regular, rather severe, headaches. My neck is extremely sensitive to even being slightly touched and even being jarred causes a headache so extreme that no medicine I have will touch it.
>
> My husband knows this, but after I said 'no more' to the abuse he has subjected me and the children to (some of the things he did to me were so degrading that, even now, I can't even think about them without feeling sick), his verbal and emotional mistreatment of the children and I escalated. He now regularly comes up and pops me or bumps me knowing what is going

> to happen and, then, if I complain, he says something like, "Oh, come on, I hardly touched you!" or "I was just playing. I couldn't have hurt you with that light pop." But the bump or the pop wasn't light and I'm left to deal with the pain for hours. That, plus the fact that, every single time we move to a new place, he can't seem to get the money together for me to see a doctor to get my blood drawn so I can get a new prescription for my medicine, leaving me to do without it for a number of months. He knows the dangers of this, but doesn't care. I know that he is still seeking ways to physically abuse me, but in a way that he can still have 'plausible deniability'.

Abusers are being enabled by the common counsel victims receive from their churches. The message the abuser gets is that, while perhaps they need to treat their victim better, nevertheless their victim is bound to them for life, regardless of whether the vows are kept or not. Abusers must be thinking, *"Alright, just as I thought! God is on my side."* And yet this no divorce for abuse position has not been consistently held by Christians in history. Consider the Westminster Confession of Faith:

> Although the corruption of man be such as is apt to study arguments unduly to put asunder those whom God has joined together in marriage: yet, nothing but adultery, or such willful desertion as can no way be remedied by the Church, or civil magistrate, is cause sufficient of dissolving the bond of marriage.... [Chapter 24]

Similarly the London Confession of Faith, 1689 (Reformed Baptist) allows divorce for adultery or desertion, as did other Reformers and many godly people who have preceded us. At least some of them considered abuse to be desertion.[136] When we come to an interpretation of Scripture that differs from the rest of the church, we *must* be cautious and humble. If we learn that people like Martin Luther or John Calvin, or the authors of the great Confessions of Faith, saw the issue differently than us, we should be very hesitant to enforce our conclusions upon others. The probability that we are right and that all of these men were in error is not at all high. It is far more likely that we are the ones in error.

Pastor Ray Sutton, in his book *Second Chance: Biblical Principles of Divorce and Remarriage*, gives an excellent, documented summary of the positions on this subject held by Christians such as Jerome, Origen, some Roman emperors

136 Roberts, *Not Under Bondage,* Appendix 2 on "Constructive Desertion."

(who professed to be Christians), and Martin Bucer.[137] No one can claim that the prevailing view of orthodox Christianity has been to reject abuse as a valid reason for divorce. Instead, quite the opposite is the case. Therefore, we should not attempt to bind the consciences of others with "maverick" views of marriage, divorce and remarriage. Only God in His Word has the right to bind the conscience. Christians do not agree on many other subjects: the use of musical instruments in worship; women and head coverings; or the precise nature of the Lord's Table. Are we so sure of our position in such matters that we are ready to enforce church discipline against those who differ from us?

What about those promises made at the wedding?

> ***Matthew 5:37*** *Let what you say be simply 'Yes' or 'No'; anything more than this comes from evil.*

Contracts. You are probably bound to more of them than you might realize. Credit cards come with them. You finance your car, buy a home with a mortgage, and enter into an employment agreement with your boss. All of these aspects of normal life involve contracts. And they all have sanctions. Blessings or curses, we might say. If I buy a new flat screen TV with my credit card, I am promising to pay the debt off in a particular time, with a specified interest rate, and if I do so, I will be blessed. I get to keep the TV. If not, well, the curses go into play! Some burly "repo man" might show up at my door, or my paycheck could be slapped with a garnishment.

For a number of years, I have wondered about one of the most important contracts human beings make. It is the marriage contract, entered into (we even use those words "entered into" at the wedding!) with *vows* recited *in the presence of God and witnesses.* My confusion about these vows originates in the fact that for the most part, the church tells people their marriage contract is non-enforceable. This is particularly evident when we consider *abuse* and the marriage vows. Consider a typical vow:

- To love.
- To honor.

137 Ray Sutton, *Second Chance: Biblical Principles of Divorce and Remarriage* (Fort Worth: Dominion Press, 1988), 12-14. Free PDF edition at http://freebooks.entrewave.com/freebooks/docs/a_pdfs/rssc.pdf.

- To cherish.
- To forsake all others.
- Until death.

Normally, at least in a Christian ceremony, these vows are expressly stated to be made "solemnly," in the sight of God, and witnessed by everyone present. And yet, unlike *every other human contract in life*, it seems that this contract can be disregarded the first day after the honeymoon with full immunity from sanctions (curses) and continued enjoyment of all privileges. Isn't, as we say, something really wrong with this picture? A spouse can, for example, never love, never honor, never cherish their wife or husband, and yet we tell the wronged party that there is nothing to be done about it. They are married, the contract is binding, and that is that. Perhaps if there is adultery, then yes, divorce is permitted. Otherwise, the defrauded party is still bound by contract. What? Say that again?

Marriage is a contract.[138] That may not sound very romantic, but *contract* is the essence of the wedding ceremony, and the vows are the means by which husband and wife enter into this contract (see Proverbs 2:17; Malachi 2:14). Each one of them states the terms: the blessings for keeping their "part of the bargain," and the curses for breaking the deal.[139] Essentially, the curse comes from the fact that the vows are recited in "the presence of God and these witnesses," acknowledging that, as the London Confession of Faith states, God is being invoked to either bless or curse us. In that respect, wedding vows *are made to God!*

> A lawful oath is a part of religious worship, wherein the person swearing in truth, righteousness, and judgment, solemnly calls God to witness what he swears, and to judge him according to the truth or falseness thereof.... Whoever takes an oath warranted by the Word of God, ought duly to consider the weightiness of so solemn an act, and therein to vow nothing but what he knows to be truth; because by rash, false, and vain oaths, the Lord is provoked, and for them this land mourns. (Chapter 23, *The London Confession of Faith*, modern language)

Today, people often want to write their own vows for their wedding. If I am the officiating minister, I discourage this or at least reserve the right to review what they propose. Why? Because I recognize that vows are to be more than mere flowery,

---

138 Instone-Brewer, *Divorce and Remarriage in the Church*, Location 366 Kindle Edition.
139 Sutton, 10.

vapory, feel-good words that evaporate as they are uttered. The vows are the terms of the contract, entered into before God. As such, they are solemn. While a wedding is indeed cause for celebration, I wonder how the atmosphere of many "party-on" ceremonies would be radically changed to a more sober sense if everyone realized just what was actually happening -- "Lord, we call upon you to bless us or curse us according to the vows we are now making." Perhaps some marriages wouldn't even take place! Is it possible that this realization is what prompted the disciples to exclaim:

Matthew 19:10 The disciples said to him, "If such is the case of a man with his wife, it is better not to marry."

Once we recognize that marriage is a contract, entered into with sober vows, we are in a position to *define* divorce – something that is often overlooked in many treatments of this subject. What we mean by "divorce" is not always as clear as we think. I am going to use two terms for clarification: 1) *destruction* of the marriage and, 2) *divorce* of the marriage:

- A marriage covenant is destroyed (made void) by willful, habitual, unrepentant breaking of the marriage vows.
- This violation of vows is what actually causes a marriage to end.
- The innocent party may then file for *divorce* and should not be condemned for doing so. Divorce then is simply the legal declaration that a marriage is over.

When the wronged spouse takes the legal means to end the marriage (i.e., files for divorce with the civil authorities) he or she is divorcing, but this is to merely acknowledge that the marriage covenant has already been rendered void by the guilty spouse's violation of the covenant terms. This means that only the victim can rightfully petition for divorce and it is only the victim who can biblically decide when the marriage has ended.[140]

What Jesus forbids, in other words, when He says, "What therefore God has joined together, let not man separate," *is the destruction of the marriage by violation of the vows.* Instone-Brewer affirms this:

> Therefore, although the breakup of a marriage is always due to sin, it is not the divorce itself that is the sin; the sin is the breaking of the vows, which causes the divorce.[141]

140 Instone-Brewer, *Divorce and Remarriage in the Church,* Location 163, Kindle Edition.
141 Ibid., Location 160

Some years ago when I was counseling a couple whose background included a history of adultery by one of them, I remember telling them, "Your marriage is over. It was destroyed by the violation of the marriage contract you made. Therefore the wronged party has the right to acknowledge this fact by filing the necessary legal papers with the civil court. You are not required to do so. You may choose to forgive and continue on in the marriage. But this is your right." In this case, the wronged spouse chose to forgive and continue in the marriage. Perhaps in cases like this it would be appropriate to recite new vows to establish a new covenant.

In the case of abuse in marriage, the abuse victim is not the one destroying the marriage when he or she decides the marriage contract has been rendered null and void. That has already been accomplished by the abuser who has refused to love, honor, and cherish as he vowed before God to do. The church continues, in many cases, to do great harm and injustice to abuse victims when we insist that if she files for divorce, she is actually the one who is effecting the destruction of the marriage and is therefore, guilty before God. All the victim is doing is *suing* for the court to recognize that the marriage contract has been broken. We even use that legal language: *suing for divorce.*

Why is it that we seem to hold credit card agreements and home mortgages in higher esteem than the marriage contract? What person in their right mind would ever enter into a contract, knowing that the other party can violate the terms to our harm, and yet there will be nothing we can do to get out of the contract?

God's Failed Marriage

God Himself, who is incapable of sin, is a divorcee.[142] Over and over again, He compares His covenant with Israel to marriage, and the violation of the terms (vows) of that covenant (entered into at Mt. Sinai) *adultery*, particularly in relation to idolatry. Ultimately, after much patient forbearing, God *divorced* His bride. He was the wounded party, the victim of broken vows. Israel destroyed the marriage, not God:

> ***Jeremiah 3:8*** *She saw that for all the adulteries of that faithless one, Israel, I had sent her away with a decree of divorce. Yet her treacherous sister Judah did not fear, but she too went and played the whore.*

142 Ibid., Chapter 3.

> ***Ezekiel 16:8*** *"When I passed by you again and saw you, behold, you were at the age for love, and I spread the corner of my garment over you and covered your nakedness; I made my vow to you and entered into a covenant with you, declares the Lord GOD, and you became mine.*
>
> ***Ezekiel 16:59*** *"For thus says the Lord GOD: I will deal with you as you have done, you who have despised the oath in breaking the covenant,*

Yes, the Lord goes on in Ezekiel 16 to promise that He will enter into a New Covenant, an unbreakable covenant, with His people one day. But the Old Covenant was broken by them, and He divorced them (also see Hosea 9:15-17). Furthermore, His New Covenant is not made with the same "bride." It is established with the Church, not with the physical, earthly Israel as in the first marriage. If we maintain that the victim of abuse who files for legal divorce is thereby guilty of sin, then we are necessarily charging God with sin! If God pronounces all divorce to be sin, then He condemns Himself, and that of course cannot ever be true of the One in whom there is not even a hint of sin.[143]

If God can righteously acknowledge a destroyed contract of marriage by divorcing Israel, why do so many Christians still insist that abuse victims cannot do the same? We state the principle once more:

> A marriage can be, and often is, destroyed when one party incurs guilt through the breaking of the marriage vows. The wronged spouse is only acknowledging this when he or she asks the civil authorities to recognize that the marriage contract is null and void.

Marriage vows (contracts) can be destroyed by: adultery or desertion. We maintain that biblical desertion is not only effected by literal leaving one's spouse, *but also by abuse.* Abuse is desertion because it is a refusal to live with one's spouse as husband or wife in the context of marriage, as defined by the vows of the marriage covenant. How the marriage contract gets destroyed may have some bearing on whether the marriage can be restored, reconciled and continued without further harm to the wronged party:

---

143 See Barbara Roberts' excellent discussion of Malachi 2:16 (*Not Under Bondage,* Chapter 8 and Appendix 7). If the reader will look in the ESV Bible, the Holman Christian Standard Bible, or the 2011 NIB, it will be noted that the phrase "I hate divorce" does not appear. Roberts explains why.

- In cases of adultery it is permissible (but not obligatory) for the wronged party to choose to remain in the marriage.
- In cases of abuse, it is usually inadvisable for the wronged party to remain in the marriage, because abuse generally gets worse over time. If a victim stays in an abusive marriage, she may find it harder and harder to muster whatever it takes to leave. All Christians need to know that abusers usually feign repentance and reformation, but it is probably only a performance to win the victim back.
- In cases where the guilty party simply deserts the innocent party by walking out, the marriage is over because the guilty party has voted with their feet.
- Victims of marital vow-breaking need to know that it is not a sin to divorce the guilty party; they are not obliged to wait interminably in hope that the guilty spouse may repent. In fact, such a divorce is actually disciplinary in nature.[144]

Is This a Lifetime Deal That is Impossible to Break?

"I remember years ago thinking that the only way out of my marriage was if William died. I used to wish that he would have a car crash and even imagined the police coming to my door to inform me and pictured myself at his funeral. I didn't think I could divorce him and still be right with God. I didn't think there was any other way to be free." (20-year abuse survivor)

The permanence view of marriage insists that the marriage contract is broken only by the death of either the husband or the wife. Every marriage is permanent, God having joined the two together into one flesh. Thus, this reasoning continues, any marriage to another person while the original spouse is still living is adultery. But there is only *one* contract or covenant that is permanent and unbreakable, and that is the New Covenant in Christ. Referring to Jeremiah's prophecy (Jeremiah 31:31ff) the Apostle writes:

> ***Hebrews 8:7-10*** *For if that first covenant had been faultless, there would have been no occasion to look for a second. For he finds fault with them when he says: "Behold, the days are coming, declares the Lord, when I will establish a new covenant with the house of Israel and with the house of Judah, not like*

144 Roberts, 39.

the covenant that I made with their fathers on the day when I took them by the hand to bring them out of the land of Egypt. For they did not continue in my covenant, and so I showed no concern for them, declares the Lord. For this is the covenant that I will make with the house of Israel after those days, declares the Lord: I will put my laws into their minds, and write them on their hearts, and I will be their God, and they shall be my people.

Why is this New Covenant impossible to break? Because it is not only established by Christ, but it includes the means for its human participants to obey it! Christ became sin, dying a substitutionary death on behalf of all who will believe in Him. Since Jesus has already fully paid the wages of sin (death), believers have assurance that they are saved from the wrath of God (Romans 5:1; 8:1). The Lord *will be* our God and we *will be* His people. It cannot fail. There will be no divorce between Christ and His bride.

But Jesus did not teach that the human marriage covenant is impossible to break. In fact, He instructed that no one *should* break it, indicating that by violation of the vows (just as with God's Mosaic Covenant with Israel) the guilty spouse separates what God has joined together. Separating what God has joined together is *always* sin. But only for the guilty spouse.[145]

Quite a number of years ago, a man called me for advice. He had committed adultery three years before, confessed this to his wife (this was his fourth marriage), and she had agreed to forgive him. He and his wife were both professing Christians, and I had known them for a long time. He said that he had learned just the night before that his wife was now involved with another man, and a heated argument ensued. He lost control of his anger and started screaming at her, and finally shouted, "*Maybe I ought to just go get my gun and blow your head off!*" Hearing this grieved me immensely and I even felt sick to my stomach to hear people whom I thought were Christians behaving in such a wicked manner. Knowing them as I did, I gave him this counsel: "Robert, your marriage is over. Leave the house now before anyone gets hurt or killed, and go file the divorce papers tomorrow."[146] And that is what he did. In such a messy, convoluted scenario as that, about the best I could accomplish with my advice

145 Ibid., 83. Roberts' discussion of the meaning of "what God has joined together."

146 In some other parts of the world, divorce proceedings cannot be filed immediately. In Australia, for example, husband and wife can separate, but only after one year can the divorce papers be filed.

was to keep a murder from happening. And sometimes in this fallen world, that is as good as we can do. Adultery and hatred had destroyed that marriage. The vows were smashed.

You Burned the Cookies, I Want a Divorce!

I sense at this point that some readers might be asking a question, and it is a fair one: Won't this view of marriage and divorce result in a kind of divorce epidemic like we see all around us? Things are bad enough with the family, aren't they, without telling people they can divorce when they believe their husband or wife has broken their wedding vows? And besides, which of us ever really keeps our wedding vows? We are all sinners.

Jesus taught us that we are to be a forgiving people, having been forgiven by God ourselves. Everyone has heard of the seventy-times-seven illustration (Matthew 18) and every Christian knows we are not to hate even our enemies, neither are we to seek vengeance when we are wronged. Christ permits a husband or wife to file for legal divorce when their spouse breaks the marriage contract, *but we are never commanded or required to do so.* We know then that for any marriage to work both parties must be quick to forgive one another. If we don't, we would all be divorced before we even leave the wedding reception!

But when a husband or wife hardens themselves in habitual, ongoing, unrepentant violation of the marriage contract, refusing to heed calls to leave off their sin, the marriage is going to be destroyed. God was quite patient and longsuffering with His bride, sinful Israel. But there came a point when He said, "Enough." Permitting divorce for abuse will not let divorce happen too easily. Barbara Roberts explains:

> Many Christians are afraid of "opening the floodgates" of excuses for divorce. However, allowing divorce for constructive desertion[147] is not the same as allowing divorce simply for "mutual incompatibility". Nor does it imply that a Christian spouse can separate in reaction to a transient incident or a light

147 When an employer wants to get rid of an employee, but does not want to actually fire him, he can create conditions in the workplace that are so unbearable that the employee is forced to resign. In a marriage, an abuser can desert his victim without ever physically leaving or without actually saying he wants a divorce. But constructively, in all practicality, he has indeed deserted her.

offense. Even in heavy offenses and repeated abuse, efforts should be made by the believer to bring the abuser to repentance. All efforts to urge a perpetrator to repent should be done with humility and a readiness to forgive.

However, it is important to be aware that most victims of abuse have already made many efforts in this direction before they seek help from a pastor or other professional. Indeed, the victim has usually borne too much for too long and the pattern of abuse has become deeply entrenched.[148]

What Did Jesus and Paul Mean Then?

We cannot present a full examination of all of the pertinent biblical passages regarding marriage, divorce and remarriage. Entire books have been written on these subjects; I will simply state what I believe is the proper interpretation and application of Jesus' and Paul's teaching.

First, consider Jesus:

Matthew 19:1-9 *Now when Jesus had finished these sayings, he went away from Galilee and entered the region of Judea beyond the Jordan. And large crowds followed him, and he healed them there. And Pharisees came up to him and tested him by asking, "Is it lawful to divorce one's wife for any cause?" He answered, "Have you not read that he who created them from the beginning made them male and female, and said, 'Therefore a man shall leave his father and his mother and hold fast to his wife, and the two shall become one flesh'? So they are no longer two but one flesh. What therefore God has joined together, let not man separate." They said to him, "Why then did Moses command one to give a certificate of divorce and to send her away?" He said to them, "Because of your hardness of heart Moses allowed you to divorce your wives, but from the beginning it was not so. And I say to you: whoever divorces his wife, except for sexual immorality, and marries another, commits adultery."*

Mark puts it like this:

Mark 10:11 *And he said to them, "Whoever divorces his wife and marries another commits adultery against her, and if she divorces her husband and marries another, she commits adultery."*

148 Roberts, 42.

For an excellent treatment of these passages, I refer the reader to two authors. 1) *Not Under Bondage: Biblical Divorce for Abuse, Adultery & Desertion,* by Barbara Roberts, and 2) David Instone-Brewer's *Divorce and Remarriage in the Church,* along with his *Divorce and Remarriage in the Bible*, provide the clearest and most accurate exposition of the central passages on marriage and divorce as seen in the cultural context in which they were written. Roberts' book is specifically written to address the common misuses of Scripture that continue to enslave victims in abusive marriages.

Paul's teaching in 1 Corinthians 7 is also a key text on the subject of marriage, divorce, and remarriage.

> ***1 Corinthians 7:10-16*** *To the married I give this charge* (not I, but the Lord*): the wife should not separate from her husband (but if she does, she should remain unmarried or else be reconciled to her husband), and the husband should not divorce his wife. To the rest I say (I, not the Lord) that if any brother has a wife who is an unbeliever, and she consents to live with him, he should not divorce her. If any woman has a husband who is an unbeliever, and he consents to live with her, she should not divorce him. For the unbelieving husband is made holy because of his wife, and the unbelieving wife is made holy because of her husband. Otherwise your children would be unclean, but as it is, they are holy. But if the unbelieving partner separates, let it be so. In such cases the brother or sister is not enslaved. God has called you to peace. For how do you know, wife, whether you will save your husband? Or how do you know, husband, whether you will save your wife?*

Once again I refer the reader to Instone-Brewer for a fuller treatment, and in particular, how Exodus 21:10-11 provides a background for interpreting Paul here in 1 Corinthians 7. Roberts deals with the Exodus passage as well, pages 61-62. Let's pull the main points out of this text.

1. In verses 10-11 Paul is addressing marriages in which both spouses are Christians.
2. In verses 12-16, Paul is dealing with a new scenario that Jesus did not address ("I, not the Lord"); namely, that of a mixed marriage between a Christian and a non-Christian. This situation may have been due to one spouse hearing the gospel and coming to faith in Christ while the other did not. A mixed marriage can also arise in other ways however. Many

abuse victims honestly believed their abuser was a Christian when they married him.[149]

3. The instruction is that if the unbeliever "consents to live with" the believer, the Christian is to remain in the marriage. In fact, they are encouraged to remain in it, unlike the situation in Ezra and Nehemiah's day when the Jews who had married pagans were required to put them away. Children in these New Testament marriages are considered "clean/holy" before God, in that, being more exposed to the faith than children whose parents are both unbelievers, they have enhanced opportunity to come to faith in Christ for themselves.
4. However, verse 15 says "But if the unbelieving partner separates, let it be so. In such cases the brother or sister is not enslaved. God has called you to peace." What does this mean and how does it apply to domestic abuse? Abusers destroy their marriages by trashing the marriage contract which included their promise to love, cherish and protect their partner. An abuser so wounds his victim, so exposes her to hardship and suffering that, despite her best efforts, the marriage bond of love and respect is destroyed. "Let it be so," tells the victim and the church to recognize and accept reality: the marriage has been destroyed and all that remains is for the wounded spouse to obtain legal recognition of this fact by obtaining a certificate declaring the marriage to be over.
5. The phrase "consent to live with" cannot be limited to a narrow, wooden definition such as "if the unbeliever agrees to remain in the same house with the Christian." As Peter seems to indicate in his use of a very similar Greek word, "to live with" means "to remain in the marriage, showing understanding and deference to one's spouse."

1 Peter 3:7 Likewise, husbands, live with your wives in an understanding way, showing honor to the woman as the weaker vessel, since they are heirs with you of the grace of life, so that your prayers may not be hindered.

It is characteristic of abusers to push his spouse/victim away while at the same time insisting that the marriage continue. Abusers abuse, and one form of their abuse is to tirelessly work to keep their victim in the marriage and under their domination. With their actions, they refuse to live amicably with their victim, yet

149 Roberts, 40-41.

claim that they don't want a divorce. We must see through all of this and recognize that the abuser in no way agrees to live with their spouse in a real marriage:

> The concept of being pleased and approvingly consenting to live in the marriage must carry the idea of respecting and honoring the believing spouse and the marriage relationship. The persistent perpetrator of abuse.... is happy to live with his wife, but only because it gives him power over her. Instead of the approval... he shows the opposite: an evil thinking towards his wife. So the command of verse 13, let her not divorce him, is not applicable.[150]

Richard Phillips in his book *The Masculine Mandate* also talks about what it means to "live with" one's spouse:.

> Peter says, "husbands, live with your wives." Most men respond, "All right, I can check that one off. We live in the same house!" But, of course, that's not Peter's point. Rather, you are to live with your wife. The word for "live with" is the Greek word that means "commune" and gives us the noun community. Peter is saying that husbands are to live with their wives in a single shared life.[151]

In other words, if the unbeliever agrees to continue in the marriage, upholding the marriage vows to which he or she originally agreed, then the Christian spouse is not to divorce the unbeliever out of some notion that it is not God's will for them to remain in a marriage with a non-Christian. But if the unbeliever chronically fails to uphold the marriage vows, then the Christian spouse is not obliged to remain in a marriage in which they are treated worse than dirt. They are free to divorce, and they should not be condemned for doing so.

We emphasize once more that abuse is a form of desertion. An abuser's conduct causes his victim to separate from the marriage. The proper legal term for this is "constructive desertion." Constructive desertion occurs when one partner's evil conduct ends the marriage because it causes the other partner to leave. *But it is the abuser who is to be construed*[152] *as the deserter, not the victim. The victim bears no blame.*

---

150 Ibid., 40-41.

151 Richard D. Phillips, The *Masculine Mandate: God's Calling to Men* (Lake Mary: Reformation Trust Publishing, 2010), 84.

152 The word "construed" relates to "constructive" - hence "constructive desertion." See Roberts, 39.

* Please note that the views on divorce and remarriage in this chapter do not necessarily reflect the views of the publisher.

1 Corinthians 7, in conjunction with Exodus 21:10-11, then, form the case for the abuse victim's right to separate from and divorce their abuser. *A Cry for Justice*, calls on pastors, Christians, and local churches to permit abuse victims to be set free.*

> Divorce was meant to be my scarlet letter, the badge of shame that would induce me to submit. Instead, I have chosen to wear my divorce now as a badge of honor and courage. (Elizabeth, abuse survivor)

CHAPTER 16

But Isn't the Bible Enough?

2 Timothy 3:14-17 *But as for you, continue in what you have learned and have firmly believed, knowing from whom you learned it and how from childhood you have been acquainted with the sacred writings, which are able to make you wise for salvation through faith in Christ Jesus. All Scripture is breathed out by God and profitable for teaching, for reproof, for correction, and for training in righteousness, that the man of God may be competent, equipped for every good work.*

Proverbs 6:6 *Go to the ant, O sluggard; consider her ways, and be wise.*

Diane is a Christian. She has a real desire to help people. Last year she learned about a series of training seminars which promised to equip a Christian to take their Bible and provide counseling to people with most any problem: alcoholism, sexual sins, marriage issues, depression, anger, and more. Diane enrolled in and completed three seminars and was awarded a counseling competency certificate. She is quite excited and is convinced that she is adequate to handle any counselee's issues. After all, she has her Bible and everything she needs is in it. She agrees, as she learned in those seminars, that the church has been wrong in using the insights and methods of secular psychology and that Christians need to take back the ministry of counseling that God's Word equips them for.

It all sounds so good, doesn't it?

And yet the sad thing is that if an abuse victim seeks out counseling from Diane, they will receive very bad and even dangerous counsel. This is not because Diane doesn't love the Word of God or desire to counsel correctly, but because

Diane has really no idea about the nature of abuse, the mentality of the abuser, or of his deceptive, manipulative, covert tactics. Diane heard nothing about these things in her seminars because most leaders of such sessions are just as uninformed about abuse as their students. Diane has never personally experienced abuse. It is a foreign world to her. To her, abuse is when someone is being disagreeable because they have been pushed to the limits and over-react with anger. If this were true, she probably would be competent to deal with the issue based upon the knowledge she has. But it isn't true. Diane is not competent to counsel.

How can this be? Why are we "missing it"? The Bible is sufficient, isn't it?

This is Elizabeth's story:

> By nature, when I married him, I would have been an easy mark for any abuser (not just the one I married). And my Christianity made it even easier.
>
> Born again at the age of 7 when I asked Jesus to come and live in my heart after hearing the gospel story at church one Sunday, I also attended Christian school in junior and senior high school and two years of college at a Baptist university. I've always counted myself blessed to have been saved to begin with, but doubly so because I was raised in a Christian home and absolutely immersed in good, fundamental Bible teaching. To this day I can still quote whole passages from Romans, the Corinthians, Galatians, Ephesians, John, Psalms, Proverbs and any number of other books. And it is a blessing, and I've needed every bit of God's word in my life.
>
> An exuberant, well-spoken and intelligent woman, raised by parents who taught me that there was nothing I couldn't do, and who loved and accepted me exactly as God made me, had you told me that I would end up in an abusive marriage I'd never, ever have believed you.
>
> I'm a firstborn pleaser and an over achiever. While not perfect by any means, I was the kid who did not openly question or defy authority, who got straight A's, who started being her church pianist at the age of 13 and helped her mom run the Sparky's program. I was the kid who did everything asked of her, and more. I will also avoid conflict at nearly all costs. I don't mind sharing my ideas and opinions, and while I think I'm entitled to them, I also believe that you are entitled to yours, and it's neither my job to argue you into submission, nor is it your job to do the same to me. My parents raised me with

love and logic, and I naively believed that adults in a relationship should be able to communicate and that people who say they love one another seek to make the other happy. That people in a marriage grow and learn from and for one another and that they never, ever hurt each other on purpose.

And that Christian upbringing? Full of sermons and practical examples of the Biblical model of male authority in the home, first by the father, then by the husband. Full of sermons about being a self-sacrificial servant to the body of Christ and to (all) other Christians. To "esteem the needs of others" as (always) greater than my own. To put myself last. That shame and fear of what others will think of you is a great way to control yourself and others. And of course that no real Christian gets divorced.

This combination of nature and nurture didn't prepare me to deal with wolves in sheep's clothing. It didn't prepare me to recognize and name abuse. It didn't prepare me for how to deal with someone who has a reprobate mind, who is unrepentant and completely reliant on narcissistic behavior and devoted only to his own welfare, well being and ego. It didn't prepare me in any way to deal with someone who lives in an alternate reality where any lie he says at the moment becomes truth to him.

What did Elizabeth miss?

The first time that I spoke to a group of people (other than my own congregation) on the topic of abuse, a pastor in the audience approached me afterward and made an excellent observation. He said, "Jeff, you are going to be accused of denying the sufficiency of Scripture." He was correct. What he meant was that I had encouraged the listeners to "wise up" in regard to the nature and tactics of abuse. I had proposed that the evangelical church is ignorant of this subject and, as a result, was far too often guilty of giving victims injustice. I advised that they read books that I recommended to them, some of which were written by secular therapists. As this pastor accurately realized, there are many Christians who reject such advice, insisting that a Christian with his Bible alone is competent to counsel anyone in any situation.[153] It is my purpose in this chapter to 1) explain what the doctrine of the sufficiency of Scripture is, 2) to

153 I express my appreciation to Pastor David Dykstra for referring me to the article by T. David Gordon, referenced in this chapter and entitled "The Insufficiency of Scripture."

propose to the reader that Scripture is *not* intended by God to be our sole source of truth *on every subject,* and, 3) to emphasize that the Bible has far more to say about abuse than we realize. Christians have simply not been seeing it.

The London Confession of Faith, 1689, addresses the sufficiency of Scripture (underlining is mine):

> The Holy Scripture is the only sufficient, certain, and infallible rule of all saving knowledge, faith, and obedience, although the light of nature, and the works of creation and providence do so far manifest the goodness, wisdom, and power of God, as to leave men inexcusable; yet are they not sufficient to give that knowledge of God and his will which is necessary unto salvation. The whole counsel of God concerning all things necessary for his own glory, man's salvation, faith and life, is either expressly set down or necessarily contained in the Holy Scripture; unto which nothing at any time is to be added, whether by new revelation of the Spirit, or traditions of men.
>
> Nevertheless, we acknowledge the inward illumination of the Spirit of God to be necessary for the saving understanding of such things as are revealed in the Word, *and that there are some circumstances concerning the worship of God, and government of the church, common to human actions and societies, which are to be ordered by the light of nature and Christian prudence,* according to the general rules of the Word, which are always to be observed.

You will notice that the phrase "the light of nature" is used twice in this section (from chapter 1 of the LCF). By "the light of nature," the writers of this confession meant *general or natural revelation.* General revelation is that revelation of God of Himself to His creatures (us) given through the creation itself. The Apostle Paul and the Psalmist both speak of this general revelation:

> *Romans 1:18-20 For the wrath of God is revealed from heaven against all ungodliness and unrighteousness of men, who by their unrighteousness suppress the truth. For what can be known about God is plain to them, because God has shown it to them. For his invisible attributes, namely, his eternal power and divine nature, have been clearly perceived, ever since the creation of the world, in the things that have been made. So they are without excuse.*

Psalm 19:1-4 *To the choirmaster. A Psalm of David. The heavens declare the glory of God, and the sky above proclaims his handiwork. Day to day pours out speech, and night to night reveals knowledge. There is no speech, nor are there words, whose voice is not heard. Their voice goes out through all the earth, and their words to the end of the world. In them he has set a tent for the sun...*

General revelation is *not sufficient* because man cannot find salvation in Christ by studying the creation. He can know that God exists, that God is God and that man is not God. He can and does realize that he owes God his thanksgiving and worship, and if he rejects this knowledge (as he does), it is sufficient *to condemn him.* But it is not sufficient to save him. This is why God *has spoken to us in His Son, the Word of God, the Lord Jesus Christ.* Christ is the ultimate and complete epiphany of God to man. This final revelation has been written down through authors who were inerrantly inspired by the Holy Spirit, and the product is the sixty six books of the Holy Scriptures.

The doctrine of the sufficiency of Scripture, as stated in the confession of faith (you will find the same doctrine in other Reformed confessions as well), maintains that the Bible contains *all things necessary for God's glory, for man's salvation, and for what we are to believe (faith) and practice (life).* The Bible is the "only sufficient, certain, and infallible rule of all saving knowledge, faith and obedience." I fully subscribe to this doctrine.

However, the men who penned this confession realized that God has also revealed Himself to man through His creation, through general revelation. The "light of nature," as they called it. They said that there are some circumstances "concerning the worship of God, and government of the church, common to human actions and societies, which are to be ordered by" this general revelation and something else they called "Christian prudence." These things are all to be so interpreted and applied that they are consistent with and never contrary to Scripture. But they are things that are not directly or even indirectly addressed in Scripture.

T. David Gordon writes that there are:

> ...circumstances concerning the worship of God, and government of the church, which are to be governed not by Scripture, but by the light of nature

and Christian prudence. Why would the divines (the theologians who wrote the confession) have added this qualification regarding the life of the covenant community (the church) if Scriptures were an otherwise complete guide for *all* of life? Are "circumstances" about automobile mechanics governed by Scripture, but circumstances regarding worship and church government *not* so governed? Of course not. Rather, this latter clause qualifies the intent of the previous, that 'faith and life" are shorthands for the beliefs of the covenant community, and the duties of the covenant community.

Gordon goes on then to apply his conclusion:

> … so I am not denying that the Scriptures contain some general instruction to the human race. I am merely denying that "faith and life" is intended to suggest that Scriptures are an adequate guide to the various particulars of our lives and callings as humans. The Bible is sufficient to guide the human-as-covenanter [i.e., the Christian] but *not* sufficient to guide the human-as-mechanic, the human-as-physician, the human-as-businessman, the human-as-parent, the human-as-husband, the human-as-wife, or the human-as-legislator….
>
> Where the big change has occurred in my own thinking has been with regard to the disastrous consequences of the common misunderstanding of the doctrine of the sufficiency of Scripture. We appear to have lost the historic Protestant understanding of the importance of Natural Revelation, and have tended to function as though such revelation were not necessary. If anything has changed, then, it is that I would now argue with equal zeal for the *in*-sufficiency of Scripture in other than religious or covenantal areas. I would want to argue now that Scripture is *not* a sufficient guide to many aspects of life, other than in the sense of providing religious direction and motivation to all of life.[154]

Does this mean that there are errors in the Bible? Certainly not.[155] When the

154 T.David Gordon Gordon, T. David. "The Insufficiency of Scripture." *Modern Reformaton* (January/February 2002): 18-23.

155 The doctrine of inerrancy applies to the original manuscripts as they were written by the inspired authors. The science of textual criticism is the discipline which gives us confidence that the Old and New Testament books that constitute our Bible are very accurate, but does not deny that there have certainly been errors made in the transmission and translation of the Scriptures. The Holy Spirit does

Bible *does* address matters, it does so inerrantly, whether those topics be direct doctrine such as justification by faith or the meaning of the cross of Christ, or subjects concerning science, psychology, mathematics and other such disciplines which describe God's creation. The idea that the Bible is in-sufficient in many aspects of life simply means that God has not spoken to us *exhaustively* about all things in the Bible, and that there are many important things that we can learn from natural revelation. Science does indeed have a place in the Christian's education, and I doubt that any reader would want to go to a physician who took his entire education about medicine from the Bible! Psychology is science. Man is properly the subject of science, just as any other created thing.

Let's consider some Scriptures that teach us some ways in which God utilizes *natural revelation* to teach us. We affirm that these methods must be subject to the truths of Scripture. God's revelation in all of its forms (special and general) will never be contradictory.

Consider, first of all, how God teaches us through *experience.*

God's Extra-biblical Instruction of His People: The School of Experience

What do the following verses tell us about a very common method God uses to teach the Christian things like endurance, hope, character, the ability to comfort others, and faith? Maturity in Christ, in other words. Listen carefully:

> ***Romans 5:3-4*** *More than that, we rejoice in our* **sufferings**, *knowing that* **suffering** *produces endurance, and endurance produces character, and character produces hope,*
>
> ***2 Corinthians 1:3-4*** *Blessed be the God and Father of our Lord Jesus Christ, the Father of mercies and God of all comfort, who comforts us in all our* **affliction**, *so that we may be able to comfort those who are in any affliction, with the comfort with which we ourselves are comforted by God.*
>
> ***2 Corinthians 1:9-10*** *Indeed, we felt that we had received* **the sentence of death**. *But that was to make us rely not on ourselves but on God who raises the dead. He delivered us from such* **a deadly peril,** *and he will deliver us. On him we have set our hope that he will deliver us again.*

---

not inspire those processes as He did the original writings.

> ***James 1:2-4*** *Count it all joy, my brothers, when you meet* **trials of various kinds,** *for you know that the testing of your faith produces steadfastness. And let steadfastness have its full effect, that you may be perfect and complete, lacking in nothing.*

These Scriptures *interpret* why God brings suffering and trials into our lives. But the initial "schoolmaster" is *suffering*. That is to say, God uses the actual experience of trials and tests, and the experience of His comfort and provision in those trials to teach us, so that we will be more perfect and complete.

The Lord Jesus Christ Himself needed this:

> ***Hebrews 2:17-18*** *Therefore he had to be made like his brothers in every respect, so that he might become a merciful and faithful high priest in the service of God, to make propitiation for the sins of the people.* **For because he himself has suffered when tempted, he is able to help those who are being tempted.**

> ***Hebrews 5:7-8*** *In the days of his flesh, Jesus offered up prayers and supplications, with loud cries and tears, to him who was able to save him from death, and he was heard because of his reverence.* **Although he was a son, he learned obedience through what he suffered.**

Until we have been trained in the school of experience, we will not be fully competent to counsel others in the same experience. We can and should learn about alcoholism, abuse, drug addiction, etc., but until we have personally entered into some aspect of the *experience* of these things, we will not truly be able to 'help those who are being tempted' by them. Is it because the Bible is not sufficient? No. It is because we do not naturally understand the nature of the thing that we are trying to bring the Scriptures to bear upon.

Now obviously this does not mean that we must become drug addicts or alcoholics before we can learn to help others struggling in those areas. But it does mean that our wisdom and ability to help such people is *greatly* enhanced when we ourselves experience some aspect of these things. The parents of a child who became addicted to drugs have experienced drug addiction in ways that they had not before this trial. In fact, I would maintain that until a person in some very personal and direct way is touched experientially by abuse, the probability of that person being truly competent to counsel and help abuse victims *is very, very doubtful.*

I can study the Bible for years, thoroughly learn all of its doctrines accurately, know the original biblical languages, and still be absolutely incompetent to bring the truth of Scripture to bear upon the issue of abuse. Experience of the thing is the link that enables us to connect the truth of Scripture to life. God taught Paul, through great suffering and hopelessness, to be able to comfort others with the comfort by which God comforted him. I cannot apply God's truth to that which I have not yet seen or understood.

The Extra-biblical Instruction of Wise People

Timothy Keller and his wife Kathy have released a new book on marriage entitled *The Meaning of Marriage: Facing the Complexities of Commitment With the Wisdom of God.* Here is a description of their sources in their own words:

> There is a third source for the material in this book, and it is the most foundational. Though this book is rooted in my personal experience of marriage and ministry, it is even more grounded in the teachings of the Old and New Testaments.... Over the last twenty-two years , we have used what we learned from both Scripture and experience to guide, encourage, counsel, and instruct young urban adults with regard to sex and marriage. We offer the fruit of these three influences to you in this book. But the foundation of it all is the Bible.[156]

The Kellers are not denying the sufficiency of Scripture. They focus upon the teachings of Ephesians chapter 5 and other biblical texts that directly address marriage. But notice carefully *that this is not the only data they present in their book.* This is a couple who have been married for thirty six years, and *they draw upon their experience*, teaching us the things that experience has taught them. Yes, their experience must be interpreted and applied in a manner consistent with Scripture. But God uses "the grey-headed" to teach the young and foolish. T. David Gordon explains this very thing:

> The biblical literature commends wisdom in the strongest terms....Yet, according to the biblical testimony, how does one acquire wisdom? Well, in part, by heeding God's commands in holy scripture (Proverbs 10:8; Ecclesiastes 12:13). But more commonly, wisdom comes from listening to advice (Proverbs

156 Timothy Keller and Kathy Keller, *The Meaning of Marriage: Facing the Complexities of Commitment with the Wisdom of God* (New York: Penguin Group, 2011), 4.

12:15; 19:20), from entertaining the opinion of a variety of people (Proverbs 11:14; 18:17; 24:6), by listening to older people (Proverbs 13:1), and by observing the natural order itself (Proverbs 6:6). Wisdom does not come easily or quickly, but through a lengthy, prolonged effort. Most importantly, it does not come exclusively, or perhaps even primarily, through Bible study. Solomon promotes listening to parents, elders, a variety of counselors, and even a consideration of ants, badgers, locusts, and lizards.[157]

The Christian and Science

And thus Solomon's words bring us back around to why I recommend that Christians read and learn about abuse from secular as well as Christian authors. The Holy Scriptures certainly teach us about sin and about its tactics, but neither exhaustively nor in completely fleshed out detail. God has not spoken in the Bible in comprehensive detail about the mentality and methods of the abusive man that we have learned in this book. That is to say, Scripture does not give word picture "for examples" for each sinful mentality or tactic it names.[158] To learn these things, God expects us to observe, to test, to interview, and to receive the experiences He providentially sends into our lives. In other words, science does indeed have a very important place in the life of the Christian and to ignore it, to somehow think of it as unholy and unnecessary, is to cut oneself off from wisdom.

Just as we listen to and learn from mathematicians, physicists, medical researchers, plumbers, automobile mechanics and a host of other experts who are not Christians, so it is time for Christians to listen to and learn from people who have studied abuse, abusers, domestic violence, sociopaths and psychopaths, victims of abuse, and other related topics. We have not been wise. We have been arrogant. And as a result, we reiterate the plight that we have left abuse victims in:

> ***Job 19:7*** *Behold, I cry out, 'Violence!' but I am not answered; I call for help, but there is no justice.*

We must not read and listen to these sources without biblical discernment.

157 T. David Gordon, *The Insufficiency of Scripture.*

158 However, if we were to go through Scripture, carefully looking for word pictures and descriptions of the abuser's mentality and tactics, and the effects of abuse on victims, we would probably find that God's Word has said much more about these subjects than we think. The problem is that we simply have not been looking with open eyes. The abuser has blinded us to his evils.

Obviously we are going to find theories and conclusions that do not correlate with God's Word, and when we do we must alter them or reject them. When a psychologist proposes her theory that human conscience is the product of eons of human evolution that enabled human societies to co-exist while those lacking conscience disintegrated and passed out of the gene pool, we reject at least the substance of this theory. Conscience originates in man as a reflection of the image of God and was present in its entirety in the first man, Adam.

But we must not permit these errors to lead us to the conclusion that we can learn nothing from a man such as Lundy Bancroft, who has studied thousands of abusive men and interviewed as many victims of those men. Christians bring no glory to God when they reject the findings of such careful, scientific, observers. In fact, we might even appear as fools in their eyes, and justifiably so.[159]

Clinton W. McLemore writes, very accurately, that psychology alone is incapable of answering man's most crucial need: being reconciled to God and fulfilling His purpose for a person's life. He adds that any idea that psychology by itself can "fix" us is a fool's notion. A man must meet Jesus Christ, the ultimate revelation of God if that man is to know God and know himself. However, as McLemore continues, psychology can help us understand how human beings think, and how they interact with one another – rightly or wrongly. If we will take that data and interpret it in the light of Scripture's teaching about sin, about the human conscience, about man's alienation from God, then this data can be a great help to us. At the same time, we must never permit science to become our religion.[160]

Inadequate Preaching

We conclude this book with a specific plea to Christian pastors. Specifically, we call upon the shepherds of Christ's flock to carefully consider what value the proposals of this final chapter might have in respect to their vital and central ministry of preaching the Word of God and applying it in counseling and

159 I do not find books such as *Psychoheresy* or *The End of Christian Psychology* by Martin Bobgan to be helpful. This approach demonizes science and often promotes an imagined, united conspiracy by psychology to discredit everything the Bible says.

160 Clinton W. McLemore, *Toxic Relationships and How to Change Them* (San Francisco: Jossey-Bass, 2003), 22-23.

pastoral settings.

I have often told my congregation that Scripture is like "condensed soup" or a "zipped computer file." We are not to run amok with unfounded applications or derivations from a passage of Scripture. We must let Scripture interpret Scripture and we must consider the entirety of the Bible's teaching to be certain our interpretation of a specific passage is accurate. This is no simple task as any student of the Word will testify. But we must "unzip" or "un-pack" the Scripture. Largely, this means that as we preach and teach God's Word to our people, we must grow in wisdom so that we will be able to provide practical illustrations and applications of that Scripture for our people. This means, if we are truly growing in wisdom as the years pass, our best preaching will come in our later years - after we have gone through those lessons of experience God brings and we then find ourselves saying as we study a passage of the Word, *"So that is what this verse means! Now I get it!"* It turns out that the Bible was sufficient after all. The insufficiency rested with us all the time.

In regard to the topic of abuse, the pulpit ministry of the evangelical church has been very, very inadequate. As we have seen in this book, there are a number of reasons for this, but perhaps the central failure is identified by the Apostle Paul:

> ***2 Corinthians 10:12*** *Not that we dare to classify or compare ourselves with some of those who are commending themselves. But when they measure themselves by one another and compare themselves with one another, they are without understanding.*

Christians, pastors, Christian counselors (I include myself here), must own up to it. We have been arrogant and we have been arrogant in our ignorance. Holding our Bible in hand and the diploma on our wall, we have looked at the abuse victim, heard her complaints, and then looked within our own selves and thoughts for the answer. Having no experience in the world in which the abuse victim lives, we nevertheless have taken *our world* and applied it to hers. We call what we are telling her "God's Word" when in fact so often it is just our own word. We may as well be listening to a speaker of a foreign language and answering her with all confidence in English.

Our sermons have been inadequate. We stop short because our wisdom is short. We preach on the great doctrines—accurately. We teach our people the details about marriage and husbands and wives, accurately. But we do not go far enough because our wisdom doesn't go far enough. We fail to paint such a clear picture of the abuser's sin that he hears us saying *"Thou art the man!"* And as a result, the abuser comfortably sits in his pew Sunday after Sunday, wearing the mask of the eminent, saintly Christian, unrevealed and untouched. And his victim hears little or no mention of her plight from the pulpit, and so she continues to suffer.

Pastors, we must become wise about abuse and abusers. We must learn how they think, how they hide, and how they operate. We must stop being respecters of persons and stop regarding "good old Joe, the pillar of the church," by the false reputation that old Joe has constructed himself and duped us with. "*What spirit is behind Joe?"* is the question. And we are not going to be able to become wise by studying the Bible by ourselves, without the help of people who are wiser than we are in a particular area. Some will be Christians, many will not. But what you will find happening as you learn is this: you will be able to apply and illustrate God's Word like never before. You will come to a fuller understanding of the psychology of sin and the ploys and schemes of the enemy. You will even understand Scripture as never before.

And your preaching will start to shake things up in your church. You will suffer. You will be opposed by abusers who have been hiding. Your church may even be split. You will be told to back off by people who claim you are unjustly targeting them. Going up against the enemy's favorite strongholds is always an intense battle. Every honest pastor knows there is "that line." The point at which, if we stop short of in our preaching, all will be peaceful and calm. *You must cross that line!* You will know when you do. And so will the evil man. Old Joe, who has perhaps enjoyed undue influence over you and through you, over the entire church, is not going to like this at all. He may come to you after a service, put his arm around your shoulder, and in a patronizing, condescending manner suggest that perhaps it would be good for you to sit down with him and discuss the direction your preaching seems to be going – for your own good, of course! You must not listen to Joe. No one man has a right to dictate the pulpit of Christ's church! This is the spirit of Diotrephes.

Something else will happen as well. Things that have been hidden for perhaps a long, long time will be brought to light. Victims of abusers will begin to be helped to come out of the bondage they have been held in for so long. Hypocrites will have to repent or "Go out from among us, because they were not of us." The weak and oppressed will begin to sense hope once again. In other words, a "cry for justice" will finally be heard and answered in your church. And only the Lord Himself knows what else He might do among you once the darkness is dispelled by the light of the truth of Christ. How many hidden things in our churches are quenching the Spirit of Christ and preventing Him from breaking out among us in revival?

May the Lord Jesus Christ our King and Savior make us wise in these things and deliver us from every evil. May our churches become pillars of the truth, defenders of the weak, and a terror to the wicked so that abuse victims, through our help, will be able to sing as David:

> ***Psalm 57:4-11*** *My soul is in the midst of lions; I lie down amid fiery beasts-- the children of man, whose teeth are spears and arrows, whose tongues are sharp swords. Be exalted, O God, above the heavens! Let your glory be over all the earth! They set a net for my steps; my soul was bowed down. They dug a pit in my way, but they have fallen into it themselves. Selah. My heart is steadfast, O God, my heart is steadfast! I will sing and make melody! Awake, my glory! Awake, O harp and lyre! I will awake the dawn! I will give thanks to you, O Lord, among the peoples; I will sing praises to you among the nations. For your steadfast love is great to the heavens, your faithfulness to the clouds. Be exalted, O God, above the heavens! Let your glory be over all the earth!*

A FINAL WORD

The Victim's Real Rescuer

We have saved the best for last. Though in some ways this book is primarily directed at pastors and church members, we expect that there might also be abuse victims reading it as well. Whoever you might be, permit us to introduce you to the real Rescuer of the oppressed. You may think that you already know Him, and some of you may. But as we have learned in *A Cry for Justice*, even well-meaning Christians sometimes misrepresent Him in some ways, especially in regard to what He thinks of abuse, abusers, and their victims. Meet the Lord Jesus Christ, the Son of God, as the following two women did. Insert yourself into their spot; substitute your own name for them. They suffered physical ailments (though Satan was apparently behind the oppression of the second), but it is very appropriate for us to conclude that Jesus sees abuse victims just as He saw and dealt with these two.

> ***Mark 5:25-34*** *And there was a woman who had had a discharge of blood for twelve years, and who had suffered much under many physicians, and had spent all that she had, and was no better but rather grew worse. She had heard the reports about Jesus and came up behind him in the crowd and touched his garment. For she said, "If I touch even his garments, I will be made well." And immediately the flow of blood dried up, and she felt in her body that she was healed of her disease. And Jesus, perceiving in himself that power had gone out from him, immediately turned about in the crowd and said, "Who touched my garments?" And his disciples said to him, "You see the crowd pressing around you, and yet you say, 'Who touched me?'" And he looked around to see who had done it. But the woman, knowing what*

had happened to her, came in fear and trembling and fell down before him and told him the whole truth. And he said to her, "Daughter, your faith has made you well; go in peace, and be healed of your disease."

Luke 13:11-17 *And there was a woman who had had a disabling spirit for eighteen years. She was bent over and could not fully straighten herself. When Jesus saw her, he called her over and said to her, "Woman, you are freed from your disability." And he laid his hands on her, and immediately she was made straight, and she glorified God. But the ruler of the synagogue, indignant because Jesus had healed on the Sabbath, said to the people, "There are six days in which work ought to be done. Come on those days and be healed, and not on the Sabbath day." Then the Lord answered him, "You hypocrites! Does not each of you on the Sabbath untie his ox or his donkey from the manger and lead it away to water it? And ought not this woman, a daughter of Abraham whom Satan bound for eighteen years, be loosed from this bond on the Sabbath day?" As he said these things, all his adversaries were put to shame, and all the people rejoiced at all the glorious things that were done by him.*

Do you see yourself in them? Consider their terrible plight:

1. They had suffered for a *long, long* time. Twelve years for the first, eighteen for the second. How long have *you* suffered?
2. The first had sought help for many years, and we can assume that the second had done the same. Mark's description is pointed and powerfully pathetic: "…[she] had suffered much under many physicians, and had spent all that she had, and was no better but rather grew worse." How many abuse victims can identify with that! How many places have *you* looked for help? Many of you have turned to your church, to your pastors, to Christian authors, and to counselors. You have spent money and resources, but their cures only made you worse.
3. The suffering was severe. The first lady bled, and bled, and bled. For twelve years, she bled. Weak. Anemic. And in her society – an outcast. Unclean, untouchable. The second had been unable to stand upright for eighteen years! *Eighteen years!* What would that be like? Some of you can imagine better than I.
4. They were ignored and passed by. Perhaps before their affliction came they were noble ladies. One had apparently had some wealth, now

entirely expended on searching for a cure. Who had they been? Like many of you, before the abuser came and sucked the life from you, they may have been bright, promising, beautiful and confident.

5. The religious establishment was opposed to them. Man was made for religion, not religion for man. They had found themselves in an *adversarial* position in their church, or in their families and friendships, rather than in an alliance of rescue and healing.

And then Jesus came.

In spite of the masses of people, all pushing the weak aside, we are told of the second woman that when Jesus saw her, *he called her over.* He is the Lord. He is the living and true God. Yet He calls people like this to come to Him, putting everything and everyone else "on hold." In front of them all, and in spite of the jealous objections of the religious leaders, Jesus *laid his hands on them.* He allowed the first to touch Him, and the second He touched (He may have done the same with the first as well). *He touched them.* And He spoke – and they were set free.

The Bible, the Word of God, records events like this *for you.* Like the first woman, who said to herself, *"If I touch even his garments, I will be made well"* – you too can touch Him by hearing His words and believing them. You touch Him, in other words, by faith. And by talking to Him!

> ***Romans 10:9-11*** *...because, if you confess with your mouth that Jesus is Lord and believe in your heart that God raised him from the dead, you will be saved. For with the heart one believes and is justified, and with the mouth one confesses and is saved. For the Scripture says, "Everyone who believes in him will not be put to shame."*

If you are a victim of abuse, and you have come to understand what is happening to you, you probably already have some experience of what it means to "confess with your mouth and believe in your heart." When an abuse victim begins to stand up and say "No more!" she experiences the cost of taking that stand. She is hated. She may suffer more intense abuse. Her friends and family members may ally with her abuser and turn against her. *When we confess with our mouth that Jesus is Lord* (that He is God), *and genuinely believe in our heart that God raised Him from the dead,* we can expect the same kinds of experiences to come our way from people who want no part of Christ. And yet, as it is with the enslavement of abuse, such confession and belief is the only way of deliverance. Christ's promise is: *everyone who believes in Him will not be put to shame.*

What is Christ's rescue going to look like for you? Well, if you are a Christian already, He is going to keep His many promises to you. He will never leave you. He will always perfectly understand you and your situation. He will come to you and comfort you just when you need it. At some point – a time known only to Him – He will set you free and He will judge your oppressor. That may happen fully or partially in this life. It *will* happen fully and in complete justice on that Day when He comes to judge the earth. He may very well bring new friends alongside you who understand abuse. But he will do good to you. That we can be sure of.

If you are not a Christian and therefore you do not know Him yet, you can be certain of this: If you cry out to Him and plead with Him to show you mercy, if you believe that He is indeed the Son of God and the only Savior of human beings, if you believe that He died on the cross for your sins and rose from the dead, then He will rescue you from the greatest abuser of all – the devil. He will come by His Spirit and take up residence in you. He will give you a new mind and heart that loves Him and that desires to obey Him. He will give you, in other words, life where there was only death before. Light where there had been darkness. And hope. Certain, unfailing, hope.

We encourage you to pick up a Bible. Get a more recent translation such as the English Standard Version, and start reading the Gospel of John. There, you will meet Jesus. You don't have to just take man's word for it. You can hear Him for yourself. He will call you. And you will live.

> *Matthew 11:28-30 Come to me, all who labor and are heavy laden, and I will give you rest. Take my yoke upon you, and learn from me, for I am gentle and lowly in heart, and you will find rest for your souls. For my yoke is easy, and my burden is light."*

> *John 10:10-11 The thief comes only to steal and kill and destroy. I came that they may have life and have it abundantly. I am the good shepherd. The good shepherd lays down his life for the sheep.*

We close with these words from Anna, who knows what it is like to be in the furnace of abuse, and to find Jesus standing there in the flames with you:

I know pain. I know the pain of being rejected by my father--who denied I was his though there was no doubt that I was. The pain of living with his drunken outrages, outrages that had me on very strong "nerve medicine" by the time I was eighteen months old; medicine that was designed to help me with the blanking out and walking into walls I was later told I had been doing. Medicine also designed to calm me down when I'd get hysterical at hearing his car pull into our driveway each evening. Medicine I had to stay on my entire childhood.

I know the fear that comes when you leave in the middle of the night in an attempt to outrun the man who wants to kill your Mama and take you-- even though he has no true love for you. I know the uncertainty and disquiet that comes from uprooting over and over and over during the very young years of your life, and the utter relief and broken heart that vie for emotional space when you hear your abuser has died. I know the very confusing pain of living with an increasingly depressed and overwhelmed mother who eventually starts taking her pain and fears out on you. The caustic words that eat at your soul. The terror at the thought of setting her off. The struggles to please a Mother who absolutely refused to be pleased. Verbal abuse that eventually bled over into other kinds of abuse. Pain that went on and on and on, increasing throughout the years. Pain that didn't stop when she finally passed.

The loneliness, confusion and pain far too deep for words that comes with an abusive marriage. The struggles to come to grips with the abuse and, finally, to confess to yourself that abuse has occurred. The never-ending ache that comes from watching your children hurt. The fear of confiding the abuse to others who just might throw it back in your face. The near-despair that comes from watching some of your own precious children go down the wrong road in a vain effort to right the many wrongs heaped on them. The drowning kind of sorrow that accompanies their rebellion, the deep heart brokenness that accompanies the cruelty of their words and accusations.

I know the emotional firestorm that erupts from hearing words of censure from supposed Christians who have no clue what you are enduring, don't give a whit for you but still feel the need to condemn and vilify because "somebody said." Or, simply because you and your family don't fit their ideals.

I know it all and more.

If I stopped here, thought about it all long enough, and wallowed in the pain, I'd be nearly as bad as those who did the abusing. I could do that. I've known those who have. Usually they end up pouring their pain out on the next generation. And on it goes. Endlessly.

I could stop and wallow except for one thing: God's grace won't let me. It's not that I'm better than those who do. It's that God's in control. It took me a long, long time to trust Him enough to even begin to understand that He is a good God, He is in control, He does a plan...even through all the pain.

That's what I want you to know. God is in charge. And He is good. He's not like your abuser. He won't lie, break or wound you. He isn't like the preachers who preach one thing from the pulpit but live quite another way everywhere else. He's not like the "good Christian folks" who refuse to listen, refuse to try to understand but love to gossip and condemn. God doesn't lie. He doesn't abuse, misuse or demand things we aren't capable of performing.

God is a good God. God is a very good God.

It bears repeating. Over and over and over. God is a wonderfully good God Who can be trusted-- even if you have never known, or have rarely known, people worthy of your trust. Once you know really Him, you will find Him far, far easier to trust than any person. Go to the pages of Scripture. Read how Jesus related to those wounded, broken ones He met along the way. Observe how tender He was, how kind. Go to the pages of the Old Testament and read about God's provision for His people. Look up the story of the Red Sea: I love that story. I've lived that story, had my own Red Sea story, many, many times. Each time God came through. Each time He delivered. Each time He proved Himself worthy of my trust.

The really great thing in all of this is that none of it depends on me. God doesn't accept me because I'm good or because I've achieved something. Abuse victims are just like everyone else in this: we're all sinners worthy of hell. Enduring abuse here doesn't give anyone a free pass to Heaven. The reason God accepts me is because He, through the blood of His Son, Jesus, has saved me from Himself. God saved me from God: from His wrath, from His condemnation, from His justice. From the Hell I so deserved. He can do it for you, too.

I am of the Reformed faith and I firmly believe God is in control. In all ways. In everything. I also know from the pages of Scripture that, when we come to Him in true repentance, confessing our sins and asking His forgiveness, He never turns us away. He's a really great God. A good God. A loving God: that's everything to those of us who have rarely known human love. Because He's a loving God and a good God, we can know for certain that He will take us in when we come to Him in our brokenness and pain. And He will never let us go. " For my father and my mother have forsaken me, but the LORD will take me in." (Psalms 27:10)

If you would like to contact us with questions, tell us your story, or find help in understanding God's Word, the Bible, you may do so on our blogsite at cryingoutforjustice.wordpress.com.

"May the Lord bless you and keep you;
the Lord make his face to shine upon you and be gracious to you;
the Lord lift up his countenance upon you and give you peace."
Sola Deo Gloria

Bibliography

Adams, Jay E. *Marriage, Divorce, and Remarriage in the Bible.* Grand Rapids: Zondervan, 1980.

Andersen, Jocelyn. *Woman Submit! Christians & Domestic Violence.* Auburndale, Florida: One Way Cafe Press, 2007.

Bancroft, Lundy. *When Dad Hurts Mom: Helping Your Children Heal the Wounds of Witnessing Abuse.* New York, New York: Berkley Books, 2004.

—. *Why Does He Do That? Inside the Minds of Angry and Controlling Men.* New York, New York: The Berkley Publishing Group, 2003.

Bancroft, Lundy, and Jay G. Silverman. *The Batterer as Parent.* Thousand Oaks, California: Sage Publications, Inc., 2002.

Bleby, Martin. *Power in Relationships: Issues of Love and Control, http://www.newcreation.org.au/books/pdf/418_Power_Relations.pdf,* 2008.

Branson, Brenda, and Paula J. Silva. *Violence Among Us: Ministry to Families in Crisis.* Valley Forge, Pennsylvania: Judson Press, 2007.

Braun, Sarah and Bridget Flynn. *Honeymoon and Hell: A Memoir of Abuse.* Kindle Edition, 2011.

Brown, Christa. *This Little Light: Beyond a Baptist Preacher Predator and His Gang.* Cedarburg: Foremost Press, 2009.

Brown, Sandra L. *How to Spot a Dangerous Man Before You Get Involved.* Alameda, California: Hunter House, Inc., 2005.

Churchill, Winston S. *The Gathering Storm.* London: Houghton Mifflin Company, 1948.

Davenport, Noa, and Schwartz, Ruth, and Elliott, Gail. *Mobbing: Emotional Abuse in the American Workplace.* Ames, Iowa: Civil Society Publishing, 1999.

De Becker, Gavin. *The Gift of Fear: Survival Signals that Protect us From Violence.* New York: Dell, 1997.

Edwards, Jonathan. *The Works of Jonathan Edwards.* Kindle. B&R Samizdat Express. February 13, 2009.

Evans, Patricia. *The Verbally Abusive Relationship.* 3rd Edition. Avon, Massachusettes: Adams Media, 2010.

Gordon, T. David. "The Insufficiency of Scripture." *Modern Reformaton,* January/February 2002: 18-23.

Greenfield, Susan. *Would the Real Church Please Stand Up!* Xulon Press, 2007.

Hare, Robert D. *Without Conscience.* New York: The Guilford Press, 1993.

Instone-Brewer, David. *Divorce and Remarriage in the Bible: The Social and Literary Context.* Grand Rapids: Wm. B. Eerdmans, 2002.

—. *Divorce and Remarriage in the Church: Biblical Solutions for Pastoral Realities (Kindle).* Downers Grove: InterVarsity Press, 2003.

Johnson, Scott Allen. *Physical Abusers and Sexual Offenders: Forensic and Clinical Strategies.* Boca Raton, Florida: Taylor & Francis, 2007.

Keller, Timothy and Kathy. *The Meaning of Marriage: Facing the Complexities of Commitment with the Wisdom of God.* New York, New York: Penguin Group, USA, 2011.

Kroeger, Catherine Clark, and Nancy Nason-Clark. *No Place for Abuse.* Downers Grove, Illinois: InterVarsity Press, 2001.

MacArthur, John. *The Divorce Dilemma: God's Last Word on Lasting Commitment.* Greenville: Day One Publications, 2009.

McLemore, Clinton W. *Toxic Relationships and How to Change Them.* San Francisco: Jossey-Bass, 2003.

Meloy, J. Reid, ed. *The Psychology of Stalking: Clinical and Forensic Perspectives.* San Diego: Academic Press, 1998.

Middleton-Moz, Jane. *Shame and Guilt: The Masters of Disguise.* Deerfield Beach, Florida: Health Communications, Inc., 1990.

Olson, Jeff. *When Words Hurt: Verbal Abuse in Marriage.* Grand Rapids: RBC Ministries, 2002.

Phillips, Richard D. *The Masculine Mandate: God's Calling to Men.* Lake Mary: Reformation Trust Publishing, 2010.

Peck, M. Scott. *People of the Lie: The Hope for Healing Human Evil.* New York: Touchstone, 1998.

Pike, Anne. *Danger Has a Face.* Outskirts Press, 2011.

Piper, John. *This Momentary Marriage.* Wheaton: Crossway Books, 2009.

Plantinga, Cornelius. *Not the Way It's Supposed to Be: A Breviary of Sin.* Grand Rapids: Wm. B. Eerdmans Publishing Company, 2010.

Pryde, Debbie, and Robert Needham. *A Biblical Perspective of What to do When You Are Abused by Your Husband.* Newberry Springs, California: Iron Sharpeneth Iron Publications, 2003.

Roberts, Barbara. *Not Under Bondage: Biblical Divorce for Abuse, Adultery & Desertion.* Victoria: Maschil Press, 2008.

Rule, Ann. *Dead by Sunset: Perfect Husband, Perfect Killer?* New York: Pocket Books, 1995.

Silvious, Jan. *Fool-Proofing Your Life.* Colorado Springs, Colorado: WaterBrook Press, 1998.

Simon Jr., George. *In Sheep's Clothing: Understanding and Dealing With Manipulative People.* Little Rock, Arkansas: Parkhurst Brothers, Inc., 2010.

Simon Jr., George K. *Character Disturbance: The Phenomenon of Our Age.* Little Rock, Arkansas: Parkhurst Brothers, Inc., 2011.

Stout, Martha. *The Sociopath Next Door.* New York: Broadway Books, 2005.

Sutton, Ray. *Second Chance: Biblical Principles of Divorce and Remarriage.* Fort Worth: Dominion Pres, 1988.

Townsend, John, and Henry Cloud. *Safe People: How to Find Relationships that are Good for You and Avoid Those that Aren't.* Zondervan, 1996.

Tracy, Steven. *Mending the Soul: Understanding and Healing Abuse.* Zondervan, 2005.

Anywhere But Here. DVD. Directed by Wayne Wang. Produced by Twentieth Century Fox. 2002.

Wilson, Sandra D. *Released from Shame: Moving Beyond the Pain of the Past.* Downers Grove: InterVarsity Press, 2002.

Wingerd, Daryl, Jim Ellif, Jim Chrisman, and Steve Burchett. *Divorce and Remarriage: A Permanence View.* Kansas City: Christian Communicators Worldwide, 2009.

Recommended Reading

In my opinion, all pastors and anyone who intends to give counsel to people asking for help with an abusive marriage, should read all of the following books (In addition to *this* book of course!). If you do so, you will find yourself becoming more and more able to recognize the mentality and tactics of the abuser and to know when you are talking to a victim of abuse. You will also have learned how to help the victim and how to avoid being duped by or enabling the abuser.

1. *Why Does He Do That?* by Lundy Bancroft. After *A Cry for Justice* (which calls your attention to the problem) turn to Bancroft. He is the best writer on this subject and this single book will take you *far* in your journey to wise up to the deceptions of abusers. Bancroft's books do contain some rough, vulgar language because he quotes abuser's' actual words.
2. *The Verbally Abusive Relationship* by Patricia Evans. This is not as detailed as Bancroft, but it is an excellent introduction, focusing on verbal abuse. It includes a very good questionnaire tool to help the reader evaluate their own relationships.
3. *When Dad Hurts Mom* by Lundy Bancroft. This is a kind of "part 2" after Bancroft's *Why Does He Do That?* It provides even more insight into abuse, focusing upon the effects on children whose mother is being abused, teaching her how she can help them. It also goes into some detail about tactics use by abusers in the court system.
4. *Fool-Proofing Your Life* by Jan Silvious. Building upon the Book of Proverbs in the Bible, Silvious teaches us that abusers (fools) are not your normal brand of sinner and cannot be handled with typical methods we might use for dealing with other people.
5. *In Sheep's Clothing* by George Simon, Jr. Simon's book, along with *Character Disturbance*, is just excellent. Like Bancroft (and Robert Hare, #7), Simon understands the mentality of the sociopath. In this book, he deals with the covert abuse and its tactics. *I love this guy!*
6. *Character Disturbance* by George Simon, Jr. Building on *In Sheep's Clothing*, Simon focuses now more upon the sociopath/psychopath; the person with no conscience. Many abusers fall into these categories. Any abuse victim reading this book is very likely to say "he is describing my situation!"

7. *Without Conscience* by Robert Hare. Robert Hare is a leader in the field of criminal and abnormal psychology. He has designed the most reliable tool used for testing for psychopaths. This is a must-read book.
8. *Not Under Bondage* by Barbara Roberts. Barbara, having come out of an abusive relationship herself, wasn't getting any help from her fellow Christians. So she set out to find for herself what the Bible really says about divorce, specifically in relation to abuse. This book will help victims throw off the unbiblical traditions they have been in bondage to and get free from their abusers. Barbara also has a website at www.notunderbondage.com where you will find many helpful resources.
9. *Released From Shame* by Sandra D. Wilson. Shame is a wicked ally of abuse. Writing from a Christian perspective, Wilson teaches us about shame, about its causes, and how to be free from it.
10. *Dead by Sunset* by Ann Rule. Yes, this is a "true-crime" story, but I recommend every young woman read it, and also anyone who is seriously interested in seeing real-life abuse by a psychopathic man named Bradly Morris Cunningham who murdered his wife right here in my home state in 1986. Free of any restraints of conscience, Cunningham devastated the lives of intelligent, talented women and just about everyone else around him. His ability to deceive and manipulate was incredible. Read this book and grow wise!
11. *The Sociopath Next Door* by Martha Stout. I found myself writing down quote after quote while reading this book. Stout introduces us to the reality that conscienceless people are far more numerous than we realize, and she helps us learn to recognize their mentality and tactics, and how we must deal with them.
12. *Divorce and Remarriage in the Church* by David Instone-Brewer. Marriage, says the author, is a contract and its terms are the wedding vows. Persistent, hard-hearted, unrepentant violation of those vows destroys a marriage and gives the wronged spouse the right to divorce. (Also see his companion volume, *Divorce and Remarriage in the Bible*).
13. *Mending the Soul: Understanding and Healing Abuse* by Steven Tracy. This book is top-notch. Written from a Christian perspective, it informs and educates us about abuse. Tracy gets the biblical doctrines of forgiveness and reconciliation *right!* That is extremely rare in all the Christian books written about forgiveness.

About the Authors

Jeff Crippen was called as pastor of Christ Reformation Church in 1993 after serving for 10 years as a pastor in Montana and Alaska. A graduate of Multnomah Biblical Seminary (MABS & MDiv), Jeff was a police officer for 12 years before entering the pastoral ministry. He has studied domestic violence and abuse since 2009. Jeff and his wife, Verla, have been married since 1971 and have a son and daughter. They live on the Northern Oregon coast with their two Labrador Retrievers, Sasha and Sadie.

Anna Wood writes and maintains several popular Christian blogs including one that deals with Domestic Abuse. A Christian and a long-time abuse survivor herself, she has a passion for helping other abuse victims come to the knowledge of what they are experiencing and finding a way to break free and thrive. Having extensive first hand knowledge of victimization, she is able to help others who haven't experienced abuse come to an understanding of what the abuse victim is facing.